Data Protection – The New Rules

Data Protection – The New Rules

Ian Long BCL, Dip EL, Dip PI
Solicitor

JORDAN PUBLISHING

Published by
Jordan Publishing (owned by LexisNexis)
Regus Castlemead
Terrace Floor
Lower Castle Street
Bristol BS1 3AG

British Library Cataloguing-in-Publication Data

A catalogue record for this book is available from the British Library.

ISBN 978 1 78473 213 4

Typeset by Letterpart Ltd, Caterham on the Hill, Surrey CR3 5XL

Printed in Great Britain by Hobbs the Printers Limited, Totton, Hampshire SO40 3WX

DEDICATION

For Deb

CONTENTS

PREFACE

Data protection has become a minefield of complex rules and regulations. Personal data is hedged around with all sorts of controls to ensure its safety from prying eyes. The new EU Data Protection Regulation will unify and strengthen the plethora of laws that affect every organisation, large and small, that handles personal data. And that includes everyone involved in handling data relating to clients, customers, employees and other individuals.

Company secretaries and directors will be responsible to see that their companies comply with these new requirements.

In April 2016 the European Parliament and the Council of Ministers finally adopted the European's Commission's proposal for the new Regulation after discussions that began in 2012. The Regulation aims to put in place a modern data protection regime that will make Europe fit for the digital age.

The Regulation will introduce a new regime for data controllers and data processors. Your customers, suppliers, employees and others will have new data protection rights. As a result you will have new requirements and obligations to meet. You must comply and be able to show that you comply. The new rules will require many changes to your business systems, policies and procedures and the entire approach of the organisation to personal data. Now is the time to prepare for the new regime.

Data Protection – The New Rules has condensed a mass of EU and UK documentation into one practical and easy-to-read manual. It guides you through all the relevant changes simply and clearly. And it sets out the current rules as well as the new ones. You will find everything you need to know in one place. The text features:

- Simple, comprehensive description of the legal and regulatory provisions;

- Detailed analysis/comment on the business requirements;

- Clear examples and case studies; and

- Sample data protection and information security policies.

Key topics include:

Fair obtaining and use of data	Transfer of data abroad
Information security	Data subject consent
Cloud computing	Direct marketing
Data access requests	Compliance framework
Big Data	Enforcement

The book is essential reading for all data controllers and data processors and anyone responsible for handling personal data.

The law is stated as at 31st May 2016.

Ian Long

ACKNOWLEDGEMENTS

The author wishes to thank all at Jordan Publishing, in particular Mary Kenny and Kate Hather, for their dedication in seeing this book through to the light of day. It was a pleasure to work with them.

The author also wishes to thank Bill and Dr Bob without whom this book would not have been written.

Thanks and love to my mum Peg who was, and is, always there for me.

TABLE OF ABBREVIATIONS

AGM	annual general meeting
BERR	Department for Business, Enterprise and Regulatory Reform
BIS	Department for Business, Innovation and Skills
CA 1948/1967/1976/1980/ 1981/1985/1989/2006	Companies Act 1948/1967/1976/1980/1981/1985/1989/2006
C(AICE)A 2004	Companies (Audit, Investigations and Community Enterprise) Act 2004
CJA 1993	Criminal Justice Act 1993
CLRB	Company Law Reform Bill
D & O insurance	Directors' & Officers' Insurance
DTI	Department of Trade and Industry
EC	European Community
EEA	European Economic Area
EGM	extraordinary general meeting
ERA 1996	Employment Rights Act 1996
EU	European Union
FCA	Financial Conduct Authority
FSMA 2000	Financial Services and Markets Act 2000
HMRC	Her Majesty's Revenue and Customs
HMSO	Her Majesty's Stationery Office
IA 1986	Insolvency Act 1986
ICTA 1988	Income and Corporation Taxes Act 1988
IoD	Institute of Directors
SFO	Serious Fraud Office
VAT	value added tax

TABLE OF CASES

References are to paragraph numbers.

TABLE OF STATUTES

References are to paragraph numbers.

TABLE OF STATUTORY INSTRUMENTS

References are to paragraph numbers.

TABLE OF EUROPEAN AND INTERNATIONAL MATERIAL

References are to paragraph numbers.

Part 1
THE CURRENT REGIME

CHAPTER 1

INTRODUCTION TO DATA PROTECTION

DATA PROTECTION

1.1 This book provides a concise introduction to data protection law and considers issues that may arise in the daily work of company directors, company secretaries and administrators. In doing so, it takes account of the fact that company directors, secretaries and administrators often have a number of functions in addition to their usual administration activities – the book includes a brief introduction on the practical effect of data protection law on the activities of commercial organisations.

1.2 Part 2 of this book provides a guide to the new regime brought about by the General Data Protection Regulation of the European Union, which will impose a new regime on companies and organisations of all kinds that hold personal data relating to their clients, customers, employees and third parties; in other words, almost every organisation that does business with individual customers or provides a service to them (see Chapter 10 et seq).

1.3 Data protection is a relatively new addition to laws that affect company administration. For this reason, it is important to keep up to date with developments as new practices and procedures become standard.

1.4 This book will be updated to reflect both changes in the law and the needs of its readers. The author would be pleased to receive (via the publisher) comments from readers as to how the book can be improved to better meet those needs.

WHAT IS DATA PROTECTION?

1.5 Driven largely by an aspiration for Europe-wide privacy rights for individuals, various legal measures culminated in a 1995 European Directive (95/46/EC) under which all Member States of the European Union, including the UK, were obliged to create new law on the 'processing of personal data'.

1.6 The Data Protection Act 1998 ('DPA' or 'the Act'), the statutory provision under which the UK implemented the 1995 Directive, came into force on 1 March 2000.

1.7   Data protection is essentially that area of the law that governs what may, and may not, be done with personal information. This information may be in electronic form (eg stored on a computer hard drive) or manual (eg paper-based) form. Although the law applies to *all* electronically processed personal data, it applies only to *some* types of paper-based records – see further **4.12**.

1.8   In the UK, data protection law is enforced by the Information Commissioner's Office ('ICO' or 'the Office'). The current Information Commissioner is Christopher Graham, who was appointed in June 2009. In April 2010, the Commissioner was given the power to impose fines on organisations for data protection breaches – up to £500,000 per breach. Since November 2011, over 100 organisations have been fined sums ranging from £60,000 to £300,000 – see further details in Chapter 9.

1.9   Data protection law is due to change over the next couple of years due to the European Commission's decision to revise and update the law, after extensive discussions with the European Parliament and the Council of Ministers. This new law is the General Data Protection Regulation ('the Regulation' or 'the new Regulation') discussed in Part 2 of this book – see Chapter 10 et seq.

1.10   The new Regulation will make it a legal requirement for some private sector organisations (such as limited companies and public limited companies) that store or use personal information to employ a qualified Data Protection Officer. Companies are well advised to prepare for this requirement by arranging for a designated member of staff to be trained in data protection matters.

1.11   The Regulation will increase the level of fines that can be imposed by the ICO, from the current £500,000 per breach of the DPA to a maximum fine of €20 million per breach of the Regulation or up to 4% of a company's/group's total annual turnover, as appropriate.

1.12   The new Regulation will also make the reporting of breaches to the ICO compulsory in certain circumstances.

TERMINOLOGY

1.13   In order to understand the scope of data protection law, it is necessary to consider four basic terms that will be used throughout this book. The definition of these terms in the is complex but it will suffice to deal with them here in general terms.

- Personal data – information that identifies a living individual, eg a person's name, address, email address, shareholding, directorships, CCTV image, photograph on a website, etc.

- Processing – any activity that can be carried out concerning personal data, eg obtaining, storing, printing, filing, copying or transferring this data to a third party.
- Data controller – any organisation that controls the processing of personal data, eg retailers, banks, insurance companies, stockbrokers, law firms, supermarkets and government departments. In fact virtually all UK organisations, including limited companies, are data controllers.
- Data subject – the individual person who is the subject of any relevant personal data.

1.14 The DPA applies only to the processing of personal data by data controllers.

WHAT DOES THE DPA DO?

1.15 Essentially the DPA does three things:

(1) It requires organisations ('data controllers') to inform the data protection regulator (the ICO) of their processing operations ('Notification').
(2) It obliges data controllers to comply with a legally enforceable code of conduct on data processing (the 'Data Protection Principles').
(3) It creates a set of enforceable expectations for individuals concerning the processing of their personal data ('Individuals' Rights').

NOTIFICATION

1.16 Companies must inform the ICO of the types of processing that they undertake. Notification can be done online at www.ico.org.uk and is subject to an annual fee of £35, or £500 – the higher fee applies to organisations:

- with a turnover of £25.9 million *and* 250 or more members of staff; *or*
- that are public authorities with 250 or more members of staff.

1.17 The register of data controllers maintained by the ICO is a public document and can be searched online – it contains a list of all the registered purpose(s) of processing for each registered data controller.

1.18 If a company does not have a Data Protection Officer, it will often be incumbent on a company director or the company secretary to notify the ICO of the company's data processing, and to maintain that register entry.

1.19 Using personal data in a company when that company is not registered is usually a criminal offence. The company, not the company secretary, will be liable for this offence.

1.20 For further details on notification, see Chapter 2.

1.21 It should be noted that the new General Data Protection Regulation will remove the requirement for notification.

DATA PROTECTION PRINCIPLES

1.22 There are eight Principles of data protection. All companies must comply with the eight Principles in respect of all personal data processing operations that they undertake, even if they are exempt from notification.

1.23 The Principles set out in the table below and discussed throughout this book are legally enforceable by the ICO by virtue of its power to issue Enforcement Notices. Failure to comply with such a Notice constitutes a criminal offence. The Principles are also enforceable, upon obtaining a court order, by any individual who suffers damage as a result of their breach by a data controller.

1.24 Although there are various exemptions from the need to comply with some of the Principles, those exemptions are rarely available in practice. Examples include processing for national security, the prevention or detection of crime, the assessment or collection of tax, the determination of examination results, and for the purposes of conducting negotiations and for management forecasting.

The Eight Data Protection Principles (Data Protection Act 1998, Schedule 1)	
(1)	Personal data shall be processed fairly and lawfully and, in particular, shall not be processed unless: (a) at least one of a set of conditions is met; and (b) in the case of sensitive personal data, at least one of a further set of conditions is also met.
(2)	Personal data shall be obtained only for one or more specified and lawful purposes, and shall not be further processed in any manner incompatible with that purpose or those purposes.
(3)	Personal data shall be adequate, relevant and not excessive in relation to the purpose or purposes for which they are processed.
(4)	Personal data processed shall be accurate and, where necessary, kept up to date.
(5)	Personal data processed for any purpose or purposes shall not be kept for longer than is necessary for that purpose or those purposes.

(6)	Personal data shall be processed in accordance with the rights of data subjects under this Act.
(7)	Appropriate technical and organisational measures shall be taken against unauthorised or unlawful processing of personal data and against accidental loss or destruction of, or damage to, personal data.
(8)	Personal data shall not be transferred to a country or territory outside the European Economic Area unless that country or territory ensures an adequate level of protection for the rights and freedoms of data subjects in relation to the processing of personal data.

INDIVIDUALS' RIGHTS

1.25 Individuals have the following rights as against any company that uses their personal data:

- To be informed by the company, upon request, whether it is processing data concerning him/her, and to be given a copy of such data.
- To prevent processing likely to cause him/her damage or distress.
- To prevent direct marketing to him/her.
- To prevent the taking of automated decisions concerning him/her.
- To have inaccurate data corrected or erased.
- To be compensated for any damage or distress caused by unlawful data processing.
- To ask the ICO to investigate the activities of any company that is processing the individual's personal data to ensure that the processing is in accordance with the requirements of the Act.

1.26 The new General Data Protection Regulation will create additional rights for individuals – see Chapter 14.

PRACTICAL APPLICATION FOR COMPANY DIRECTORS, COMPANY SECRETARIES & ADMINISTRATORS

1.27 Companies will use (or 'process') a number of types of personal data about a range of individuals on a daily basis. The following is a list of the most common types of individual about whom personal data will be processed:

- staff (including former staff);
- prospective staff (job applicants);
- customers;

- prospective customers (most commonly this information is contained in the 'marketing database');
- contractors (including agency staff and consultants);
- suppliers; and
- shareholders.

1.28 Where the company director or company secretary performs a compliance role, it will be incumbent on him/her to ensure that all processing of personal data is undertaken in accordance with the requirements of the DPA. Because the definition of 'processing' is very wide, virtually everything that may be done with personal data in the business will fall within the remit of the Act, and so must comply with the eight Data Protection Principles.

REMAINING CONTENT OF THIS PART

1.29 In the remaining chapters of this Part, the following topics will be considered:

- The notification system and the exemptions from requirement to notify (Chapter 2).
- The 'fair and lawful processing' requirement, including rules for direct marketing and for using sensitive personal data (Chapter 3).
- The right of individuals to gain access to a copy of the data held on them by any company (Chapter 4).
- Other rights of individuals (Chapter 5).
- The security requirement, including the need for contracts for outsourced operations (Chapter 6).
- Export of personal data outside the EU (Chapter 7).
- Other obligations of data controllers (Chapter 8).
- Enforcement and compliance (Chapter 9).

CHAPTER 2

NOTIFICATION SYSTEM

2.1 Data protection law requires that all companies (unless they are exempt – see below) must register themselves as being 'data controllers' with the ICO. The register entry must list the types of personal data processed by the company, as well as the types of processing undertaken (for basic definitions of 'processing', 'personal data' and 'data controller' – see **1.13**. An annual fee is payable to maintain the register entry.

2.2 The register of data controllers is a public document and can be inspected online at www.ico.org.uk. A search of the register will reveal the name of the registered company, its data protection registration number, the date of expiry of its current registration and the type(s) of processing registered as undertaken by that company.

NEED TO NOTIFY

2.3 The obligation on companies to notify derives from s 17 of the DPA, which provides that:

> '...personal data must not be processed unless an entry in respect of the data controller is included in the register maintained by the Commissioner ...'

2.4 Certain types of processing are exempt from the need to notify – see **2.18** et seq below. However, it is most important for company directors and company secretaries to realise that the Data Protection Principles – see **1.22** above – apply to all uses of personal data by the company, even if this use is exempt from the notification requirement. This means that the Commissioner can take action against companies for breaching one or more Principles as a result of processing that was not notified or was not required to be notified.

HOW TO NOTIFY

2.5 Notification can be undertaken either online, at www.ico.org.uk, or by telephone by calling 0303 1231113 or 01625 545 745. In each case the company will be asked for certain information – see **2.10** et seq below. (A *Data Protection Breach Notification Form* is at Appendix 3 to this book.)

2.6   The relevant individual at the company (often a director or the company secretary) will then be sent a copy of the draft register entry and be given an opportunity to amend it before it becomes available for public inspection. Data controllers should ensure that all their automated (ie computer-based) processing (unless exempt – see **2.18** et seq below – is covered in their register entry.

2.7   Manual (purely paper-based) data processing operations do not need to be notified, but companies may volunteer to include their manual processing within their register entry.

2.8   The notification fee is £35 (or £500 for larger organisations) and the register entry will be maintained for 1 year. Roughly 2 months before the expiry of the registration, the ICO will contact the company to invite renewal – a further fee is payable each year. Only one register entry is permitted per company.

2.9   Where a company is part of a group structure, each company within the group will require its own register entry, unless that member of the group is exempt from registration. Further advice can be obtained from the ICO.

WHAT TO NOTIFY

2.10   The registering company will be asked for its name, address, contact information and company registration number. The company must then make some general statements about the types of processing undertaken.

2.11   The general statement includes information on the purposes of processing (eg for staff administration, marketing, credit referencing, fundraising, trading in personal information), the types of data subjects whose data are being processed (eg staff, shareholders, customers, agents), the classes of data processed (eg personal details, employment details, family and social circumstances), the persons to whom the data may be disclosed (eg prospective employers, financial institutions, the media) and the countries to where data may be transferred if those countries are located outside the European Economic Area (see **2.12** below). In each case the data controller is given an opportunity to select from a list of available options. Most types of organisation have their own standard registration templates on the Commissioner's website – however, the information contained in the standard template for organisational types should be checked to ensure that it accurately reflects the data processing activities being carried on.

2.12   When companies are considering whether they send personal data outside the European Economic Area (the 27 EU countries plus Norway, Iceland and Liechtenstein), they should bear in mind the need that some organisations have to book foreign hotel rooms or airline tickets for their employees – in doing so, they will necessarily send the names (and other information) of staff to the foreign country in question. Where organisations transfer personal data to several countries, or where there is some uncertainty as to which countries receive personal data, they should list 'worldwide' in their register entry.

2.13 Companies are additionally expected to make a 'security statement'. This consists of a series of questions to which the company must answer either 'yes' or 'no'. It should be noted that there are no adverse consequences of answering the standard questions with a 'no'. However, where data controllers find that their answers are in the negative, they should be aware that their processing may breach the seventh Data Protection Principle – see **11.77** et seq below.

2.14 It should be remembered that if the data controller's processing activities change after a notification has been made, there is a duty to inform the ICO of this change as soon as possible – companies should not wait until the expiry of their 'notification year' before informing the Office of the change.

CRIMINAL OFFENCES

2.15 Prosecutions by the ICO for breaching the notification and related requirements of the Act take place in local magistrates' courts. The Commissioner's Annual Report – published each July and available for free download from the ICO website – lists the organisations that have been prosecuted in the previous year.

2.16 As far as the notification regime is concerned, it is generally a criminal offence to:

- process personal data without a register entry;
- process personal data in a manner that is incompatible with the register entry; or
- fail to notify the ICO of changes to the registrable particulars.

2.17 By virtue of s 61 of the DPA, a director, manager, company secretary or other officer of a corporate body may be prosecuted for the same offence as that which has been proved against the corporate body if he or she has been involved in the offence by way of some connivance or neglect.

EXEMPTIONS

2.18 Certain types of person or organisation are exempt from the notification requirement. In the main, these exemptions do **not** apply to corporate bodies that use computers to process personal data and that operate with a view to profit.

2.19 Certain types of processing are exempt from the requirement to notify, namely processing undertaken only for one or more of the following:

- national security;
- staff administration;
- advertising, marketing and public relations; and
- accounts and records.

2.20 However, the exemption from the requirement to notify will be lost where processing is undertaken for one of the purposes listed at **2.21** below. Accordingly, most companies will not be exempt from the notification requirement and the annual fee.

NON-EXEMPT PURPOSES

2.21 Where a company processes personal data for any of the purposes listed below, the company will be unable to claim an exemption from the notification requirement. Most companies will process personal data for one of more of these purposes. The company must list each relevant reason for processing in its notification with the ICO.

- Accounting and auditing
- Administration of justice
- Administration of membership records
- Advertising marketing and public relations for others
- Assessment and collection of taxes and other revenue
- Benefits, grants and loans administration
- Canvassing political support amongst the electorate
- Constituency casework by politicians
- Consultancy and advisory services
- Credit referencing
- Crime prevention and prosecution of offenders
- Debt administration and factoring
- Education
- Fundraising
- Health administration and services
- Information and databank administration
- Insurance administration
- Journalism and media
- Legal services
- Licensing and registration
- Pastoral care

- Pensions administration
- Policing
- Private investigation
- Processing for not-for-profit organisations
- Property management
- Provision of financial services and advice
- Realising the objectives of a charitable organisation or voluntary body
- Research
- Trading/sharing in personal information.

CONCLUSION

2.22 Notification is important, not least because it is a criminal offence to process personal data without a corresponding register entry. Prosecutions for failure to notify are taken against the company, not against any individual within the company.

2.23 It must be remembered, however, that notification is not the complete picture. By making an appropriate notification to the ICO, the company is merely complying with one obligation in the DPA. Data controllers must then go on to comply with the Data Protection Principles – it is important to bear in mind that notification does not exempt data controllers from compliance with other obligations in the Act, nor does it constitute a licence or permission to process personal data for the registered purpose(s).

2.24 The requirement for notification will be abolished under the new General Data Protection Regulation, which is expected to come into force in the UK in 2018. The Regulation is discussed in Part 2 of this book.

CHAPTER 3

FAIR AND LAWFUL PROCESSING

3.1   Unless a relevant exemption applies (which is rare), all processing of personal data by UK companies must comply with the eight Data Protection Principles – see **1.22** above. A substantially similar set of rules applies to all personal data processing carried out by all companies located in all Member States of the European Union.

3.2   The first, and perhaps the most important, principle is that companies must use personal data both fairly and lawfully, and that at least one of a set of pre-conditions for processing must exist.

FIRST PRINCIPLE DEFINED

3.3   The first Data Protection Principle provides as follows:

'Personal data shall be processed fairly and lawfully and, in particular, shall not be processed unless –

(a)   at least one of a set of conditions is met, and
(b)   in the case of sensitive personal data, at least one of a further set of conditions is also met.'

3.4   The first Principle therefore requires three things:

(1)   that personal data be processed *fairly* – see **3.6** below;

(2)   that personal data be processed *lawfully* – see **3.13** below; and

(3)   that at least one of a set of *conditions* applies to every instance of personal data processing – see **3.15** below.

3.5   In addition, when processing sensitive personal data – see **3.33** et seq below – an organisation must be able to show that the relevant processing operation benefits from one of a set of further legitimising conditions. Accordingly, for the storage and use of sensitive personal data, there are four requirements under the first Principle.

FAIR PROCESSING

3.6   In determining whether a company's processing of personal data is 'fair', the DPA requires that particular regard must be paid to the method by which the data were or are obtained. Part II of Schedule 1 to the Act indicates that it is likely that processing will not be fair where the person from whom data are obtained is 'deceived or misled' as to the purposes of processing.

Fair collection statement

3.7   Personal data are not to be regarded as having been obtained fairly unless, at the time of the obtaining, or very soon afterwards, a statement regarding a company's use (and/or proposed use) of the data is made 'readily available' to the relevant data subject(s). It should be noted that this requirement is not one of consent – there is no need for the relevant individual to 'sign off' on the statement or even to acquiesce in it. Further, the individual may never have seen the statement – this is fine provided that the statement was readily available to the individual. The statement that must be supplied is known as a 'fair collection statement' (sometimes called a 'privacy notice') and consists of the following information:

- the identity of the data controller (ie the company name);
- the purpose(s) of the processing; and
- any further information that is necessary, having regard to the specific circumstances in which the data are or are to be processed, to enable processing in respect of the data subject to be fair.

3.8   The requirement to provide the 'fair collection statement' applies whether or not the data were obtained from the data subject. However, where the data were obtained from someone other than the data subject, eg by way of list rental, there is an exemption from the need to provide the information where to do so would constitute 'disproportionate effort'. The ICO has indicated that all circumstances will be taken into account in determining what is 'disproportionate' in this context, including the nature of the personal data, the likely duration of their retention and the cost to the data controller involved in making the information available.

3.9   The requirement to provide the 'fair collection information' will not apply where the company received personal data from another data controller in circumstances where that other data controller had informed the relevant data subject(s) of the transfer and of all the relevant information about the new data controller before the transfer took place.

Sample fair collection statement

3.10   The following is a basic sample fair collection statement for staff data. Such a notice may appear in the staff handbook or attached to a New Staff Details form, or elsewhere.

'XYZ Ltd will use the information supplied by you for all purposes associated with the administration of the employer/employee relationship, including the monitoring of our communications facilities to check for compliance with our relevant policies.

We will transfer part of the information we hold on you to third parties where we are required to do so by operation of law. We may also transfer information to third parties where such transfer forms part of the administration of the employer/employee relationship. We may transfer your information to companies and organisations that carry out processing operations on our behalf, such as payroll companies and brokers.

You are entitled to see a copy of the personal data that we hold on you. Should you wish to see the information we hold, please contact [name of Data Protection Officer or relevant HR Officer or company secretary] on extension [number] or at [email address].'

3.11 *Note:* The above example is a basic precedent and will not suit all companies. It should be amended to reflect the processing that is actually carried out by the company. If appropriate, legal advice should be sought before any new 'fair collection' statement is implemented. Fair collection statements should not contain opt-in and opt-out devices for marketing purposes – see 3.22 et seq below.

3.12 For the collection of *customer* information, a different statement – with different content – will be required.

LAWFUL PROCESSING

3.13 To process personal data in compliance with the first Principle, the data controller must process the data 'lawfully'. This means that a company must observe general legal obligations of the UK – both statutory and common law, including all requirements of the Companies Acts (except where such requirements conflict with those contained in the DPA).

3.14 Of particular relevance will be the laws of confidence (especially that arising between the data subject and the company), *ultra vires* (where an action is taken that is outside the scope of the organisation's powers) and, in appropriate circumstances, Art 8 of the European Convention on Human Rights (the right to privacy).

LEGITIMISING CONDITIONS

3.15 All personal data processing (including the obtaining and transferring of personal data) will generally be unlawful unless one of the six legitimising conditions shown in the table below exists. It should be noted that the requirement to have one of these conditions to legitimise all instances of personal data processing is additional to, and separate from, from the obligation described at 3.7 above to provide a 'fair collection statement'.

	The Conditions for Processing Personal Data **(Data Protection Act 1998, Schedule 2)**
(1)	The data subject has given his/her consent to the processing.
(2)	The processing is necessary: (a) for the performance of a contract to which the data subject is a party; or (b) for the taking of steps at the request of the data subject with a view to entering into a contract.
(3)	The processing is necessary for compliance with any legal obligation to which the data controller is subject, other than an obligation imposed by contract.
(4)	The processing is necessary in order to protect the vital interests of the data subject.
(5)	The processing is necessary: (a) for the administration of justice; (b) for the exercise of any functions conferred on any person by or under any enactment; (c) for the exercise of any functions of the Crown, a Minister of the Crown or a government department; or (d) for the exercise of any other functions of a public nature exercised in the public interest by any person.
(6)	The processing is necessary for the purposes of legitimate interests pursued by the data controller or by the third party or parties to whom the data are disclosed, except where the processing is unwarranted in any particular case by reason of prejudice to the rights and freedoms or legitimate interests of the data subject.

3.16 Although some of the six conditions in the table are relatively self-explanatory, others require further explanation, as set out below.

CONSENT

3.17 The first, and most controversial, of the legitimising conditions is consent. Although 'consent' is not defined in the DPA, the European Directive, upon which the Act is based, states that it means:

'... any freely given specific and informed indication of his wishes by which the data subject signifies his agreement to personal data relating to him being processed.'

3.18 The word 'signify' indicates the need for some active communication between the parties and means that the non-response to a communication from a data controller cannot constitute consent.

3.19 The words 'freely given' mean that there can be no element of coercion on the individual to give consent. Further, nothing must be conditional on the giving of consent, eg a job with the company. Accordingly, data protection consent provisions cannot be included within an employment contract.

3.20 Consent is viewed as a last resort for most types of processing, not least because the Commissioner has indicated that he is not keen on organisations relying on consent generally, particularly in the context of processing staff data. Further, it must be borne in mind that it is inherent in the nature of consent that it can usually be withdrawn by the data subject at any time. However, consent will often be the only available option for certain types of processing, one of which is direct marketing.

3.21 There is some controversy surrounding the issue of whether 'implied' consent can be acceptable. In some cases it may be appropriate to rely on implied consent although it will not be lawful in other cases. Legal advice should be sought before relying on implied consent.

Consent & direct marketing

3.22 Certain types of processing, notably direct marketing, can perhaps be legitimised only by obtaining some form of 'consent'.

3.23 Consent may be obtained by a number of methods. Use of an opt-out clause is particularly common with commercial organisations. An example of such a clause is:

☐ **Please tick the box if you do not wish to be contacted in the future about products/services that we believe may be useful to you.**

3.24 It is important that such a clause is drafted to take account of all the anticipated uses of the personal data by the organisation concerned. It may be for example that an organisation wishes only to send marketing information concerning its own products or services to its customers. On the other hand, the organisation may wish to transfer copies of its customer database to 'carefully chosen' third parties.

3.25 Another type of clause is the 'opt-in' type – this will successfully take consent only where the individual ticks the box to show that he assents to the processing described. An example of an opt-in clause is as follows:

☐   **Yes, I am happy for my email address to be provided to your carefully chosen business partners so that they can send me details of their products and services.**

3.26 Companies should note that the law is complex in the area of direct marketing. Readers wishing to learn more about legitimising direct marketing are referred to a standard legal text, such as *Data Protection – a practical guide to UK and EU law* by Peter Carey (Oxford University Press).

Direct marketing by email

3.27 When using electronic communications (emails, text messages, MMS, etc), to promote the products or services of a company, it must be borne in mind that European Directive 2002/58/EC and Directive 2009/136 – implemented in the UK by the Privacy and Electronic Communications (EC Directive) Regulations 2003 and 2011 – generally require (with one important exception) *opt-in* consents.

3.28 Thus 'opt-in' consent – see **3.25** above – must now be obtained prior to conducting all email marketing (eg emails to customers or potential customers informing them of the organisation's products/services) except where:

(1)   the sending company obtained the electronic contact details from the intended recipient in the context of a sale or negotiations for the sale of a product or service;

(2)   the marketing relates to the sender's own similar/products services; and

(3)   opt-outs (unsubscribe opportunities) were provided at the point of data collection and on each subsequent marketing communication.

3.29 These rules effectively render the email list rental business unlawful in the vast majority of cases – organisations should buy lists of email addresses for marketing purposes only in very exceptional circumstances and only where they obtain clear warranties concerning the legality of their use for marketing purposes.

3.30 Further, opt-in consents will usually need to be obtained prior to conducting email marketing campaigns unless there is some prior course of dealings with the intended recipients of the communication.

3.31 The law in this area is complex. Readers are advised to seek legal advice before sending marketing emails and text messages.

LEGITIMATE INTERESTS

3.32 The ICO recommends that two tests be applied to establish whether this condition may be appropriate in any particular case – both tests must be satisfied. The first is the establishment of the legitimacy of the interests pursued by the company or the third party to whom the data are to be disclosed. The second is whether the processing is unwarranted in the particular case by reason of prejudice to the rights and freedoms or legitimate interests of the data subject. The latter test is weighted in favour of the individual, as opposed to the company, by the fact that, due to the protective nature of the legislation, the interests of a data subject will usually override those of the data controller.

SENSITIVE PERSONAL DATA

3.33 There are further restrictions on the processing of 'sensitive personal data'. In order to use this data in a company, the company must have at least one of a set of pre-defined reasons to do so. Sensitive personal data is defined as any information that gives an indication of one or more of the factors shown in the box below.

Sensitive Personal Data

(a) the racial or ethnic origin of the data subject;

(b) his/her political opinions;

(c) his/her religious beliefs or other beliefs of a similar nature;

(d) whether he/she is a member of a trade union;

(e) his/her physical or mental health or condition;

(f) his/her sexual life;

(g) the commission or alleged commission by him/her of any offence.

3.34 Schedule 3 to the DPA contains a set of legitimising reasons for the processing of sensitive personal data – see **3.37** below. Member States of the European Union are permitted to create further exemptions – the UK has created a further 10 such exemptions in the form of secondary legislation. Companies should (as part of a data protection compliance review or otherwise) ensure that they are aware of all the types of sensitive personal data that they process. Any processing of sensitive personal data that is not needed for the proper or desired operation of the organisation should cease.

3.35 As with non-sensitive personal data, organisations should try to find a legitimising condition other than consent. If explicit consent is the only likely candidate, then it must be borne in mind that 'explicit' in this context means fully informed and freely given consent (see above for the meaning of 'freely given'). This will require specific detail being given to the data subject on the precise uses for the data and any disclosures of the data that may be made by the data controller. Explicit consent cannot be obtained by way of an 'opt-out' clause, although an 'opt-in' clause will often suffice – see **3.25** above.

3.36 A full list of the reasons to use sensitive personal data appears at **3.37**. Readers wishing to obtain further detail on the scope of the reasons are directed to Schedule 3 to the Act, the Data Protection (Processing of Sensitive Personal Data) Order 2000 and Guidance from the Information Commissioner, as well as the standard texts on data protection law.

Sensitive personal data – legitimising conditions

3.37   The following is the list of 'reasons' specified by the Act for the lawful processing of sensitive personal data. Those shown in bold are likely to be the most relevant for private companies:

- **Explicit consent of the data subject**
- **Compliance with employment law obligations**
- Vital interests of the data subject
- Processing by not-for-profit organisation
- Information made public by the data subject
- **Legal advice and establishing or defending legal rights**
- Public functions (administration of justice, etc)
- Medical purposes
- **Records on racial equality**
- **Detection of unlawful activity**
- Protection of the public
- Public interest disclosure
- Confidential counselling
- Certain data relating to pensions
- **Religion and health data for equality of treatment monitoring**
- Legitimate political activities
- **Research activities that are in the substantial public interest**
- Police processing
- Processing by elected representatives

Sensitive personal data about staff

3.38   For most companies, the most common occurrence of sensitive personal data processing will arise in the context of staff information. Sickness and injury records will always constitute 'sensitive personal data'. According to the June 2005 version of the Employment Code (available from the ICO website at www.ico.org.uk), these records should, where possible, be kept separate from other records – eg records relating to the *fact* that a worker is absent and the length of absence should be kept separately from records relating to the *reason* for the absence. The latter will constitute sensitive personal data, thus bringing into play the higher level of protection for this data.

3.39 According to the ICO, access to sensitive personal data should be restricted to those members of staff who require access to carry out their functions and who have received appropriate training in data protection.

CONCLUSION

3.40 The first Data Protection Principle is perhaps the most difficult for companies to comply with. The first Principle not only requires that information be supplied to the data subject at the point of acquisition but also that all processing comply with appropriate conditions. Accordingly, care should be taken to ensure that all personal data processing complies with the above requirements.

CHAPTER 4

RIGHT TO ACCESS PERSONAL DATA

4.1   The most important of the rights of an individual in data protection is the right to make a 'data subject access request'. This right enables an individual to gain access to a copy of all the personal data held about him/her by any UK organisation. For smaller companies without a compliance officer or data protection officer, dealing with an access request will often fall to a director or the company secretary.

4.2   An access request can be made by any person, although usually it will be made by someone about whom the company is processing personal data, for example a member of staff, a former member of staff, job applicant, director, shareholder or customer.

4.3   One of the most common types of complaint to the ICO is from individuals who have made an access request and have not received the documentation that they were expecting. Accordingly, the handling of subject access requests is one of the most important aspects of data protection for companies to get right.

FORM OF SUBJECT ACCESS REQUEST

4.4   The DPA does not specify any particular method of request for data subject access, save that it be 'in writing' – it is clear that this includes email. It also includes a request made via social media, eg Facebook or Twitter.

IDENTITY OF REQUESTOR

4.5   A company need not comply with the request where it is uncertain as to the identity of the person making it. The company may request reasonable identification proof. It is suggested that, where a data subject sends a personally signed letter to a data controller, that will in most cases constitute sufficient identification. However, there may be occasions when compliance with a subject access request that has been made by signed letter may be inappropriate, and may even constitute a breach of the DPA. This will be especially true in circumstances where it is reasonably likely that the request had come from someone other than the person whom it purports to be from. Additional identifying documentation may be requested, such as a photocopy of a driving licence or passport.

FEES & TIME LIMIT

4.6   A company may, if it chooses to do so, make a charge for subject access but that fee must not usually be more than the statutory maximum amount of £10. It should be noted that the new General Data Protection Regulation will limit the ability of companies to charge a fee – see Chapters 11 and 14.

4.7   Companies have 40 days from the date of the receipt of the request in which to comply with the request. Where the company makes a charge for access, the 40-day period does not start until the fee is paid.

EXTENT

4.8   The right of subject access is extremely wide-ranging and may involve the company in many man-hours to find the relevant information. Unless a relevant exemption applies – see **4.27** below – an individual is entitled to see his/her personal data contained in all locations, including the locations shown in the table below:

Possible locations for Personal Data within the Company (non-exhaustive list)	
Appraisal records	Disciplinary records
Minutes of Board Meetings	Sickness records
Marketing information	Performance review notes
Emails stored on any system in the workplace	Interview notes
References received from third parties	Customer files/CRM systems
Register of Directors	Register of Members

4.10   It should be noted that an individual is entitled to see only his/her own personal data. Accordingly, he/she will not be able to see any information that relates to anyone else – see further under 'Third Party Data' at **4.24** below.

OBLIGATIONS OF COMPANIES

4.9 By virtue of the right to make a subject access request, any individual is able to contact any UK organisation and request to know whether that organisation is processing personal data concerning him/her. By virtue of s 7 of DPA, an organisation processing any such data must give the individual a description of:

(i)   the personal data of which that individual is the data subject;

(ii)   the purpose(s) for which they are being or are to be processed; and

(iii) the recipient(s) or class(es) of recipient(s) to whom they are or may be disclosed.

4.10 Further, the individual is entitled to have communicated to him/her in an intelligible form, the information itself, as well as the source of that information. Where any processing of the individual's personal data is undertaken by some automated means, he/she is entitled to be informed of the logic involved in the decision-taking – see Chapter 5.

4.11 Generally the obligation to provide 'subject access' will be met by gathering together all the personal data held on the requesting individual, and providing him/her with a copy of it.

PAPER RECORDS

4.12 In addition to the right of an individual to see all electronically held personal data, the right of subject access also obliges companies to supply copies of certain paper records. All paper-based records that form part of a 'relevant filing system' are included within the ambit of a data subject access request.

4.13 A 'relevant filing system' is defined as:

> 'Any set of information relating to individuals to the extent that, although the information is not processed by means of equipment operating automatically in response to instructions given for that purpose, the set is structured, either by reference to individuals or by reference to criteria relating to individuals, in such a way that specific information relating to a particular individual is readily accessible.'

4.14 The key requirement is that the method of filing (structuring) must make for easy access to particular data. If a record can be found within a reasonable time, it is likely that the manual filing system is within the scope of the Act.

4.15 The definition of 'relevant filing system' was narrowed somewhat by the court decision in *Durant v The Financial Services Authority*.[1]

---

[1]   [2003] EWCA Civ 1746.

In this case the Court of Appeal sought to limit the ambit of data protection law relating to manual files to those systems that allow access to information almost as easily as electronic ones – in other words, the system would need to be highly structured and easily searchable.

PRACTICAL STEPS FOR COMPANIES

4.16 All organisations must be in a position to comply with a subject access request. This is likely to mean an investigation by a relevant officer, perhaps the company secretary, of existing data processing systems – the purpose of this is:

(1)   to establish relevant knowledge as to the location of all personal data processed within the company, and

(2)   to discover the nature of the personal data held with a view to purging any unlawfully held data or data that the company would rather not disclose should it receive an access request.

4.17 HR departments will be particularly concerned to ensure that records held are in compliance with the eight Data Protection Principles. These departments often have massive quantities of paper stored in manual files by alphabetical reference to employees' surnames. Managers should ensure that all files are kept up to date and do not contain material that should not be seen by employees or, often more importantly, former employees.

4.18 A data subject access request made to a company will be deemed to relate to all the personal data held by the company on the requesting individual. However, an individual may by virtue of s 7(7) of DPA expressly limit his/her application to certain data.

4.19 The obligation on a data controller to supply the personal data to the data subject in an intelligible form will usually be complied with by sending copies of all relevant files. Where codes have been employed by the controller, the data subject should be given either a decoded version or the key. However, a physical copy of the data does not have to be made available to the data subject where:

(a)   the supply of such a copy is not possible or would involve disproportionate effort, or

(b)   the individual agrees otherwise.

4.20 There is no definition of 'disproportionate effort' in the Act, but it is likely to require more than mere inconvenience. It should be remembered that, even where a copy of the data does not have to be supplied (eg due to disproportionate effort), the remaining requirements to provide appropriate descriptions, the logic behind automated decisions and information as to the data source, still remain.

4.21 The requirement on data controllers to disclose the source of the personal data is not accompanied in the legislation by a parallel obligation to keep records of the source. Of course it is possible that the latter obligation will be inferred, either by the ICO or the court, from the presence of the requirement to disclose.

4.22 In order to thwart those nuisance applicants who make repeated subject access requests, a company is relieved from the obligation to comply with a second or subsequent request from the same individual where a 'reasonable time' has not elapsed since the last request.

4.23 For problematic access requests, or where one or more of the exemptions is likely to apply, companies should seek legal advice.

THIRD PARTY DATA

4.24 There will be circumstances where compliance with a subject access request would lead to the disclosure of another individual's personal information. In these circumstances the company may have the option to withhold this data. However, the company may disclose third party data where either:

- the third party has consented to the disclosure, or
- it is reasonable in the circumstances to make the disclosure.

4.25 Where an employee (or former employee) requests to see his/her file, the question arises as to whether the employee is entitled to see his/her 'appraisal' documents. On the one hand the employee would not be entitled to see these documents as they disclose third party data (the name and opinions of the person who carried out the appraisal). On the other hand the employee already knows the identity of the appraiser (as he/she was presumably present at the appraisal) and so it would be reasonable to make the disclosure.

4.26 In most cases any document that contains third party data should be disclosed with the third party data blocked out or redacted.

EXCEPTIONS

4.27 There are a number of exceptions to the obligation on companies to disclose personal data following a subject access request. The most significant are listed below:

- Confidential references – the author/giver of a confidential reference is exempt from the need to disclose that reference.
- Prevention/detection of crime (eg certain CCTV images).

- Legal professional privilege (eg communications with the company's lawyers regarding an employee or customer).

- Management forecasting – personal data used for this purpose is exempt from disclosure for as long as the management forecasting activity continues.

- Negotiations – personal data used for this purpose is exempt from disclosure for as long as the negotiations continue.

4.28 The precise scope of these exemptions is complex and companies are advised to seek legal advice when considering using an exemption unless the exemption is clear.

CHAPTER 5

OTHER RIGHTS OF INDIVIDUALS

5.1   In addition to the data subject access right, individuals have further rights under the DPA. UK companies are under an obligation to process data in such a way as to be compatible with these rights. The sixth Data Protection Principle provides:

> 'Personal data shall be processed in accordance with the rights of data subjects under this Act.'

CESSATION OF PROCESSING

5.2   Any individual can request a company to cease, or not begin, the processing of personal data of which he/she is the data subject on the ground that:

'(a)   the processing of those data … is likely to cause substantial damage or substantial distress to him or another, and

(b)   that damage or distress is or would be unwarranted.'

5.3   However, the right to request the cessation of processing does not apply where the processing being undertaken is with the consent of the data subject, or necessary for the performance of a contract with the data subject, or necessary for compliance with a legal obligation; or necessary to protect the vital interests of the data subject.

5.4   Once a data controller receives a request for the cessation of processing, it must respond to the data subject in writing within 21 days. The response must either outline the data controller's intention to comply with the request or explain why the request is unjustified.

5.5   The right to cessation of processing is enforceable by court order where the data controller refuses to comply.

DIRECT MARKETING

5.6   Direct marketing ('the communication of any advertising or marketing material that is directed to particular individuals') takes many familiar forms such as posting brochures, commercial emails, and cold calling. It also includes online advertising that has been specifically targeted to a particular individual, eg banner advertisements on websites that appear only to certain users (behavioural advertising).

5.7 The DPA gives an absolute right to individuals to require any UK organisation to stop sending direct marketing materials. The right must be exercised in writing to the data controller and is enforceable by court order where the data controller fails to comply.

5.8 A company receiving a request for cessation of direct marketing should immediately alter its records to ensure that the requesting individual is not sent further materials. Ideally the individual should be informed that his/her request has been actioned. The details of the requester can be retained on the company's marketing database to ensure that he/she is not targeted in future.

AUTOMATED DECISIONS

5.9 There are two main rights in respect of 'automated decisions' (those decisions that are taken based solely on processing that has been undertaken by automated means and that substantially affect the data subject).

5.10 The first is the right of an individual to request that no automated decisions are taken about him/her for the purpose of evaluating matters relating to him/her. Such matters might, for example, be credit worthiness (automated credit scoring), reliability (automated time recording systems) or performance at work (automated performance indicators).

5.11 The second right is that an individual is entitled to be informed when an automated decision has been taken. This right applies only in the absence of any request having been received by a data controller for the cessation of automated decision-taking. Any data controller that takes an automated decision must inform the relevant individual as soon as reasonably practical that such a decision has been taken. The individual has 21 days in which to require the data controller to retake the decision by alternative means (ie with some human intervention).

5.12 Where the individual sends this notice (known as a 'data subject notice') to the data controller, a further period of 21 days arises during which the data controller must write to the individual concerned specifying the steps it intends to take to comply with the notice.

5.13 Neither the right of an individual to request that no automated decisions are taken concerning him/her, nor the obligation on a data controller to inform him/her that an automated decision has been taken, applies to an 'exempt decision'.

5.14 An exempt decision is one where one of the conditions from each of the following two lists is present. The first list is the following:

(a) the decision is taken in the course of steps taken for the purpose of considering whether to enter into a contract with the data subject; or
(b) the decision is taken in the course of steps taken with a view to entering into such a contract; or
(c) the decision is taken in the course of steps taken in the course of performing such a contract; or
(d) the decision is authorised or required by or under any law.

The second list contains the following two alternatives:

(a) the effect of the decision is to grant a request of the data subject; or
(b) steps have been taken to safeguard the legitimate interests of the data subject (for example, by allowing him/her to make representations).

5.15 As with the other rights, the right to have a decision retaken by non-automated means is enforceable by court order.

5.16 It should be remembered that, where an individual makes a data subject access request (see Chapter 5), he/she is entitled to be informed of the logic involved in automated decision-taking. In most cases this will require data controllers to explain in general terms how the relevant software operates and what criteria are taken into account in drawing any relevant conclusions.

COMPENSATION

5.17 Compensation may be claimed by any person who suffers damage as a result of the contravention by the data controller of any provision of the DPA.

5.18 Compensation may also be claimed where a person suffers distress as a result of the data controller's contravention of the DPA. However, to obtain compensation for distress an individual must show either that he/she has suffered damage or that the contravention relates to processing for one of the following purposes:

• journalism;
• art;
• literature.

5.19 In a court action for compensation for damage and/or distress, it is a defence for the data controller to show that all reasonable care was taken to comply with the provision concerned. Applications to court for compensation are extremely rare due to the expense involved.

RECTIFICATION, BLOCKING, ERASURE & DESTRUCTION

5.20 The confusing terminology that comprises the right to 'rectification, blocking, erasure or destruction' means that an individual is entitled to have any inaccuracies corrected in relation to data held by any data controller.

5.21 This right is enforceable by court order. Usually a data subject would become aware of inaccuracies in data, either where he/she has received some communication from a data controller or where he/she has made a subject access request.

CONCLUSION

5.22 Organisations must ensure that their processing activities are carried out in compliance with the rights of individuals. An assessment should be undertaken to determine whether any 'automated decisions' are made and there should be a system in place whereby checks on the accuracy of data are made on a regular basis.

5.23 Organisations must ensure that their customer and prospective customer databases are set up in such a way that an individual's details can be deleted from mailing lists for direct marketing purposes where he/she makes a request for direct marketing to stop.

CHAPTER 6

SECURITY AND OUTSOURCING

6.1 The seventh Data Protection Principle requires that all personal data processing be undertaken in a secure environment. This requires 'appropriate' measures to be adopted to ensure that unauthorised processing does not occur and that data are not accidentally lost, stolen or destroyed.

6.2 Arising out of the security requirement in the DPA is an obligation on companies to ensure that all staff who use personal data are adequately trained in data protection. The ICO has stressed the need for staff training, and indeed the majority of fines that have been imposed by the Commissioner against companies have been for breach of the security requirement. For junior staff the training will often to be to a basic level and may consist of a short course or appropriate reading. Senior staff and heads of departments will be expected to undertake more in-depth training, including refresher sessions.

PRACTICAL IMPLICATIONS OF SECURITY

6.3 Many of the provisions that should be adopted by companies are 'common sense' and include using anti-virus protection, firewalls and passwords for restriction of access to secure areas. Others are less familiar and will include vetting of all organisations with which the company does business, carrying out data security surveys, adopting 'clear desk' policies and using encryption technologies for the transfer of personal data to third parties. For further advice, companies should consult a data security specialist. (See *A Practical Guide to IT Security* at **Appendix 6.**)

NOTIFICATION OF DATA SECURITY BREACHES

6.4 At present there is no legal obligation in the UK to inform customers whose data have been lost or stolen in a 'security breach', eg a successful hacking or data theft event. However, the new General Data Protection Regulation will require organisations that have suffered a security breach to inform all of their customers of the breach; laws have already been passed in most states of the United States in an attempt to:

(1) encourage compliance with security obligations; and

(2) provide those potentially affected by a breach with relevant knowledge.

The new law will also require breaches to be notified to the ICO.

OUTSOURCING OF DATA PROCESSING

6.5   Special rules apply to the situation where a company engages another company to carry out certain operations or functions on its behalf.

6.6   Where processing of personal data is carried out by a third party company (known as a 'data processor') on behalf of the company, the company must:

(a)   choose a data processor that provides sufficient guarantees in respect of the technical and organisational measures governing the security of the processing to be carried out; and

(b)   take reasonable steps to ensure compliance with those measures.

6.7   Data controllers must also enter into a written contract with data processors, which must contain specific requirements – see **6.10** below.

6.8   Data controllers remain responsible under the DPA for the processing carried out by their data processors. Data processors have no DPA obligations themselves in respect of the processing they carry out on behalf of the data controller.

Examples of data processors

6.9   The following types of third party service providers are 'data processors':

- call centres
- debt collectors
- database management companies
- mailing houses
- payroll providers
- website hosting companies
- confidential waste management agents
- outsourced IT providers.

(This is a non-exhaustive list.)

Checklist for use of data processors

6.10 Companies that outsource one or more forms of data processing should:

(1) Ensure there is a contractual obligation on the data processor that the processing is undertaken only in accordance with the company's instructions.

(2) Ensure that the processing by the data processor is undertaken only for the purpose(s), and in the manner, stated in the contract.

(3) Ensure that all staff at the data processor are adequately trained in data security measures.

(4) Ensure there is a contractual obligation on the data processor to implement specific security measures, both in terms of physical security and technical security such as protection from corruption by virus; and to consult the organisation before changing any such measures.

(5) Ensure the company has rights of access to and inspection of the processor's premises and systems to ensure that security measures are being implemented.

(6) Restrict the data processor's ability to sub-contract any of its obligations.

(See *Outsourcing: A Guide for Small and Medium-Sized Businesses* at **Appendix 5.**)

CHAPTER 7

EXPORT OF PERSONAL DATA

7.1 The eighth Data Protection Principle prevents, subject to exceptions, the sending of personal data to destinations that are not within the European Economic Area – the list of countries within the EEA is shown in the table below.

7.2 The exceptions to this rule include transfers to those countries that have adequate data protection legislation (the shortlist of such 'safe' countries comprises Switzerland, Guernsey, Jersey, the Isle of Man, Canada and Argentina) and where the exporter and importer have contractually agreed to treat the data in accordance with standard provisions. A further exception, known as 'safe harbor', was agreed by the US and the EU in 2000 to allow transfers of personal data from Europe to certain companies within the US but this agreement was declared invalid by the European Court of Justice in October 2015. The court decided in the case of *Maximillian Schrems v Data Protection Commissioner* (Court of Justice of the European Union, Case C-362/14) that safe harbor was a voluntary scheme only and allowed the US authorities to gain access to personal data in breach of the fundamental right to privacy.

7.3 The new General Data Protection Regulation will introduce a new regime for the transfer of personal data outside the EU – see Chapter 12.

EEA Countries

Austria	Greece	Norway
Belgium	Hungary	Poland
Bulgaria	Iceland	Portugal
Croatia	Ireland	Romania
Cyprus	Italy	Slovak Republic
Czech Republic	Latvia	Slovenia
Denmark	Liechtenstein	Spain
Estonia	Lithuania	Sweden
Finland	Luxembourg	United Kingdom
France	Malta	
Germany	Netherlands	

CHAPTER 8

OTHER OBLIGATIONS OF DATA CONTROLLERS

INTRODUCTION

8.1   The most important obligations in data protection law have been discussed in previous chapters. In terms of compliance, those obligations are likely to be the most costly in terms of time and cost. The remaining obligations can be stated simply – they are those that derive from the second, third, fourth and fifth Data Protection Principles.

SPECIFIC & COMPATIBLE PURPOSES

8.2   The second Data Protection Principle provides that personal data shall be obtained only for one or more specified and lawful purposes, and shall not be further processed in any manner incompatible with that purpose or those purposes. Accordingly, data obtained for one purpose should not be used for another purpose.

ADEQUACY, RELEVANCE & EXCESSIVENESS OF DATA

8.3   By virtue of the third Data Protection Principle, organisations must not hold data about individuals that is excessive for the purpose(s) for which the information was acquired or is held – this makes it essential for organisations to make clear statements to individuals as to the reasons for holding personal data. Organisations should also review the forms (both online and offline) on which they collect personal data to review the information requested and to make a determination as to whether the entirety of all such information is actually needed.

Data must also be adequate and relevant to the purpose(s) of processing.

ACCURACY

8.4   The fourth Data Protection Principle requires that all data held on individuals must be accurate and up to date. This is an ongoing obligation and organisations should have in place an effective procedure for ensuring the accuracy of all data.

DATA RETENTION

8.5   The fifth Data Protection Principle requires that personal data must not be kept for longer than is necessary for their purpose(s). Organisations will therefore need to determine how long their data will be needed and should implement a procedure for rolling data destruction, as necessary. The table below shows a few examples of possible retention periods for various types of personal data relating to employees.

Type of Information	Possible Retention Period
Job applicants' data (where applicant is unsuccessful)	Four months from the recruitment decision
Annual leave information	One year from end of the year in which the annual leave was taken
Disciplinary records	Six years after conclusion of the disciplinary process
Salary details	Two years after the worker has left employment
Accidents on the premises	Three years from the date of the accident

CHAPTER 9

ENFORCEMENT AND COMPLIANCE

ENFORCEMENT REGIME

9.1 There are various powers of enforcement available to the ICO, including the power to request information on the methods that a company has adopted to store, use and transfer personal data and the power to require remedial action where processing operations do not comply with the law. These powers are discussed in detail in Chapter 16.

9.2 Of most significance perhaps is the power of the ICO to fine organisations for data protection breaches. Since April 2010 the Commissioner has been able to fine companies up to £500,000 per breach. The new General Data Protection Regulation will dramatically increase the fines that may be levied – up to €20 million (£14.8 million approx.) or up to 4% of a company's global annual turnover, as appropriate.

9.3 In November 2010 the ICO imposed the first two fines. Hertfordshire County Council was fined £100,000 for sending two faxes containing sensitive personal data to the wrong recipients. In the same month an employment agency, A4e, was fined £60,000 for allowing an employee to take home an unencrypted laptop containing personal data (the laptop was stolen from the employee's house in a burglary).

COMPLIANCE PROGRAMME

9.4 All organisations must consider how they will implement an appropriate data protection compliance programme. The elements of a compliance programme or framework are discussed in Chapter 15. Most organisations (except the smallest companies) will need to appoint a person who will have responsibility for data protection within the company. In the case of medium and larger sized companies, this will be a full-time role. The Data Protection Officer or Compliance Officer should be a relatively senior appointment within the organisation, and will require appropriate training to perform the role.

9.5 An initial audit is advisable, particularly where a company is addressing data protection issues for the first time. Audits can be carried out by internal personnel if they have sufficient expertise. Alternatively, there are many suppliers of audit services, including the larger law firms and specialist data protection services providers.

Part 2

THE NEW REGIME

CHAPTER 10

DATA PROTECTION – THE NEW RULES

EXECUTIVE SUMMARY

10.1 The new General Data Protection Regulation will transform the data protection landscape for companies and organisations of all kinds that hold personal data in relation to clients, customers, employees and third parties. The Regulation has been negotiated over the last four years between the various EU institutions and the Member States, and was finalised in April 2016. It will come into force on 25 May 2018. This book sets out the new rules provided by the Regulation as approved by the Council of Ministers, the European Parliament and the European Commission. The Regulation will repeal the DPA and the EU Directive 95/46/EC on which the DPA is based. It will apply to all business sectors.

(1) Consent to processing of personal data must be informed and explicit. Prior to giving consent, the individual concerned, ie the data subject, must be informed of his/her right to withdraw it at any time. However, a company should not rely solely on consent to legitimate its data processing: the overriding principle is that the company as the data controller should treat data subjects fairly. Even before the company starts data processing, it must fully inform the data subject so that he/she can decide whether to consent or not. In the event of a dispute, the company must be able to show the data subject consented. And the request for consent must be presented in a manner that is 'clearly distinguishable from the other matters in an intelligible and easily accessible form, using clear and plain language'.
This means that consent will become harder to obtain and, in the event of a challenge, defend.

(2) The respective positions of the parties are relevant to the question whether consent is freely given. Consent will not be a valid ground for the processing if there is a 'clear imbalance' between the data subject and the data controller, and this imbalance makes it unlikely that consent was freely given in the circumstances. Consent will also be regarded as not freely given if the data processing consists of separate and distinct operations, each of which would require a specific consent. Likewise if the performance of a contract is stated to be dependent on the data subject's consent, where this is not so and he/she cannot obtain the same services from another party without consent.

Accordingly, the default cannot be that the data subject has consented to the processing, in the absence of some indication by him/her to that effect.

(3) The Regulation provides that extensive information must be given to data subjects regarding the processing of their personal data, including: the identity and contact details of the data controller; the purpose(s) and 'legal basis' of the data processing; any third party to whom the data may be disclosed; whether the controller intends to transfer the data to a country or international organisation outside the EU; and the right of the data subject to access the data, to have it rectified if necessary or erased, to object to the data processing, and to transfer the data to another data controller in a suitable format.

Companies will have to be to be open and transparent in their dealings with clients, customers, employees and suppliers.

(4) This requirement as to transparency is a specific obligation of the data controller, who must take 'appropriate measures to provide any information relating to the processing of personal data to the data subject in an intelligible and easily accessible, using clear and plain language'. The information may be given verbally or in writing. If verbally, the controller must take particular care as to the identity of the data subject: identity is harder to establish on a phone call than in writing. Transparency extends to the purpose(s) of the processing. Where the controller intends to process the data for some purpose(s) other than that/those for which it was obtained, ie 'further processing', the controller should so inform the data subject.

(5) Regardless of whether a company is operating as a data controller, ie determines the purpose(s) and means of the data processing, or a data processor, ie operating on behalf of the data controller and on its instructions, the company will be liable for breach of relevant provisions of the new Regulation. Accordingly, companies that provide data processing services, including cloud services, will be liable to data subjects in addition to any sanction that may be imposed by the Information Commissioner's Office (ICO).

(6) The Regulation introduces a specific 'right to be forgotten', subject to certain exceptions. The data controller must erase any personal data without undue delay in the following circumstances:

- if the controller no longer requires the data for the original purpose(s) for which it was obtained;
- if the data subject withdraws his/her consent to the data processing and there are no other legal grounds for it;
- if the data subject objects to the processing and there are no overriding legitimate grounds for it or the processing is for direct marketing purposes;
- if the processing has not been done lawfully;
- the data must be erased for compliance with a legal obligation of the company.

Companies must have appropriate procedures to allow individuals to be forgotten.

(7) If the controller has disclosed the data to other parties, eg a subcontractor, it must make contact with them in order to protect the data subject's right to be forgotten. The Regulation obliges the controller to take reasonable steps to 'inform controllers which are processing the data, that the data subject has requested the erasure by such controllers of any links to, or copy or replication of that personal data'. In determining what steps to take, the controller may take into account the available technology and the cost of implementation.

(8) The new Regulation aims to make it easier for data subjects to switch from one service provider to another and so requires data controllers to make the relevant data available in a format that facilitates the transfer. The Regulation provides for the portability of personal data relating to the data subject from one data controller to another in a 'commonly used and machine readable format'. *Companies will have to ensure that all data is in a suitable format.*

(9) The new Regulation sets limits on the extent to which companies can create a personal profile of an individual for marketing or other purpose. 'Profiling' is defined as:

> 'any form of automated processing of personal data consisting of the use of personal data to evaluate certain personal aspects relating to a natural person, in particular to analyse or predict aspects concerning that natural person's performance at work, economic situation, location, health, personal preferences, reliability, behavior, location or movements.'

In scope are decisions made by a company based solely on automated processing, including profiling, that produce 'legal effects' concerning the data subject or significantly affect him/her. The Regulation allows profiling only in certain circumstances to protect customers from improper or unlawful use of their data. Profiling is prohibited if it does not include appropriate measures to safeguard the rights of the data subject, including his/her right to be consulted, and is not:

- necessary to enter into or perform a contract with the data subject;
- expressly authorised by law; or
- done with the data subject's explicit consent and appropriate safeguards. This consent can be withdrawn at any time. In the event of a dispute, the onus is on the company to show that the data subject consented to the profiling.

(10) The Regulation makes provision for 'Big Data' in the form of further processing of personal data, and sets out the factors to be considered as to whether the purpose(s) of any further processing is/are compatible with the original purpose(s). Personal data must be collected for specified, explicit and legitimate purposes and not further processed in a way incompatible with those purposes; however, further processing of personal data for archiving purposes in the public interest or scientific, statistical or historical purposes is not considered incompatible with the original purpose(s). A separate consent will be required for any further processing that is incompatible with the original purpose(s), unless the further

processing is for archiving, statistical, research or historical purposes. However, the Regulation also provides that further processing by the same data controller is permitted on the grounds of the legitimate interests of the controller or a third party if these interests override the interests of the data subject(s) in the circumstances. This will oblige the controller or third party, as the case may be, to establish why they need to process the data further to the original purpose(s) and whether it outweighs the interests of the data subject(s) involved.

The company will have to balance the business need to process the data further against the interests of the individual(s) concerned.

(11) 'Data protection by design' is a new concept introduced by the Regulation and requires the company to put in place 'appropriate technical and organisational measures' to protect personal data. 'Data protection by default' is also new and requires the company to ensure that, by default, only personal data may be processed that is necessary for the purpose(s) of the processing. Likewise, access to personal data must be limited to those people who need to have access to it.

(12) Extensive record-keeping is required by the new Regulation in order to demonstrate compliance. What is good business practice in any event is now a legal requirement. The new Regulation obliges the company to keep proper records of all its data processing operations. These records must include the following information:

- name and contact details of the data controller, ie the company, and any joint controller, and the data protection officer, if any;
- purpose(s) of the data processing, including the legitimate interests of the data controller if the processing is based on those interests;
- categories of data subjects and the personal data relating to them;
- categories of third parties to whom the data may be disclosed, including any third party in a country or international organisation outside the EU;
- if applicable, the categories of personal data transferred or to be transferred to countries or international organisations outside the EU;
- if possible, the anticipated timeframe for erasure of categories of personal data; and
- technical and organisational measures to secure the data.

The company must not only comply but be seen to comply.

(13) The company must carry out a 'data protection impact assessment' in the case of 'high risk' processing of personal data. This is any processing that involves new technology or has not been subject to an assessment previously or has become necessary due to the passage of time since the initial processing, ie further processing not envisaged at that time. The new Regulation introduces a specific requirement to consult the supervisory authority in certain circumstances, even before any data processing starts. Accordingly, the controller must consult with the ICO as the UK supervisory authority prior to the processing if the impact

assessment indicates that a high risk exists 'in the absence of measures to be taken by the controller to mitigate the risk'.

(14) The new Regulation gives a central role to an individual called a 'data protection officer' (DPO). The company may appoint a DPO or may be obliged to do so by EU law or the law of a Member State. Among other things, the DPO will be responsible to advise the company of its data protection obligations and monitor its compliance with them. He/she will also be the contact point for any dealings with the ICO and with the public. His/her qualifications for the job are based on expertise and knowledge of data protection requirements. He/she must be independent, must report to senior management of the company and cannot be dismissed except for gross misconduct or incompetence. The DPO may be either an employee or a consultant on an outsourced basis.

The company will have to consider appointing a DPO, not just for compliance reasons, but for business reasons and to be seen as a good corporate citizen.

(15) The Regulation allows a supervisory authority, the ICO in the UK, to levy considerable fines for breaches of specific provisions. These can amount to €20 million (£14.8 million approx.) or up to 4% of a company's total worldwide annual turnover in the preceding financial year, as appropriate. Breaches include:

- failure to process personal data fairly and lawfully or without the data subject's consent;
- failure to implement 'appropriate measures' to safeguard the interests of data subjects;
- failure of a data controller to ensure that a processor implements these measures in working on its behalf (see 'Key definitions' at **10.24** et seq below);
- failure to notify the ICO of a personal data breach or to inform the data subject(s) affected;
- failure to carry out a data protection impact assessment for 'high risk' processing or to consult with the ICO prior to the processing as required.

The company faces heavy penalties for any breach of the new Regulation.

INTRODUCTION

10.2

'Directive 95/46/EC is repealed.'

'This Regulation shall be binding in its entirety and directly applicable in all Member States.'

With these two simple sentences, buried at the end of a 260-page document, the European Union will flatten the sprawling mass of rules and regulations that govern the use of personal data. This document is the new EU Regulation on the subject of data protection. From the wreckage of the past will arise a magnificent new tower block, bristling with antennae and assorted projectiles that show real intent. And the intention is to destroy the disjointed laws and practices of 28 EU Member States and replace them with a single coherent statement of how personal data should be protected in Europe. This statement is in the form of the General Data Protection Regulation ('the Regulation' or 'new Regulation') that sets out the rights of EU citizens as well as the responsibilities of companies and organisations that hold information about them.

10.3 Directive 95/46/EC ('the Directive' or 'the 1995 Directive') is the basic law that has governed data protection in Europe to date. However, the EU has recognised that the Directive is outdated in the internet age and needed a complete overhaul to protect the personal data of individuals. The Directive and the 1981 Convention for the Protection of Individuals with regard to Automatic Processing of Personal Data ('the 1981 Convention') were implemented in the UK, with various amendments, by the ('DPA' or 'the Act'). The new Regulation will replace the 1995 Directive, the 1981 Convention and the DPA. As stated above, it has been agreed by the Council of Ministers, the European Parliament and the European Commission and will come into force on 25 May 2018.

10.4 Data protection is now more important than ever for large and small organisations. Private companies and public bodies hold vast amounts of personal data about their clients, customers, employees and suppliers. As a result, the Information Commissioner's Office ('ICO' or 'the Office') and the supervisory authorities in other EU countries closely monitor these organisations to ensure compliance with their data protection obligations. The stated mission of the ICO is to promote openness and transparency in dealing with personal data, and to uphold data privacy for individuals. (See www.ico.org.uk for information about the ICO.)

10.5 The ICO has substantial powers of enforcement, including substantial fines, and is not afraid to use them. It imposed a fine of £50,000 on Prudential Assurance in 2012 for mixing up data relating to two customers. Prudential had failed to keep their customers' data accurate and up to date, in breach of a principle of data protection. (The data protection principles are discussed in Chapter 11.) One of the customers involved had complained to Prudential over a long period of time but nothing was done to rectify matters. The ICO commented:

> 'We hope this penalty sends a message to all organisations but particularly those in the financial sector, that adequate checks must be in place to ensure people's records are accurate. Staff should also receive adequate training on how to manage and maintain them, with any concerns fully investigated in order to ensure problems are addressed at an early stage.'

10.6 The ICO is not the only authority in the UK with powers of enforcement in this area. Zurich Insurance was fined £2.3 million by the Financial Services

Authority (now the Financial Conduct Authority) in 2010 due to the loss of personal data relating to 46,000 customers.

10.7 Many of the provisions of the new Regulation are clear and self-explanatory, some are less so. But clear or not, they will impose a heavy burden on data controllers throughout the EU. They will require those who hold personal data to comply with specific (and many new) obligations as to the collection, storage, rectification, disclosure, transfer and deletion of data. This in turn will make it necessary for appropriate contracts to be put in place for any outsourcing arrangements between data controllers and data processors working for them in order to ensure adequate safeguards for personal data. These arrangements may provide for the outsourcing of various functions such as payroll or debt collection. In addition to regulatory sanctions for breach of the Regulation, data controllers and data processors face the prospect of court action by aggrieved customers in the form of a claim for compensation or other remedies. (These remedies and other rights of data subjects are discussed in Chapter 14.)

10.8 This book explains what companies are obliged to do and how they can comply with these new obligations. It describes the background to the new data protection regime. It analyses the legal and regulatory obligations, and the business requirements that flow from them. The relevant legislation is as follows:

- the DPA;
- the Privacy and Electronic Communications (EC Directive) Regulations 2003-15 ('PECR');
- other regulations made under the DPA; and
- the new Regulation.

10.9 The book is aimed primarily at those who are responsible for data protection in companies that process personal data in the course of their business.

Background

10.10 Data protection is all about privacy as a fundamental right of the individual. The EU Charter of Fundamental Rights 2000 recognises this fundamental right:

'1.   Everyone has the right to the protection of personal data concerning him or her.

2.   Such data must be processed fairly for specified purposes and on the basis of the consent of the person concerned or some other legitimate basis laid down by law. Everyone has the right of access to data which has been collected concerning him or her, and the right to have it rectified.

3.   Compliance with these rules shall be subject to control by an independent authority.'[1]

10.11   In the digital age the collection and storage of personal data are essential – as are the risks of this data falling into the wrong hands. Personal data is used by organisations of all kinds, including transfer from one country to another, both inside and outside the EU. There are no borders online and personal data may be sent anywhere around the world, from York to New York. One of the recitals, ie introductory sections, of the new Regulation specifically recognises the importance of cross-border flows of data:[2]

'The economic and social integration resulting from the functioning of the internal market has led to a substantial increase in cross-border flows of personal data. The exchange of personal data between economic and social, public and private actors, including natural persons, associations and undertakings across the Union increased.' (Recital 5)

10.12   Data protection rules have been in place in Europe since 1995 but Member States have differed in the way they implement the 1995 Directive. This has led to inconsistencies across the EU, which in turn create complexity, uncertainty and administrative costs. It has become apparent that the rules need to be streamlined and modernised to reflect today's online environment. One of the recitals to the new Regulation (Recital 9) recognises that:

'Differences in the level of protection of the rights and freedoms of natural persons, in particular the right to the protection of personal data, with regard to the processing of personal data in the Member States may prevent the free flow of personal data throughout the Union. Those differences may therefore constitute an obstacle to the pursuit of economic activities at the level of the Union, distort competition and impede authorities in the discharge of their responsibilities under Union law.'

The new Regulation

10.13   In January 2012 the European Commission proposed a comprehensive reform of the EU's data protection rules. This reform is the General Data Protection Regulation that was agreed between the various EU institutions in January, 2016. Among other objectives, the Commission sought to strengthen online privacy rights and boost Europe's digital economy. It stated that technological change and globalisation had profoundly changed the way that personal data is collected, accessed and used. The 1995 Directive was introduced before the advent of cloud computing, social networking, mass data storage and threats to data security. Furthermore, as stated above, the EU Member States implemented the rules in widely different ways. The Commission believes that a single law will do away with the current fragmentation and costly administration, with possible savings for business of

---

[1]   Article 8.
[2]   Note: recitals in the Regulation operate to clarify and interpret the relevant Articles.

€2.3 billion per annum. The new Regulation aims to boost consumer confidence in online services, providing growth in jobs and innovation throughout Europe.

10.14 In October 2013 the European Parliament backed the Commission's proposals and, indeed, strengthened them in certain respects. At the same time European heads of state committed to new data protection legislation at a meeting that focused on the digital economy, innovation and services. In a statement after their meeting the European Commission stated:

> 'Data is the currency of today's digital economy. Collected, analysed and moved across the globe, personal data has acquired enormous economic significance. According to some estimates, the value of European citizens' personal data has the potential to grow to nearly €1 trillion annually by 2020. Strengthening Europe's high standards of data protection is a business opportunity.'

10.15 The recent experience of a large US company revealed that the opposite is also true. A high standard of data protection represents a business opportunity but a data security breach can result in enormous costs and lost revenue. In March 2014 it was reported that a hacking incident at a major US retailer, Target, affected approximately 70 million customers in November and December 2013. The breach cost the company US$61 million in the first quarter of 2014 (*New York Times*, 14 March 2014).

10.16 Recent incidents of hacking and loss of data in the UK and other countries have focused public attention on the importance of data protection in all our lives. In particular, revelations by the US whistleblower, Edward Snowden, about data gathering operations of the US government have featured prominently in the media. The EU has raised concerns about access to personal data of EU citizens by the National Security Agency (NSA) in the US. The EU Commissioner for Justice, Vivian Reding, who is responsible to implement the new Regulation, made the following remarks to the European Parliament in December 2013:

> 'The Snowden revelations have affected trust in our transatlantic relationship. The [European] Commission immediately took a firm stance, saying clearly that mass surveillance [by the NSA] is unacceptable ... We made sure that the rights of EU citizens were part of the debate in the US ... Asking for data held by private companies located in the EU directly should only be possible under clearly defined, exceptional and judicially reviewable situations.'

10.17 Accordingly, the new Regulation seeks to update the 1995 rules to guarantee privacy rights in the future. Key changes include:

- A single set of rules across the EU. Unnecessary administrative requirements will be removed, eg the current obligation on companies and public bodies to notify their data protection activities every year to the supervisory authority, which in the UK is the ICO.

- Greater responsibility and accountability for all those who process personal data. For example, companies and public bodies should notify the ICO of any serious data breach as soon as possible.

- Wherever an individual's consent is required for data to be processed, the new Regulation requires that consent has to be given explicitly rather than assumed.

- Individuals will have easier access to their data and be able to transfer it from one service provider to another more easily.

- A 'right to be forgotten' will help individuals to manage data protection risks online, eg they can insist that an organisation delete their data if there is no legitimate reason to keep it.

- The powers of data protection authorities in Member States will be strengthened to enforce the new Regulation. They will be able to levy fines on companies that break the rules. Fines can amount to €20 million (approximately £14.8 million) or up to 4% of the global annual turnover of a company, as appropriate.

10.18   The Commission believes that a regulation rather than a directive is the most appropriate legal instrument to define the framework for the protection of personal data in the EU. The Explanatory Memorandum that accompanied the draft Regulation gives the reasons why: 'The direct applicability of a Regulation in accordance with Article 288 of the Treaty on the Functioning of the European Union ... will reduce legal fragmentation and provide greater legal certainty by introducing a harmonised set of core rules, improving the protection of fundamental rights of individuals and contributing to the functioning of the Internal Market.'

10.19   As stated above, the original proposal for a regulation was made by the Commission in January, 2012. The text of the new Regulation was prepared by the Civil Liberties, Justice and Home Affairs Committee of the European Parliament in October 2013 and approved by the Parliament in March 2014 and adopted by the Council of Ministers in June 2015. The European Data Protection Supervisor made further recommendations in July 2015 and these were finally agreed by the various EU institutions, including the European Commission, before final approval of the text in April 2016. This book is based on the final approved version of the text.

10.20   The Regulation recognises that although it is directly applicable in Member States, it may be adapted by them to reflect 'constitutional, organisational and administrative structures' in each country (Recital 19).

10.21   Specifically, Member States may introduce laws to apply relevant provisions of the Regulation to the processing of personal data to comply with a legal obligation, perform a task carried out in the public interest or in the exercise of official authority or to provide for specific requirements for processing for the purposes of freedom of expression, access to official documents, use of public information or a national ID number (Art 1.2a).

10.22 The main objective of the new Regulation is to protect the right to the protection of personal data as one of the citizen's fundamental rights and freedoms. However, it recognises (in Recital 3a) that every right has its limits:

> 'The right to the protection of personal data is not an absolute right; it must be considered in relation to its function in society and be balanced with other fundamental rights, in accordance with the principle of proportionality. This Regulation respects all fundamental rights and observes the principles recognised in the Charter of Fundamental Rights of the European Union as enshrined in the Treaties, notably the right to respect for private and family life, home and communications, the right to the protection of personal data, the freedom of thought, conscience and religion, the freedom of expression and information, the freedom to conduct a business, the right to an effective remedy and to a fair trial as well as cultural, religious and linguistic diversity.'

10.23 Accordingly, the Regulation lays down rules relating to the protection of personal data on the one hand and rules relating to the free movement of personal data on the other (Art 1.1). A balance must be struck between protecting the data and allowing it to move freely in the interests of individuals and organisations alike.

Example

Cheap Stores has its head office in London with shops operating under franchise in 14 other Member States. Data relating to customers is collected in every shop and transferred to head office where the data is processed in various ways. One of these is to compile a database for direct marketing. The data protection laws of the UK would therefore apply to these activities. However, the shops are responsible for processing their customers' personal data for purposes of day-to-day shopping, eg payments. To that extent the shops are subject to the law of the relevant Member State where each one is located. Among other requirements, each shop must notify its data processing operations to the data protection authority of that Member State, if notification is required by the law of that State (as is the case in the UK). Abolition of the requirement to notify, as provided by the new Regulation, will mean that neither head office nor the franchisees will be subject to this or similar local requirements and instead will have a single set of requirements to comply with.

Key definitions

10.24 As stated above, the new Regulation builds on the data protection rules first established throughout Europe by the 1995 Directive. The Regulation adds to the rules set out in the Directive and DPA, and the definitions and principles that underlie them. A clear understanding of these definitions and principles is essential to achieve compliance with the legal obligations and business requirements of the Regulation.

10.25 The fundamental definition is *personal data*. This is data that refers to a living individual who can be identified from the data either by itself or together with other information in the possession of the data controller.

Example

A company holds information in records stored on microfiche. These records do not identify individuals by name but have a unique reference that matches a reference in a card index system to identify the individuals concerned. Accordingly, the information held on the microfiche is personal data for data protection purposes.

10.26 The scope of the new Regulation is wide. It applies to the 'processing of personal data wholly or partly by automated means and to the processing other than by automated means of personal data which form part of a 'filing system' or are intended to form part of a filing system' (Art 2(1)). Accordingly, it applies to personal data held in computer or manual files. The only qualification is that the manual files must form part of a filing system. This is similar to a 'relevant filing system' as defined by the DPA 1998. Data that is not filed in a system, eg alphabetical or numerical, is out of scope. The territorial scope is equally wide. The Regulation (in Art 3(2)) applies to processing of personal data by a controller outside the EU where the processing relates to:

'(a) the offering of goods and services, irrespective of whether a payment by the data subject is required, to such data subjects in the Union; or
(b) the monitoring of their behaviour as far as their behaviour takes place within the European Union.'

10.27 Accordingly, the key element is the location or residence of the individual concerned in the EU, regardless of the location or residence/place of business of the controller. Even if the individual does not live or work in the EU, the Regulation applies if the processing monitors his/her behaviour while there, eg on holidays.

10.28 Below are definitions of the key terms used in the DPA and/or the new Regulation (where no definition appears below of an equivalent term in either set of rules, none has been provided):

- 'Data' is defined by the DPA as information that is either processed on computer equipment or recorded in some way with the intention that it be processed on computer equipment, or recorded in a 'relevant filing system' or with the intention that it be so recorded. Information that is an 'accessible record' is also information even if it is not processed or recorded, as is information that is recorded and held by a public authority (DPA, s 1(1)).

- 'Data concerning health' is defined by the Regulation as 'personal data related to the physical or mental health of a natural person, including the provision of health care services, which reveal information about his or her health status' (Art 4(15)).

- 'Relevant filing system' for purposes of data is defined by the DPA as a set of information about individuals that is structured so that specific information about any particular individual is readily accessible (s 1(1)). This covers manual or paper records that allow access to information about particular individuals. For example, if employee John Smith's salary details are kept in a folder marked 'Salaries' with tabs in alphabetical order, his details are readily accessible by looking under the 'S' tab.

- 'Filing system' is defined by the Regulation as any structured set of personal data that is accessible according to specific criteria 'whether centralised, decentralised or dispersed on a functional or geographical basis' (Art 4(6)).

- 'Accessible record' for purposes of the DPA's definition of data is a record of an individual's health or condition, or a record of a student's education by a local education authority or a special school, or a record held by a local authority for purposes of housing or social services (s 68(1)).

- 'Personal data' is defined by the DPA as any data about a data subject who can be identified from the data either by itself or in conjunction with other information in the possession, or likely to come into the possession, of a data controller, and includes any expression of opinion about the data subject or intention of the data controller in respect of the data subject (s 1(1)). This 'other information' may or may not be personal data itself, eg a reference number for each individual that does not identify him/her by itself but does so if matched with other records that link the reference number to the individual concerned; *personal data* is defined by the new Regulation as any information relating to an identified or identifiable 'natural person', ie an individual. An identifiable person is someone 'who can be identified directly or indirectly in particular by reference to an identifier such as a name, an identification number, location data, online identifier or to one or more factors specific to the physical, physiological, genetic, mental, economic, cultural or social identity of that natural person' (Art 4(1)).

- 'Sensitive personal data' is defined by the DPA as personal data relating to a data subject's criminal record, health, race, politics, religion, sex life or trade union membership (s 2). This is a special category because of its very nature and the potential for discrimination against the individual concerned.

- 'Data subject' is defined by the DPA as an individual who is the subject of personal data; it is defined by the Regulation as an identified or identifiable person, 'one who can be identified, directly or indirectly, in particular by reference to an identifier such as a name, an identification number, location data, unique identifier or to one or more factors specific to the physical, physiological, genetic, mental, economic, cultural or social or gender identity of that person' (Art 4(1)).

- 'Consent of the data subject' is defined by the Regulation as 'any freely given, specific, informed and unambiguous indication of the data subject's wishes by which he or she , by a statement or by a clear affirmative action, signifies agreement to the processing of personal data relating to him or her' (Art 4(11)).

- 'Data controller' is defined by the DPA 1998 as a person who determines the purposes for which and the manner in which any personal data is processed (s 1(1)); this person may be a company, an organisation or an individual such as a sole trader. Similarly, the Regulation defines a *controller* as an individual or organisation that 'determines the purposes and means of the processing of personal data' (Art 4(7)).

- 'Data processor' is defined by the DPA as any person other than someone who processes personal data on behalf of a data controller (s 1(1)). The Regulation defines a *processor* as an individual or organisation that processes personal data on behalf of a controller (Art 4(8)), eg in an outsourcing arrangement. However, an employee of the data controller/controller is not a data processor/processor acting on its behalf as he/she is not an independent party.

- 'Processing' is defined by the DPA as obtaining, recording or holding personal data or carrying out any operation or set of operations on the data (s 1(1)). The Regulation defines *processing* as any operation performed on personal data, whether automated or not, including collection, recording, organisation, adaptation or alteration, storage, retrieval, consultation, use, disclosure, making available, alignment or combination, restriction, erasure or destruction of the data (Art 4(2)). So, effectively, every operation on personal data is in scope of both the DPA and the new Regulation.

- 'Restriction of processing' is defined by the Regulation as 'the marking of stored personal data with the aim of limiting their processing in the future' (Art 4(3)).

- 'Recipient' is defined by the Regulation as an individual or organisation to whom personal data is disclosed, 'whether a third party or not' (Art 4(9)), ie whether the data relates to the individual or organisation concerned or another party.

- 'Personal data breach' is defined by the Regulation as 'a breach of security, leading to the accidental or unlawful destruction, loss, alteration, unauthorised disclosure of or access to personal data transmitted, stored or otherwise processed' (Art 4(12)).

- 'Genetic data' is defined by the Regulation as 'all personal data relating to the genetic characteristics of a natural person that have been inherited or acquired which give unique information about the physiology or the health of that natural person, resulting in particular from an analysis of a biological sample from the natural person in question' (Art 4(13)).

- 'Biometric data' is defined by the Regulation as 'any personal data resulting from specific technical processing relating to the physical, physiological or behavioural characteristics of a natural person which allows or confirms the unique identification of that natural person, such as facial images, or dactyloscopic data' (Art 4(14)). (Dactyloscopic data relates to fingerprints.)

- 'Profiling' is defined by the Regulation as 'any form of automated processing of personal data consisting of using those data to evaluate personal aspects relating to a natural person, in particular to analyse and predict aspects concerning that natural person's performance at work, economic situation, health, personal preferences, or interests, reliability, behaviour, location or movements' (Art 4(4)).

- 'Main establishment' in the case of a controller is defined by the Regulation as the place of its central administration in the Union 'unless the decisions on the purposes and means of the processing of personal data are taken in another establishment of the controller in the Union' (Art 4(16(a))). In the case of a processor, the main establishment is likewise the place of its central administration in the Union, and if it has no such place, where the main processing activities are carried on (Art 4(16(b))).

- 'Enterprise' is defined by the Regulation as an individual or organisation 'engaged in an economic activity irrespective of its legal form including partnerships or associations regularly engaged in an economic activity' (Art 4(18)).

- 'Binding corporate rules' are defined in the Regulation as 'personal data protection policies which are adhered to by a controller or processor established on the territory of a Member State for transfers or a set of transfers of personal data to a controller or processor in one or more third countries within a group of undertakings or group of enterprises engaged in a joint economic activity' (Art 4(20)). These rules may be used to allow the transfer of data outside the EU – see **12.62** et seq below.

- 'Cross-border processing of personal data' is defined by the Regulation as taking place either (a) as part of the activities of establishments in more than one Member State of a controller or processor in the Union, or (b) as part of the activities of one establishment of a controller or processor in the Union but which 'substantially affects ... data subjects in more than one Member State' (Art 4(23)(b)).

10.29   The new Regulation makes it clear that the data protection regime does not apply to all kinds of personal data but only to data that identifies or may identify an individual. Anonymous data is therefore out of scope.

10.30   Recital 26 provides:

'The principles of data protection should apply to any information concerning an identified or identifiable natural person. Personal data which has undergone pseudonymisation, which could be attributed to a natural person by the use of additional information, should be considered as information on an identifiable natural person. To determine whether a person is identifiable, account should be taken of all the means reasonably likely to be used, such as singling out, either by the controller or by any other person to identify the individual directly or indirectly. To ascertain whether means are reasonable likely to be used to identify the individual, account should be taken of all objective factors, such as the costs of and the amount of time required for identification, taking into consideration both available technology at the time of the processing and technological development. The principles of data protection should therefore not apply to anonymous data, which is information that does not relate to an identified or identifiable natural person or to data rendered anonymous in such a way that the data subject is not or no longer identifiable. This Regulation does therefore not concern the processing of such anonymous data, including for statistical and research purposes.'

10.31 What does 'pseudonymisation' mean? According to the new Regulation, it means data that cannot identify an individual without additional information. The data refers to him/her by another name or in some other way. For example, data relating to Joe Bloggs is said to anonymised if it does not identify him or refer to him in any way but aggregates his data with data relating to others. However, data that does not identify him but refers to him as Customer 123 is said to be 'pseudonymised', on the basis that the data refers to him but does not identify him. Personal data contains identifiers such as name, address and date of birth. When it is pseudonymised the various identifiers are removed and replaced by one pseudonym, eg Customer 123. This allows processing of personal data on a large scale. The Regulation defines pseudonymisation as:

> 'the processing of personal data in such a way that the data can no longer be attributed to a specific data subject without the use of additional information, as long as such additional information is kept separately and subject to technical and organisational measures to ensure non-attribution to an identified or identifiable person.' (Art 4(5))

10.32 Accordingly, the pseudonymisation of data is recognised by the Regulation as a means of reducing the risks for data subjects and yet enabling controllers and processors to meet their obligations.

10.33 In May 2014 the EU's Article 29 Working Party, an advisory group on data protection, published a paper on the techniques involved in anonymising personal data (*Opinion on Anonymisation Techniques*, Opinion 05/2014). Anonymisation is the process of turning data into a form that does not identify individuals and where identification is not likely to take place. This allows for a much wider use of the information. The Article 29 paper notes that anonymity is interpreted differently across the EU, and differences exist as to what is considered an acceptable level for the risk of re-identification of a data subject. It discusses the two main anonymisation techniques, namely randomisation and generalisation, and considers the strengths and weaknesses of each technique based on three criteria:

(1) Is it possible to identify an individual?
(2) Is it possible to link records relating to an individual?
(3) Can information be inferred concerning an individual?

10.34 The Article 29 paper also looks at pseudonymisation, noting that it is not a method of anonymisation, but rather reduces the ability to link a 'dataset', ie a set of personal data, to the original identity of a data subject, and is therefore a useful security measure.

10.35 A code of practice introduced by the ICO in 2012 shows that anonymisation of personal data is both possible and desirable (see *Anonymisation: managing data protection risk* (Nov 2012), which is available from the ICO website at www.ico.org.uk). Anonymisation ensures the availability of data resources, whilst protecting the personal data of individuals. Anonymisation is of particular relevance at present in view of the increasing amount of information available through 'Open Data' initiatives and through individuals posting their own personal data online in various forms of social media such as Facebook and Twitter. However, for anonymisation to be effective there must be a clear understanding of what constitutes personal data. The use of anonymised data where appropriate has several advantages over personal data. These include protection against inappropriate disclosure of personal data, and fewer legal restrictions. Disclosure of anonymised data is not a disclosure of personal data – even if the data controller holds the key to allow re-identification of the data subject.

10.36 Organisations should ensure that they have in place an effective data protection framework, including an appropriate governance structure – see **15.19** et seq below – to manage their anonymisation processes. They should carry out a thorough risk analysis at the initial stage of producing and disclosing anonymised data on the likelihood and potential consequences of re-identification of a data subject. The risk of re-identification will differ according to the way the anonymised information is disclosed, shared or published. In cases where the consequences of re-identification of anonymised data could be significant – for example, because it would leave an individual open to damage, distress or financial loss – organisations should seek the data subject's consent for the disclosure of the data explaining its possible consequences, and adopt a more rigorous form of risk analysis and anonymisation.

10.37 Spatial information including GPS data and map references such as Google Maps may constitute personal data. There is no simple rule for handling this kind of data. The approach taken will depend on related information that is available and the size of the dataset. In order to avoid disclosure of personal data, and to reduce re-identification risk for some types of spatial information, the ICO has guided that the organisation should consider removing certain elements such as house numbers or street names. Small numbers in small geographical areas obviously present an increased risk.

CHAPTER 11

GENERAL PRINCIPLES

11.1 The DPA and the new Regulation provide for the general principles of data protection as set out below. These are similar but not identical as between the two sets of rules.

PRINCIPLE 1

11.2

> 'Personal data shall be processed fairly and lawfully and, in particular, shall not be processed unless (a) at least one of the conditions in Schedule 2 is met, and (b) in the case of sensitive personal data, at least one of the conditions in Schedule 3 is also met.'[1]

> 'Personal data must be processed lawfully, fairly and in a transparent manner in relation to the data subject ("lawfulness, fairness and transparency").'[2]

11.3 Accordingly, fair and lawful processing is a key element of this first principle of data protection. What does 'fair' mean in this context? It requires that a data controller is open and transparent about how it uses personal data. This is particularly important where an individual can decide whether or not to do business with the data controller. If the individual knows from the start what his/her data will be used for, he/she can make an informed decision about whether to proceed with the relationship. An assessment of whether personal data is being processed fairly will depend partly on how the data was obtained. If the individual was deceived or misled, this is obviously unfair.

11.4 Lawful processing of personal data is processing that complies with applicable legal and regulatory requirements. Depending on the nature and extent of the processing, data controllers may need to take legal advice in order to satisfy themselves that the relevant requirements are complied with. At least one of the following conditions must be complied with in order to process personal data 'fairly and lawfully'(DPA, Sch 2):

- the individual to whom the data refers has consented to the processing;

---

[1]   DPA 1998, Sch 1, Part I.
[2]   Regulation, Art 5(1)(a).

- the processing is necessary for something to be done at the individual's request to allow him/her to enter into a contract with the data controller, or for the contract to be performed;

- the processing is necessary because of a legal obligation that applies to the data controller (other than an obligation imposed by a contract);

- the processing is necessary to protect the individual's 'vital interests', ie a life or death matter such as access to his/her medical history for treatment for serious illness or injury;

- the processing is necessary for administering justice or for exercising a statutory or public function; or

- the processing is in pursuit of the data controller's 'legitimate interests'.

Example

A bank is unable to locate a customer who has stopped making repayments on a loan. The customer has moved house without informing the bank of his new address. The bank engages a debt collection agency to find the customer and seek repayment of the loan. It discloses the customer's personal data to the agency for this purpose. Although the customer has not consented, the disclosure is made for purposes of the bank's legitimate interests, ie to recover the loan.

11.5 The new Regulation goes to some length to explain what is meant by 'lawful and fair' processing in accordance with Principle 1. Transparency is at the heart of it. Indeed the relevant provision is worth quoting in full as a comprehensive statement of the general principles of data protection.

11.6 Recital 39 provides:

'Any processing of personal data should be lawful and fair. It should be transparent to natural persons that personal data concerning them are collected, used, consulted or otherwise processed and to what extent the personal data are or will be processed. The principle of transparency requires that any information and communication relating to the processing of those personal data be easily accessible and easy to understand, and that clear and plain language is used. That principle concerns, in particular, information to the data subjects on the identity of the controller and the purposes of the processing and further information to ensure fair and transparent processing in respect of the natural persons concerned and their right to obtain confirmation and communication of personal data concerning them which are being processed. Natural persons should be made aware of risks, rules, safeguards and rights in relation to the processing of personal data and how to exercise their rights in relation to such processing. In particular, the specific purposes for which personal data are processed should be explicit and legitimate and determined at the time of the collection of the personal data. The data should be adequate, relevant and limited to what is necessary for the purposes for which they are processed. This requires, in particular, ensuring that the period for which the data are stored is limited to a strict minimum. Personal data should be processed only if the purpose of the processing could not reasonably be fulfilled by other means. In order to ensure that the personal data are not kept longer than necessary, time limits should be established by the controller for erasure or for a periodic review. Every reasonable step should be taken to ensure that personal data which are inaccurate are rectified or deleted. Personal data should be processed in a manner that ensures appropriate security and confidentiality of the personal data, including for preventing unauthorised access to or the use of personal data and the equipment used for the processing.'

Example

A mail-order operator sends its regular customers a range of catalogues of books and records, and has done so for many years. It decides to start selling CDs and DVDs as well. If it sends catalogues of these products to its regular customers, this is likely to be regarded as fair and not surprising by customers who have an established relationship with the company and have bought its products over the years. However, they might well be surprised to receive a brochure for skiing holidays offered by another company. This will be regarded as unfair: customers did not consent to their data being shared with another company for marketing purposes.

11.7 If the information is 'sensitive personal data', there are more stringent requirements that apply and at least one of the conditions below must also be met (DPA 1998, Sch 3):

- the individual to whom the data refers has given his/her explicit consent to the processing;
- the processing is necessary for the data controller to comply with employment law, ie as employer of the data subject(s);
- the processing is necessary to protect the individual's 'vital interests' where his/her consent cannot be reasonably obtained, or those of another individual where the first individual's consent has been unreasonably withheld;
- the processing is carried out by a not-for-profit organisation and does not involve disclosing personal data to a third party, unless the individual consents;
- the individual has deliberately made the information public;
- the processing is necessary in relation to legal proceedings, for obtaining legal advice, or otherwise to establish or exercise legal rights;
- the processing is necessary for administering justice, or for exercising a statutory or public function;
- the processing is necessary for medical purposes, and is undertaken by a health professional or by someone who is subject to a duty of confidentiality;
- the processing is necessary to ensure equality of opportunity, and is carried out with appropriate safeguards for the rights of individuals.

11.8 Accordingly, the individual's consent must be obtained for the data to be obtained and processed for the relevant purpose(s). Unless this has been done clearly, and preferably in writing, it will depend on the circumstances as to whether a valid consent has been obtained. Consent is not defined in the DPA. However, the new Regulation defines consent as 'freely given, specific, informed and unambiguous indication of the data subject's wishes by which he or she by a statement or by a clear affirmative action, signifies agreement to the processing of personal data relating to him or her' (Art 4(11)). For an individual to 'signify' his/her agreement, there must obviously be some communication between the parties. He or she may indicate consent other than in writing, but a data controller should not infer consent if an individual does not respond to a communication, eg failure to return a form or respond to a request for consent.

11.9   Consent must also relate to the age and capacity of the individual and to the particular circumstances. If a data controller intends to continue to hold personal data after the relationship with the individual has ended, the consent should specify this. And while in most cases the consent will last for as long as the processing to which it relates, the individual may withdraw consent at any time, depending on the nature of the consent and the circumstances in which the data is being processed. The withdrawal of consent does not affect any processing already done on the basis of the consent that had been given.

11.10   The DPA makes a distinction between the consent required to process personal data and the 'explicit' consent required to process sensitive personal data. Accordingly, the individual's consent need not be explicit in all cases but at the very least must be clear and unambiguous. It should specify the details of the processing, the kind of personal data involved, the purpose(s) of the processing, and any specific effects of the consent, eg that disclosures may be made to certain third parties. A data controller should not rely on an individual's consent as the sole basis to legitimate its processing. The view of the ICO is that it is more important to treat individuals fairly rather than proceed only on the basis obtaining their consent.

11.11   The new Regulation recognises the special case of *sensitive personal data*. As stated above, this is personal data relating to a data subject's criminal record, health, race, politics, religion, sex life or trade union membership (DPA, s 2). This is a special category because of its very nature and the potential for discrimination against the individual concerned (Recital 51):

> 'Personal data which are, by their nature, particularly sensitive in relation to fundamental rights and freedoms, deserve specific protection as the context of their processing may create important risks for the fundamental rights and freedoms ... Those personal data should also include personal data revealing racial or ethnic origin, whereby the use of the term 'racial origin' in this Regulation does not imply an acceptance by the Union of theories which attempt to determine the existence of separate human races ..... Such personal data should not be processed unless processing is allowed in specific cases set out in this Regulation, taking into account that Member States law may lay down specific provisions on data protection in order to adapt the application of the rules of this Regulation for compliance with a legal obligation or for the performance of a task carried out in the public interest or in the exercise of an official authority vested in the controller.

In addition to the specific requirements for such processing, the general principles and other rules of this regulation should apply, in particular as regards the conditions for lawful processing.'

11.12 However, the Regulation also recognises that derogations or exemptions may be allowed from the general prohibition on the processing of sensitive personal data in certain circumstances. These are discussed at **13.2** et seq below.

11.13 Many of the conditions for fair and lawful processing of personal data depend on the processing being 'necessary' for the relevant purpose(s). It will only be regarded as necessary if the data controller cannot achieve the purpose(s) by any other reasonable means.

Example

A company decides to outsource its payroll function to a specialist payroll provider, and for that purpose transfers the personal data of employees to the provider. While it is 'necessary' for the company to process employees' personal data in the course of its business, it is not necessary to transfer this data to a third party, and so the company would have to obtain consent, or show that it has a 'legitimate interest' to be able to process its employees' personal data in this way.

11.14 What about 'privacy notices' that are sometime used to inform individuals about the use of their personal data? The DPA does not define fair processing but it does provide that, unless a relevant exemption applies, personal data can only be processed fairly if certain information is given to the individual concerned, eg In a privacy notice. The law gives organisations some discretion in how they provide fair processing information. The oral or written statement that individuals are given when information about them is collected is called a 'privacy notice'. In general terms, the notice should state:

- name of the organisation and, if not based in the UK, the name of its UK representative;
- the purpose(s) for which the organisation intends to process the information; and
- any extra information required for individuals in the circumstances to enable the information to be processed fairly.

11.15 For example, if it is intended to disclose information to another organisation, fairness requires that the individual(s) concerned is/are informed unless he/she is likely to expect this disclosure. It is also recommended practice to tell the individual(s) how they can access the relevant information about them, as this may help them to find inaccuracies or omissions.

11.16 The ICO has issued a Privacy Notices Code of Practice to help organisations to draft clear privacy notices and to ensure they collect information about individuals fairly and transparently. The Code explains that the duty to give a privacy notice is strongest when the information is likely to be used in an unexpected, objectionable or controversial way, or when the information is confidential or particularly sensitive. (See www.ico.org.uk for details of the Code.)

Case study

The case of *Innovations (Mail Order) v Data Protection Registrar*[3] in 1993 concerned the issue of the timing and manner of informing the data subject as to the proposed use of his personal data. The company claimed that a subsequent notice of use was sufficient. The Data Protection Tribunal rejected this claim as the company wished to use the data for a different purpose (the sale of a mail order list) and had deliberately withheld the notice until the list had been sold so as to force customers to opt out at that stage if they wished. The Tribunal decided this was unfair.

11.17   The new Regulation provides for prior disclosure of information to data subjects about the processing of their personal data. The required information is set out at **14.6** et seq below.

PRINCIPLE 2

11.18

'Personal data shall be obtained only for one or more specified and lawful purposes, and shall not be further processed in any manner incompatible with that purpose or those purposes.'[4]

'Personal data shall be collected for specified, explicit and legitimate purposes and not further processed in a way incompatible with those purposes; further processing of personal data for archiving purposes in the public interest, scientific, historical research purposes or statistical purposes shall in accordance with Article 89(1) not be considered incompatible with the initial purposes ("purpose limitation").'[5]

11.19   The data controller must ensure that the data subject is informed of the use and disclosure of his/her data, which can only occur with his/her consent or if permitted/required by law. Any use or disclosure must be necessary for the purpose(s) or be compatible with it/them. A useful test suggested by the ICO is whether a data subject would be surprised to find out about a particular use or disclosure of his/her data. Any data processing by a data processor on the controller's behalf must also be undertaken in compliance with this principle (and the other principles if applicable). This requires that, as a minimum, any such processing takes place subject to a contract between the controller and the processor that specifies the conditions for the processing, the security

---

[3]   Case DA/92 31/49/1.
[4]   DPA 1998, Sch 1, Part 1.
[5]   Regulation, Art 5(1)(b).

arrangements, and arrangements for deletion or return of the data upon completion or termination of the contract. The controller must take 'reasonable steps' to ensure compliance by the processor with these requirements.

11.20 What is meant by 'lawful'? This refers to statute and to common law, whether criminal or civil. If the processing of personal data involves committing a criminal offence, the processing will obviously be unlawful. However, processing may also be unlawful if it results in:

- breach of a duty of confidence. Such a duty may be stated, or it may be implied by the content of the information or because it was collected in circumstances where confidentiality is expected – medical or banking information, for example;
- the organisation exceeding its legal powers or exercising those powers improperly;
- infringement of copyright;
- breach of contract;
- breach of industry-specific laws or regulations;
- breach of the Human Rights Act 1998 (the Act implements the European Convention on Human Rights, which, among other things, gives individuals the right to respect for private and family life, home and correspondence);
- breach of the new Regulation.

11.21 This Principle aims to ensure that organisations are open about their reasons for obtaining personal data, and that what they do with the data is in line with the reasonable expectations of the individuals concerned. There are clear links with other data protection principles, in particular Principle 1, which requires personal data to be processed fairly and lawfully. Obviously, in order to comply with this Principle 2 as to purpose(s) of the processing, the organisation must know what data or categories of data are held and the relevant purposes(s). In practice, an organisation must:

- be clear from the outset about why it is collecting personal data and what it intends to do with the data;
- comply with the DPA's fair processing requirements – including the duty to give privacy notices to individuals when collecting their personal data;
- consult with the ICO if required in the case of 'high risk' processing as identified by a data protection impact assessment; and
- ensure that, if the organisation wishes to use or disclose the personal data for any purpose that is additional to, or different from, the originally specified purpose, the new use or disclosure is fair.

Example

A GP discloses his patient list to his wife who runs a travel agency, so that she can offer special holiday deals to patients needing to recuperate after surgery.

Disclosing the information for this purpose would be incompatible with the purposes for which it was obtained. The GP will need to get prior consent to use or disclose personal data for a purpose that is additional to, or different from, the purpose for which it was originally obtained.

11.22   The new Regulation (in Recital 50) specifically provides for the further processing of personal data as referred to in Principle 2:

'The processing of personal data for purposes other than those for which the personal data were initially collected should be allowed only where the processing is compatible with those purposes for which the data were initially collected. In such a case, no legal basis separate from that which allowed the collection of the data is required. If the processing is necessary for the performance of a task carried out in the public interest or in the exercise of official authority vested in the controller, Union or Member State law may determine and specify the tasks and purposes for which the further processing should be regarded as compatible and lawful. Further processing for archiving purposes in the public interest, scientific or historical research purposes or statistical purposes should be considered as compatible lawful processing operations. The legal basis provided by Union or Member State law for the processing of personal data may also provide a legal basis for further processing. In order to ascertain whether a purpose of further processing is compatible with the purpose for which the personal data are initially collected, the controller after having met all the requirements for the lawfulness of the original processing, should take into account, inter alia: any link between those purposes and the purposes of the intended further processing, the context in which the personal data have been collected, in particular the reasonable expectations of data subjects based on their relationship with the controller as to their further use; the nature of the personal data; the consequences of the intended further processing for data subjects; and the existence of appropriate safeguards in both the original and intended further processing operations.'

11.23   Accordingly, the Regulation provides that further processing of the data by the same controller may be permitted by the laws of a Member State if it is compatible with the original processing, based on the factors specified in Recital 50 above. (Any such law must be a necessary and proportionate measure in a democratic society to safeguard national/public security, defence, protection of data subjects' rights, pursuit of legal proceedings, investigation of criminal offences or professional misconduct, and exercise of official functions in the public interest – Art 6(4)). However, regardless of whether the further processing is compatible or not, it is permitted if the data subject consents to it:

'Where the data subject has given consent or the processing is based on Union or Member State law which constitutes a necessary and proportionate measure in a democratic society to safeguard, in particular, important objectives of general public interest, the controller should be allowed to further process the personal data irrespective of the compatibility of the purposes...' (Recital 50)

11.24   In the absence of consent, accordingly, the controller must establish whether the further processing is compatible with the original purpose(s) and on that basis that it may further process the data. The criteria are set out in Recital 50 above and in Art 6(4)(a)-(e) below:

- any link between the original purpose(s) and that/those of the intended further processing;
- the context in which the data was obtained, in particular the relationship between data subject and controller;
- the nature of the data, eg whether it includes a special category of personal data, including sensitive personal data, or whether data related to criminal convictions and offences are processed;
- possible consequences of the intended further processing for the data subject(s) involved; and
- whether appropriate safeguards are in place, including encryption or pseudonymisation.

PRINCIPLE 3

11.25

'Personal data shall be adequate, relevant and not excessive in relation to the purpose or purposes for which they are processed.'[6]

'Personal data must be adequate, relevant and limited to what is necessary in relation to the purposes for which they are processed ("data minimisation").'[7]

In almost identical terms as set out above, the DPA and the new Regulation require that the organisation only collects the personal data it needs for whatever purpose(s) it has specified. It also requires that the data is sufficient for the purpose(s) for which it was obtained in the first place. These requirements have to do with data adequacy and data minimisation – that is, the data is adequate for the relevant purpose(s), and the minimum necessary for that/those purpose(s). In practice, the organisation should ensure that:

- it holds personal data about an individual that is sufficient for the purpose(s) for which it holds the data in relation to him/her; and
- it holds no more information than it needs for that/those purpose(s).

11.26 What is meant by 'adequate, relevant and not excessive'? Neither the DPA nor the Regulation defines these words but they need to be considered in the context of the purpose(s) for holding the personal data, and separately for each individual concerned. Accordingly, in order for the organisation to assess whether it holds the correct amount of personal data, it must first be clear about why it holds and uses the data. This may differ from one individual to another. As stated above, the organisation can only keep the minimum amount of data required for the relevant purpose(s) and must have appropriate procedures in place to ensure this is the case. In order to comply, the

---

[6] DPA 1998, Sch 1, Part 1.
[7] Regulation, Article 5(1)(c).

organisation should decide on specific criteria to assess what is adequate, relevant, and not excessive, and apply those criteria to each data item.

Example

A debt collection agency is engaged to locate a debtor. It collects information on several people with a similar name. The agency should delete most of this information, keeping only the minimum data needed to form a basic record of any person they have removed from their search. It is permitted to keep this small amount of information so that any such person is not contacted again.

11.27 What about the adequacy and relevance of professional opinions? Neither the DPA nor the new Regulation provides for the right of an individual to demand that an organisation delete an opinion about him/her because it may be based on irrelevant information, or has not taken account of information that may be important. The right to request deletion of the data – the so-called 'right to be forgotten' – applies in circumstances specified in the Regulation – see **14.44** et seq below. However, the record of an opinion should contain enough information to interpret it correctly. For example, it should state the date and the author's name and occupation/position. If an opinion is likely to be contentious or sensitive, or if it will have a significant impact when disclosed, it is even more important to state the circumstances or the evidence it is based on. An individual has the right of rectification under the new Regulation (Art 16(1)) if the opinion is inaccurate, as in the case of any inaccurate data.

Example

A GP's record of a medical opinion about Susan's condition consists of a letter from her consultant. The hospital file contains greater detail about her condition. In this case the record of the consultant's opinion held by the GP should contain enough information to enable the more detailed records to be located.

PRINCIPLE 4

11.28

'Personal data shall be accurate and, where necessary, kept up to date.'[8]

'Personal data must be accurate and, where necessary, kept up to date; every reasonable step must be taken to ensure that personal data that are inaccurate, having regard to the purposes for which they are processed, are erased or rectified without delay ("accuracy").'[9]

Accordingly, both the DPA and the new Regulation impose obligations on controllers to ensure the accuracy of all personal data. The data must also be kept up to date where necessary. This requirement is closely linked with

---

[8] DPA 1998, Sch 1, Part 1.
[9] Regulation, Art 5(1)(d).

Principle 3 that personal data must be adequate. Data that is accurate is likely to be adequate as well. Although it sounds straightforward, the law recognises that it may not be practical to double-check the accuracy of every item of personal data. Accordingly, the ICO has guided that the organisation should:

- take reasonable steps to ensure the accuracy of any personal data it obtains;
- ensure that the source of any personal data is clear; and
- consider whether it is necessary to update the information.

11.29 Neither the DPA nor the Regulation defines 'accurate' but they do provide for the right of an individual to have inaccurate date corrected. In any event it will usually be obvious whether information is accurate or not. For example, if an individual has moved house from London to Glasgow, a record showing that he currently lives in London is obviously inaccurate. But a record showing that he once lived in London remains accurate even though he no longer lives there.

11.30 There can often be uncertainty about whether it is appropriate to keep records of things that happened that should not have happened. Individuals understandably do not want their records to be tarnished by, for example, a fine or other penalty that was later cancelled. However, the organisation may legitimately want its records to accurately reflect what actually happened. Keeping a record of a mistake and its correction might also be in the individual's interests. For example, it would be in a bank customer's interests that the bank keeps a record of correcting an overcharge on the account in the event of any dispute about the account balance at a later date.

Example

A company dismisses an employee for gross misconduct after a series of events that have severely affected the business. The sacked employee contests the dismissal and an Employment Tribunal decides it was unfair and orders that he be reinstated. He then demands that all references to his dismissal in the company's records are deleted. However, the record of his dismissal is accurate. Although the Tribunal decided that he should not have been dismissed, the fact remains that he was.

11.31 Does personal data always have to be up to date? This depends on what the information is used for. If it is used for a purpose that relies on it remaining current, the information should be kept up to date. For example, employee payroll records should obviously be updated when there is a pay rise. Similarly, records should obviously be updated for a customer's change of address so that letters are sent to the right place. Where information is held only for statistical, historical or other research reasons, however, updating the information might defeat the purpose of holding it.

11.32 The controller must have appropriate procedures in place to review data on a regular basis to ensure it is fit for the purpose(s) for which it is used. The controller has a duty of care to a data subject to ensure that decisions affecting him/her are made on the basis of accurate information. Office procedures must be adequate to ensure high levels of data accuracy. According to the ICO, these should include periodic reviews and audits, to ensure that each data item is kept up to date. However, the accuracy requirement does not apply to back-up data, ie data that is backed-up at a point in time and kept only for the specific purpose of replacing 'live' data in the event of its loss or destruction.

11.33 It may be impractical to ensure the accuracy of personal data that someone else provides. The DPA provides (in Sch 1, Part 2) that even if the organisation holds inaccurate personal data, it will not be considered to have breached the requirement for accuracy if:

- the data has been accurately recorded as it was provided by the third party;
- reasonable steps have been taken to ensure the accuracy of the information; and
- if the individual concerned has challenged the accuracy of the information, this is clear to those who access it.

11.34 As to what are 'reasonable steps', this will depend on the circumstances and, in particular, the nature of the personal data and what it will be used for. If the data will be used to make decisions that could significantly affect the individual concerned or others, there is a correspondingly greater need for accuracy. This may require independent verification. For example, an employer will obviously need to check the details of a job applicant's education, qualifications and work experience if it is essential for a particular job, and will need to verify at least some of this information.

11.35 Of course, an individual may challenge the accuracy of information held about them. For example, he/she may be able to provide solid proof that a date of birth has been recorded incorrectly. In that event the data should be corrected or at least marked as being challenged by the individual concerned. The latter will offer some defence against an allegation that the controller has acted in breach of this principle of data protection if the data turns out to be inaccurate. If the individual is not satisfied that appropriate action has been taken to ensure that the accuracy of his/her data, he/she may take legal action for a court order to rectify, block, or destroy the data.

Case study

In *Law Society v Kordowski*,[10] the Law Society obtained an injunction from the High Court against the defendant to prevent him from publishing a website similar to a website called 'Solicitors from Hell' that he had published before. One of the grounds for the injunction was that the personal data on the site was inaccurate.

---

[10] [2011] EWHC 3185 (QB).

11.36 What about the accuracy of opinions? An expression of an opinion about an individual is classified as his/her personal data. In determining whether the opinion is accurate, the difficulty is that personal experiences and preferences can affect someone's opinion of someone else. So any opinion should be clearly recorded as such and whose opinion it is.

11.37 Some records may appear to be opinions but are in fact statements of fact and not opinion. For example, financial institutions often use credit scores to help them decide whether to provide credit. A credit score is a number that summarises the historical information in a credit report and quantifies the risk involved in granting credit to an individual. These scores are based on a statistical analysis of data rather than on a subjective opinion of his/her creditworthiness.

11.38 A medical opinion is obviously a sensitive matter. It is often impossible for a doctor to conclude with certainty whether a patient is suffering from a particular condition. An initial diagnosis or opinion may prove to be incorrect after further examination. This does not necessarily mean that the opinion should be deleted. If the patient's records accurately reflect the diagnosis at the time, the records are not inaccurate because they reflect the doctor's opinion at a particular time. However, in the event of legal action, if the court is satisfied that an expression of opinion is based on that inaccurate data, it can order deletion of all the data, including the expression of opinion.

PRINCIPLE 5

11.39

> 'Personal data processed for any purpose or purposes shall not be kept for longer than is necessary for that purpose or those purposes.'[11]

> 'Personal data must be kept in a form which permits identification of data subjects for no longer than is necessary for the purposes for which the personal data are processed; personal data may be stored for longer periods insofar as the personal data will be processed for archiving purposes in the public interest or scientific or historical research purposes or statistical purposes in accordance with Article 89(1) subject to implementation of the appropriate technical and organisational measures required by the Regulation in order to safeguard the rights and freedoms of the data subject ("storage limitation").'[12]

11.40 Ensuring that personal data is deleted when no longer required will reduce the risk that it will become inaccurate, out of date or irrelevant. It will also reduce the task of keeping the data safe and secure. Deleting the data too soon, however, may put the controller at a disadvantage if it is required for

---

[11]   DPA 1998, Sch 1, Part 1.
[12]   Regulation, Art 5(1)(e).

business purposes or to defend a claim, and may also cause great inconvenience to individuals to whom the data relates.

11.41   The data controller can only keep the relevant data for as long as is necessary and must have appropriate procedures in place to delete it when the purpose(s) has/have been completed. Controllers must be clear about the length of time that data will be kept and the reason(s) why it is being kept. Personal data collected for one purpose cannot be kept once that purpose has ceased (and, of course, cannot be used for a separate purpose without the data subject's consent or unless permitted/required by law). Controllers should have a defined policy on retention periods for all items of personal data, and appropriate procedures to implement the policy.

11.42   What determines how long the data should be kept? Personal data will need to be retained for longer in some cases than in others. It will depend on:

- the value of the information;
- the risks and liabilities associated with keeping the information; and
- the degree of difficulty in ensuring that it remains accurate and up to date.

11.43   How long the data should be kept will also depend on the purpose(s) for which it was obtained and is being used. For example, if it is necessary to hold the data in order to perform a public function or comply with employment law, it should be kept for as long as that purpose applies. On the other hand if the data has only a short-term value, as in the case of a straightforward purchase of a household item, it may have to be deleted within a matter of days. If the data relates to provision of a service such as a financial or professional service that spans months or years, the data may need to be retained for an equivalent period of time.

> *Example*
>
> A bank holds personal data about its customers. The data includes the names, addresses, dates of birth and other information that are required by the bank. These are required in order to provide financial services and also for security in compliance with the bank's data protection obligations. It is therefore right and proper that the bank should retain and use this data while the customer operates an account. But even after an account has been closed the bank may need to retain some or all of the data for legal or business reasons, e g anti-money laundering.

11.44   There may often be good reason for keeping personal data, e g for historical, statistical or research purposes. The DPA provides that personal data held for these purposes may be kept indefinitely as long as it is not used in connection with decisions affecting particular individuals, or in a way that is likely to cause damage or distress. The new Regulation provides for retention and use of personal data for these purposes if permitted by the laws of the Member States and provided that 'technological and organisational measures' are applied to protect the data (Art 89(1)). This does not mean that the information may be kept forever – it should be deleted when it is no longer needed for the relevant purposes. The surrounding circumstances will also need to be taken into account. If personal data has been obtained because of a relationship between the controller and the individual concerned, eg supply of professional services, the controller should consider whether it needs to keep the data when the relationship ends, ie the professional services are no longer required.

Example

Joe is a GP's former patient who has moved house. When the relationship ends, the doctor must decide what personal data to keep and what to delete. The doctor may not need to delete all the data; some may be kept to confirm that Joe was a patient and relevant details such as medical diagnosis and treatment that could arise in the event of a claim.

11.45 Legal and regulatory requirements are also relevant in determining the length of time to keep certain records, eg income tax, audit or health and safety. It may also be determined by reference to professional requirements and industry-standard practices. For example, the ICO has decided that credit reference agencies may keep consumer credit data for 6 years.

11.46 What should happen to personal data at the end of its shelf life, ie the retention period? At the end of the period it should be reviewed and deleted, unless there is some reason to keep it. This will require the controller to carry out a formal periodic review of data for this purpose. However, there is a significant difference between permanently deleting a record and merely archiving it. If a record is archived or stored offline or offsite, this will reduce the risk of misuse or mistake. But if it is appropriate to delete the record this should be done and it should also be deleted from any back-up system that holds the record.

11.47 A controller's obligations may extend beyond the period during which it needs to hold the personal data. The controller must dispose of the data safely and securely when no longer required. Clients or customers of a company that goes out of business, for example, are entitled to expect that their personal data will be processed in accordance with the relevant requirements. However, it may depend on the circumstances as to who the controller is.

Example

A company that operates as a high street retailer goes into liquidation, due to a sharp downturn in business. The board of directors no longer controls the company's assets, including the database of customers, which pass to the liquidator. As the liquidator now controls the database that contains personal data relating to customers, he/she becomes the controller in relation to that data. Accordingly, he/she must comply with data protection requirements in any sale of the database.

PRINCIPLE 6

11.48

> 'Personal data shall be processed in accordance with the rights of data subjects under the Acts.'[13]

The above statement of principle in the DPA has no equivalent in the new Regulation.

The rights of data subjects referred to above, as they are stated in the DPA and the Regulation, consist of the following:

- right of access to their personal data;
- right against enforced access, ie to be forced to access personal data and provide it to a third party such as a prospective employer;
- right to object to processing likely to cause or that is causing damage or distress;
- right to prevent processing for direct marketing;
- right to object to decisions being taken by automated means;
- right to have inaccurate personal data rectified, blocked, or destroyed; and
- right to 'judicial remedies', including the right to claim compensation for damages caused by a breach of the DPA or the Regulation, as the case may be.

11.49 The Regulation provides for the additional right of data subjects to 'data portability', ie access to the data in a 'structured, commonly used and machine-readable format' for transfer to another controller (Art 20(1)). However, the right to have the data transferred to another controller only applies where this is 'technically feasible' (Art 20(2)). Accordingly, the individual is entitled to receive the data in a certain format but not to require the controller to transfer the data if it is not feasible to do so.

Subject access request

11.50 This is the first right that arises from Principle 6 and it refers to the right of an individual to request a copy of the personal data that a controller holds about him/her. The right includes the following:

- to be told whether any personal data is being processed;
- to be given a description of the personal data, the reason(s) why it is being processed, and whether it will be given to any other party;
- to be given a copy of the data; and
- to be given details of the source of the data where this is known.

---

[13] DPA 1998, Sch 1, Part 1.

11.51 An individual can also request information about the reasons behind any automated decisions, such as a computer-generated decision to grant or deny credit. The controller must respond to a subject access request promptly and in any event within 1 month. However, some types of personal data are exempt and so cannot be obtained by making a subject access request. The right of access to personal data is discussed in detail at **14.6** et seq below. In order to comply with a request for access, the controller should have appropriate procedures to ensure retrieval and checking of relevant paper and computer records.

11.52 The individual is entitled to access only his/her own personal data, and not data relating to other people. He/she has the right to see the data rather than the documents or records that include that information. This is the distinction between data and records that contain the data. The same data may be contained in several records or documents and so not every record has to be provided to the individual concerned as long as the relevant data is provided. For example, it may be easier to provide a spreadsheet of relevant data rather than a printout of multiple documents or computer screens.

11.53 What is a valid subject access request? For a request to be valid, it should be made in writing, which includes email or fax. Requests may also be made by way of social media, eg Facebook or Twitter. A data controller is not obliged to respond to a verbal request but would be well advised to do so and should at least explain to the individual concerned how to make a valid request. If a disabled person finds it impossible or unreasonably difficult to make a subject access request in writing, the controller should make a reasonable adjustment for the individual under the Equality Act 2010 (in Northern Ireland, the Disability Discrimination Act 1995). This could include treating a verbal request for information as though it were a valid subject access request. The controller may also be obliged to respond in a particular format that is accessible to the disabled person, such as Braille, large print, email or audio. A standard form of request will make it easier for the controller to recognise a subject access request and make it easier for the individual to include all the data that he/she requires to see but any request in writing must be considered as a valid request, whatever the format.

11.54 The controller is not obliged to explain the contents of the personal data sent to the individual. The DPA requires that the data is in 'intelligible form' (s 7(1)(c)) and the new Regulation requires 'meaningful information about the logic involved in any automated processing, as well as the significance and the envisaged consequences of such processing for the data subject' (Art 15(1)(h)). It should be capable of being understood by the average person but this does not necessarily mean that the data is provided in a form that is intelligible to the individual who has made the request. He/she may or may not be able to understand the data, and the controller cannot be expected to know his/her capacity to understand it.

11.55 The data controller may not charge a fee for dealing with the request – the new Regulation has abolished fees for subject access requests – except in certain circumstances relating to health data or health records. The normal maximum fee is £10 but there are different fee arrangements for organisations that hold credit, health or education records. The new Regulation defines health data as data that relates to the 'physical or mental health of a natural person, including the provision of health care services, which reveal information about his or her health status' (Art 4(16)). For the purposes of the DPA, a 'health record' is a record which consists of information relating to the physical or mental health or condition of an individual; and has been made by or on behalf of a health professional in connection with the care of that individual (s 68(2)). 'Health professionals' include registered medical practitioners, dentists and nurses and clinical psychologists (s 69). Information that forms part of a health record about a living individual is the personal data of the individual it relates to, regardless of the form in which it is held. This means that a subject access request can be made for health records kept in manual form, eg on paper or in a GP's medical notes, as well as for health records kept electronically. A maximum fee of between £10 and £50 may be charged to respond to a request for health records. The precise amount of the maximum fee depends on how the records are held. A charge up to £10 applies to request for health records if they are held in electronic form only. A charge of up to £50 applies to a request for health records held either entirely or partly in paper form.

According to the Regulation, if an individual makes a request by 'electronic means', eg email, the data must be provided in a 'commonly used electronic form', ie soft copy such as a Portable Document Format (PDF) – Art 15(3).

11.56 A controller must confirm a number of details before responding to a request. First, it must establish to its own satisfaction that the person making the request is the individual to whom the personal data relates. This is to avoid data about one individual being sent to another, either accidentally or as a result of deception. Unless the controller knows the individual personally, it is reasonable to ask the person making the request to verify his/her identity. Secondly, the controller must be clear as to the extent of the subject access, ie the amount of data that has been requested. In some cases, personal data may be difficult to retrieve and collate. However, it is not acceptable for the data controller to delay responding to a request unless it has reasonably requires more information to find the relevant data.

11.57 A subject access request may be a made by a third party on behalf of an individual to whom the data relates. This may be a solicitor or other professional acting on behalf of their client. The controller must be satisfied the third party is authorised to act on behalf of the individual concerned on the basis of a written authority to make the request or a general power of attorney. According to ICO guidance, if the controller has reason to believe the individual may not understand what information would be disclosed to the third party acting on his/her behalf, it may respond directly to the individual instead.

11.58 It may happen that an individual does not have the mental capacity to manage his/her own affairs. Although there is no specific provision for this in the Act, other provisions may apply to this situation. The Mental Capacity Act 2005, or the Adults with Incapacity (Scotland) Act 2000, allows a third party to exercise subject access rights on behalf of an individual with a mental incapacity. It is reasonable for a data controller to assume that an attorney with authority to manage the property and affairs of an individual will have the appropriate authority to make a subject access request.

11.59 A response to a subject access request may include information that relates both to the individual making the request and to someone else. The DPA provides that a data controller is not obliged to comply with a request if to do so would mean disclosing information about another individual who can be identified from that information, except where:

- the other individual has consented to the disclosure; or
- it is reasonable in the circumstances to respond to the request without that individual's consent, eg where it is possible to redact or delete data relating to him/her from the data provided in response to the request (s 7(4)).

11.60 The data controller is not obliged to supply a copy of the data in permanent form if it would involve 'disproportionate effort' to do so (s 8(2)). Neither the DPA nor the Regulation defines a disproportionate effort but it is clear that there is scope for assessing whether complying with a request would involve so much work as to outweigh the individual's right of access to their personal data. However, this exception to the right of access only applies in the most exceptional of cases and in particular applies in respect of *supplying* a copy of the relevant information in permanent form. Accordingly, the controller cannot refuse to deal with a subject access request just because it believes that locating the information in the first place would involve disproportionate effort.

Example

An organisation decides for operational reasons that it would involve disproportionate effort to supply copies of Geoff's records in permanent form. Rather than refuse the request, the organisation agrees with Geoff that it would be preferable if he visited their premises and viewed the original documents. It is also agreed that copies will be provided of any relevant documents that he would like to take away.

11.61 What about repeated or unreasonable requests? Neither the DPA nor the new Regulation limits the number of subject access requests an individual can make. However, they do allow some discretion for data controllers when dealing with requests that are made at unreasonable intervals. The controller is not obliged to comply with an identical or similar request to one that it has already dealt with, unless a 'reasonable interval' has elapsed between the first request and any subsequent request (s 8(3)). The Regulation provides that a controller can refuse requests that are 'manifestly unfounded or excessive, in particular, because of their repetitive character' (Art 12(5)). However, the onus is on the controller to show this is the case. In making a decision, the controller should consider the following:

- the nature of the data (is it particularly sensitive?);
- the purpose(s) of the processing – whether the processing is likely to cause detriment to the individual; and
- how often the data is altered – if the data is unlikely to have changed between requests, the controller may decide that it is not obliged to respond to the same request twice.

11.62 If the information has been added to or changed since the last request, the controller needs to consider whether it only has to provide the new or updated information. However, the DPA provides that data must be provided by reference to the data in question at the time when the request is received (s 8(6)). (The new Regulation does not provide for any specific reference point.) Accordingly, the controller is obliged to provide a full response to the request and not merely provide data that is new or has been amended since the last request. In practice, the controller should attempt to negotiate with the individual concerned to limit the scope of the access request to the new or updated information. If he/she insists upon a full response the controller must provide all the relevant information.

Right to object

11.63 The DPA refers to the 'right to prevent processing' (s 10) and is the second right associated with Principle 6. An individual has the right to object to processing of his/her personal data if it causes or is likely to cause unwarranted and substantial damage or distress but only in certain circumstances. The new Regulation provides for a wider right to object and this is discussed further at **14.30** et seq below. In particular, the individual concerned may object even if the processing is for the legitimate interests of the controller. Accordingly, in certain circumstances the controller must not carry on the processing of personal data. The individual's right to object to processing only applies to his/her own personal data, so it cannot prevent the processing of personal data relating to someone else. Of course, an individual may still make an objection to processing on behalf of another person, ie as an authorised third party acting on his/her behalf.

11.64 The individual who wants to exercise this right to prevent processing must put his/her objection in writing and state what they require the controller to do or stop doing. Article 6(1)(a)–(d)) provides that he/she has no right to object to processing if:

- he/she has consented to the processing;
- the processing is necessary in relation to a contract that the individual has entered into, or because the individual has asked for something to be done so he/she can enter into a contract;
- the processing is necessary because of a legal obligation that applies to the controller (other than a contractual obligation);
- the processing is necessary to protect the individual's 'vital interests';
- the processing is necessary for the performance of task carried out in the public interest; or
- the processing is necessary for the purposes of the legitimate interests of the controller unless these interests are overridden by the 'interests or fundamental rights of the data subject'.

Example

A mobile phone company receives a request to remove a customer's details from its database. This should be treated as an objection to processing. The customer explains that using his personal data for credit referencing is causing distress and has led to him being refused a credit card. The company does not have to comply with this request because the credit referencing is necessary to put into effect the contract that the customer has signed. Accordingly, the right to prevent processing does not apply. However, it would be good practice for the company to write to the customer to explain why it does not have to comply with the request.

Direct marketing

11.65 The third right that arises from Principle 6 is the right to object to processing for direct marketing. Individuals have the right to prevent their personal data being processed for this purpose. An individual can, at any time, give the data controller written notice to stop using his/her data, and the controller must comply with this notice within a reasonable period – 28 days is reasonable, according to the ICO.

11.66 What is meant by direct marketing? The marketing in question must be directed at a particular individual or individuals – junk mail that is not addressed to someone in particular but to 'The Occupier', eg leaflets or flyers, is not direct marketing and so is outside the scope of the DPA and the new Regulation. This is because the data does not relate to a particular individual. However, to be considered direct marketing the method of communication may be by email, fax, phone text message or letter. And direct marketing does not just refer to selling goods or services. It includes promoting political or social campaigns such as those of a political party or charity. Accordingly, the controller must stop any promotional activity directed at a particular individual or individuals, using their personal data, if they send a written notice to that effect.

11.67 It may or may not be clear from his/her notice whether the individual requires the data controller to delete his/her data. An individual may ask a controller to remove or delete his/her data from its marketing database but the ICO has guided that in general it will suffice to follow the standard practice of keeping enough information about him/her to ensure that his/her marketing preferences are complied with in future, rather than deleting the data completely. This will also ensure that the controller complies with any industry-specific requirements as to how long personal data should be kept.

11.68 Data controllers must comply with a range of duties in using personal data for direct marketing, eg the duty to process personal data fairly and lawfully as per Principle 1 of the data protection principles. Accordingly, controllers must ensure that data subjects are aware that their personal data may be used to send marketing material and how the material will be sent, ie by post, phone or email. They must be informed at the outset that they have the right to object (Art 19(4)). The right to prevent the use of personal data for direct marketing is expressed in the form of an 'opt out'. Unless the data subject opts out of receiving marketing material, the controller may continue to send it. However, best practice is to provide the data subject with an opportunity to object to any future contact at the time of collecting personal data from him/her, such as during a phone call or browsing a website or signing an application form for a product or service, as required by the new Regulation. The rules as to direct marketing are discussed further at **12.27** et seq below.

11.69 The ICO has guided that when sending direct marketing by post controllers should screen their mailing lists against lists held by the Mailing Preference Service (MPS). Individuals can register with MPS to reduce the amount of direct marketing mail they receive. There is no legal obligation to check the MPS before sending direct marketing but many reputable organisations do so. However, the position is quite different with the Telephone Preference Service (TPS). There are rules to prevent controllers from making sales phone calls to a subscriber who has instructed otherwise. Furthermore, subscribers can register with the TPS to prevent unsolicited phone calls. A controller cannot make an unsolicited call to any number listed on the TPS. Registration with the TPS does not override any specific consent that an individual has given to a particular controller.

Automated decision-making

11.70 The right of subject access allows an individual access to information about the reasoning behind any decision affecting him/her that was made by automated means. This is the fourth right derived from Principle 6. Both the DPA (s 12(1)) and the new Regulation (Recital 77) provide for additional rights that relate to automated decision-making. Accordingly, an individual can give written notice requiring the data controller not to make any automated decisions using his/her personal data. Even if he/she has not given notice, an individual should be informed when such a decision has been made, and he/she can request the controller to reconsider a decision made by automated means.

These rights can be seen as safeguards against the risk that a decision could be made by the controller that would damage the individual concerned, without any human intervention.

11.71 The rights in respect of automated decisions only arise if two requirements are met. First, the decision has to be made using personal data that is processed solely by automatic means. For example, an individual applies for a personal loan online: the bank's systems use algorithms and automatic credit scoring to provide an immediate decision. Secondly, the decision must have a 'significant effect' on the individual concerned: in the case of credit scoring the decision will have a significant effect. The right to object is discussed further at **14.30** et seq below.

11.72 Some decisions are exempt from the application of these rights against automation. These include decisions authorised or required by legislation, eg to prevent fraud or tax evasion, or made in relation to a contract with the individual concerned at his/her request, or decisions made with the data subject's consent. However, even in these cases he/she has the right to express a view and to contest any decision made in this way (Art 22(3)).

Inaccurate personal data

11.73 A data subject has the right to request a controller to rectify, or correct, any inaccurate data (Art 16(1)). This is the fifth right arising from Principle 6. This right of rectification/correction is discussed at **14.44** et seq below.

Right to compensation/judicial remedy

11.74 As the sixth right that arises from Principle 6, an individual who suffers loss and damage due to the controller's breach of duty has the right to claim compensation or a 'judicial remedy'. The breach may have caused 'material or non-material damage' (Art 82(1)), which suggests that non-financial loss such as reputational damage may be included. Indeed, some recent court cases in the UK courts shows that compensation may be awarded where no financial loss has occurred. In many cases a breach of the DPA or the new Regulation will not cause a financial loss but it may be distressing for an individual that his/her personal data has been processed improperly. The controller has a defence if it can show that it was not responsible for the damage. This is a higher burden of proof than before. The courts have required the data subject to establish his/her case on the 'balance of probabilities' and to prove the controller was responsible, whereas in a compensation claim for data protection it seems the defendant must prove it was not responsible.

11.75 What is the amount of compensation that a controller would have to pay? Unfortunately there are no guidelines as to appropriate compensation, and the court will decide on the facts of the case, unless of course, the case is settled by agreement between the parties. The right to claim compensation/judicial remedies is discussed below at **14.61** et seq and **14.66** et seq respectively.

Data portability

11.76 This is the seventh and final right related to Principle 6 and requires that a data controller provide the data subject with his/her personal data in a standard machine-readable format so that it can be transferred to another controller (Art 20(1)). This right is discussed at **14.54** et seq below.

PRINCIPLE 7

11.77

> 'Appropriate technical and organisational measures shall be taken against unauthorised or unlawful processing of personal data and against accidental loss or destruction of, or damage to, personal data.'[14]

> 'Personal data must be processed in a way that ensures appropriate security of the personal data, including protection against unauthorised or unlawful processing and against accidental loss, destruction or damage, using appropriate technical or organisational measures ("integrity and confidentiality").'[15]

The data controller must have appropriate security procedures in place to ensure that personal data is protected against unauthorised access, alteration, disclosure or destruction. A minimum standard of security would include: restricted access to central IT servers in a secure location; restricted access to personal data on a 'need to know' basis; password-protected computer systems; comprehensive and secure back-up procedures for computer data; staff awareness of the controller's data security procedures; secure disposal of waste paper and other material. What is appropriate will depend on the circumstances of the data controller, who should adopt a 'risk-based approach' to determine the level of security required to protect personal data. In particular, the controller must:

- implement security measures to fit the nature of the personal data it holds and the loss and damage that may result from a security breach;
- establish who in the organisation is responsible for information security;
- ensure both physical and technical security, supported up by robust policies and procedures and well-trained staff; and
- be in a position to respond to any breach of security promptly and effectively.

11.78 Advances in technology have enabled organisations to process more and more personal data. This has obvious benefits for data subjects if controllers are collecting and sharing personal data in accordance with the principles of data protection but it also gives rise to security risks. The more data that is processed and shared the greater the risk of loss or misuse of the data.

---

[14] DPA 1998, Sch 1, Part 1.
[15] Regulation, Art 5(1)(f).

Principle 7 relates to the security of every aspect of the processing of personal data. Accordingly, the security measures put in place should ensure that:

- only authorised personnel can access, change or delete personal data;
- these personnel act within the scope of their authority; and
- if personal data is accidentally lost, changed or deleted, it can be recovered to prevent any damage or distress to the individuals concerned.

Case study

In April 2014 a private investigator was convicted of obtaining personal details of individuals by deception and trickery. A company called ICU Investigations acted for various companies to trace individuals for payment of outstanding debts. By pretending to be the individuals they were trying to trace, ICU Investigations obtained their personal details unlawfully and without their consent. The company was fined £20,000. The ICO commented: 'This fine and confiscation order is not only a justified punishment ... but also a powerful deterrent to anyone thinking they can profit from illegally blagging personal data. People have the right to have their personal data kept securely.'

11.79 What level of security is required? Both the DPA and the new Regulation provide that a controller must have security that is 'appropriate' to the nature of the relevant data and the harm that might result from its improper use, or from its accidental loss or destruction. An assessment of the appropriate security measures should include new technology and the costs involved. Ultimately, the appropriate level of security will depend on the risks involved in processing the data. 'Appropriate measures' are discussed further at **12.41** below.

11.80 Information security is not just about physical and technological security but also requires that the appropriate management and organisational security is in place to protect personal data. This should be based on a strong culture of security within the organisation. It is recommended practice to identify a person in the organisation with day-to-day responsibility for information security. He/she should have the necessary authority and resources to fulfil this responsibility effectively.

11.81 It is vital that the controller's staff understand the importance of protecting personal data; that they are familiar with its security policy; and that they operate the security policy and relevant procedures effectively. The DPA requires the controller to take reasonable steps to ensure the reliability of anyone who has access to personal data. Accordingly, the controller must provide appropriate training to include:

- duties under the DPA and the Regulation, and restrictions on the use of personal data;

- responsibilities of all personnel to protect personal data, including the possibility of a criminal offence if they try to access or disclose data without authorisation;

- the appropriate procedures to identify callers and visitors;

- the dangers of people trying to obtain personal data by deception; and

- any restrictions on use by personnel of the organisation's information systems.

11.82 Information security is not all about technology. Breaches of security are often due to theft or loss of equipment or to abandonment of old computers or paper records. Physical security includes basic items such as solid doors and locks, good quality alarm systems, security lighting or CCTV. It also includes how the organisation controls access to the premises, supervises all visitors, disposes of waste and secures all portable devices such as laptop computers and mobile phones. All information on these devices should be password-protected and encrypted. Paper waste should be collected in secure bins and shredded at the end of each week.

11.83 An organisation may decide to use a third party processor to process personal data on their behalf on an outsourced basis, eg payroll or debt collection. A *processor* is someone who processes personal data on behalf of a controller other than as an employee (see 'Key definitions' at **10.24** et seq above). In this case the controller is responsible for compliance with the DPA and the Regulation, and the processor likewise under the terms of a contract that must be put in place between the parties. Accordingly, the controller must (Art 28):

- use a processor that provides adequate safeguards for security of the data;

- take reasonable steps to ensure that those security measures are put into practice; and

- put in place a written contract setting out what the processor is authorised to do with the data.

11.84 What should happen in the case of a breach of security? The breach may be due to a theft, a deliberate attack on the data controller's systems, the unauthorised use of personal data by a member of its staff, or from accidental loss or a systems failure. The ICO expects data controllers to have a written policy on breaches of information security (for a sample Information Security Policy, see FP 13.2).

11.85 According to the ICO, there are four important elements to any breach management plan:

'1. Containment and recovery – the response to the incident should include a recovery plan and, where necessary, procedures for damage limitation.

2. Assessing the risks – you should assess any risks associated with the breach, as these are likely to affect what you do once the breach has been contained.

In particular, you should assess the potential adverse consequences for individuals; how serious or substantial these are; and how likely they are to happen.

3. Notification of breaches – informing people about an information security breach can be an important part of managing the incident, but it is not an end in itself. You should be clear about who needs to be notified and why. You should, for example, consider notifying the individuals concerned; the ICO; other regulatory bodies; other third parties such as the police and the banks; or the media.

4. Evaluation and response – it is important that you investigate the causes of the breach and also evaluate the effectiveness of your response to it. If necessary, you should then update your policies and procedures accordingly.'[16]

11.86 There is a legal obligation on controllers in the new Regulation to report any breach of security likely to cause a 'high risk' for data subjects (Art 31(1)) within 72 hours. Examples are risk of fraud, identity theft and financial loss. (There is no such legal obligation in the DPA.) However, the ICO expects to be informed of any serious breach – relevant factors include the potential loss or damage to individuals, the amount of data and sensitivity of the data.

Case study

The Belfast Health & Social Care Trust had stored sensitive personal data consisting of patient and staff records for several years at a disused site prior to June 2012. At that time, trespassers gained access to the site on several occasions to photograph the records, which were then posted on the internet. The ICO found there had been a serious contravention of the Trust's data protection obligations:

> '[T]he data controller failed to take appropriate technical and organisational measures against accidental loss of personal data such as carrying out a full inspection of the site and making an inventory of the records at the outset; maintaining the integrity of the buildings that held any records; having the appropriate CCTV systems; intruder alarms; security lighting and a sufficient number of security guards to secure a 26 acre site pending its decommissioning. The Commissioner is satisfied that the contravention is of a kind likely to cause substantial distress. Confidential and sensitive personal data was subject to unauthorised access and put at risk of loss due to the inappropriate technical and organisational measures taken by the data controller. [The controller] failed to take reasonable steps to prevent the contravention.'

---

[16] *The Guide to Data Protection* (ICO, December 2014).

PRINCIPLE 8

11.87

> 'Personal data shall not be transferred to a country or territory outside the European Economic Area unless that country or territory ensures an adequate level of protection for the rights and freedoms of data subjects in relation to the processing of personal data.'[17]

The European Economic Area (EEA) comprises the EU Member States in addition to Liechtenstein, Norway and Iceland. There is no equivalent statement of principle in the new Regulation but it provides for transfer of data to countries and territories outside the EU.

11.88 The transfer of personal data outside the EEA in accordance with Principle 8 brings into play some of the other data protection principles. For example, fair and lawful processing of personal data will require the data controller to inform individuals about disclosure of their personal data to third parties abroad, if that is the case. Information security will also be relevant to the transfer of data.

11.89 Data controllers should ask the following questions to determine if this principle applies to a proposed transfer of data:

- Is there a need to transfer personal data abroad?
- If so, is the data being transferred to a country outside the EEA or will it just be in transit through a non-EU country, ie the destination is elsewhere? Personal data added to a website that may be accessed in a country outside the EU amounts to a transfer of data for this purpose.
- Has the controller complied with all data protection principles and not just Principle 8?
- Is the transfer to a country on the European Commission's list of countries or territories that provide adequate protection for the 'rights and freedoms of data subjects' in connection with the processing of their personal data? Transfers may be made to any country or territory in respect of which the Commission has made a positive finding in this regard.
- If the transfer is to a country or territory in respect of which the Commission has not made a positive finding, such as the United States, have 'appropriate safeguards' been put in place to protect the data? In the case of data transfers to the United States, the voluntary Safe Harbor scheme introduced in 2000 was declared invalid by the European Court of Justice in October 2015 as not providing an adequate level of protection.
- Does the personal data consist of passenger name record information (PNR)? An agreement made between the EU and the US in July 2007 to regulate the transfer of PNR from European airlines to the US Department of Homeland Security is regarded as providing adequate protection for the

---

[17] DPA 1998, Sch 1, Part 1.

rights of the data subjects. There are also arrangements in place between the European Commission, Canada and Australia. If the recipient of the data is not in a country approved by the Commission, the controller must determine whether the proposed transfer will provide an adequate level of protection for the data to be transferred.

- Can the controller determine that the level of protection for data subjects' rights is adequate in all the circumstances? If not, can it put in place appropriate safeguards to protect the rights of the data subjects whose data is to be transferred?

11.90 Appropriate safeguards may be put in place in a number of ways including standard data protection clauses, *binding corporate rules*, or various contractual arrangements either standing alone or in conjunction with approved codes of conduct or approved certification mechanisms (Art 46(2)). These will enable the transfer to take place in the absence of a positive finding by the Commission as regards the country or territory where the data is to be sent. These safeguards are discussed at **12.41** below.

11.91 A comprehensive risk assessment must be carried out by the controller if factors such as the nature of the data and the country or territory involved indicate that the transfer is 'high risk'. In that event the controller must consider the extent to which the country in question has adopted data protection standards in its law; whether it is possible to ensure that the standards are achieved in practice, eg a code of conduct, and whether there is an effective procedure for individuals to enforce their rights or obtain compensation in the event of a breach. The ICO has produced a guide to assist data controllers – 'Assessing adequacy for international data transfers' on the ICO website (www.ico.org.uk).

Nb the new General Data Protection Regulation will introduce specific requirements for the transfer of personal data outside the EU and these are discussed in Chapter 12.

Example

Alan travels outside the EU regularly with a laptop containing personal data relating to his job. His employer is the data controller in this instance. Provided the information stays under Alan's control on the laptop, and the employer has an effective procedure to deal with security and the other risks of using portable devices, it is reasonable for the employer to decide that adequate protection exists.

ACCOUNTABILITY

11.92 A company must not only comply with the general principles above but must be able to show that it complies. This underlines the importance of proper record-keeping.

'The controller shall be responsible for, and be able to demonstrate compliance with, [the principles stated in] paragraph 1 [Art 5(1)] ("accountability").' (Art 5(2))

EXEMPTIONS

11.93 The new Regulation provides for certain exemptions from one or more of the General Principles set out above. This is to strike a balance between the right of data subjects to protection of their personal data, and freedom of expression and information. Accordingly, the Regulation provides that Member States may allow exemptions for 'the processing of personal data for journalistic purposes or the purpose of academic, artistic or literary expression' (Art 85(2)). These exemptions, insofar as they affect specific categories of personal data, are discussed in Chapter 13 and as they affect the rights of data subjects are discussed under 'Compliance' at **15.1** et seq below.

11.94 The following exemptions are provided for by the DPA and may survive implementation of the new Regulation.

Legal obligation/legal requirement

11.95 Any restrictions on processing do not apply if the processing is required to comply with a statutory obligation or a rule of law or court order (DPA, s 35). Accordingly, personal data may be disclosed to third parties if the data controller is required to disclose it by law, regulation or court order. For example, an employer is required by law to disclose details of employees' pay to the Inland Revenue for the correct deduction of income tax. The employer may disclose this information irrespective of any objection that an employee may raise. It is recommended practice for a data controller to inform data subjects if it is likely that certain kinds of personal data may be disclosed to third parties by law.

Case study

The Health and Social Care Information Centre (HSCIC) was directed by the NHS in 2015 to undertake a collection of workforce data from providers of NHS services such as GP practices and hospitals. NHS service providers were required to supply information to HSCIC, which includes personal data of their staff. The ICO received complaints that this was excessive and unlawful and in breach the DPA. The relevant legislation provides HSCIC with the power to request the information to fulfil its obligation under the direction of the NHS. In April 2015, the ICO expressed the view that the service providers were not in breach of the DPA in disclosing this information to HSCIC as it is a disclosure required by s 35(1) of the Act. However, in providing this information, the service providers were still required to provide fair processing →

information to their staff to explain what the HSCIC will be doing with their information and what information will be shared.

LEGAL PROFESSIONAL PRIVILEGE/LEGAL ADVICE OR PROCEEDINGS

11.96 The right of access does not apply to documents passing between a client and his/her legal advisers that are subject to privilege (or its equivalent in Scotland), ie documents that relate to legal proceedings (DPA, s 35 and Sch 7, para 10). As regards legal advice or proceedings, any restrictions on processing do not apply if the processing is required for the purpose of the data controller obtaining legal advice or in the course of legal proceedings, current or pending, to which the data controller is a party or where the controller is a witness.

REFERENCES

11.97 Personal data is exempt from the right of access by a data subject of an individual's right of access if it consists of a confidential reference that the data controller gives in connection with an employee (DPA, Sch 7, para 1). The reference may be about the employee's education, training or performance.

MANAGEMENT INFORMATION

11.98 Personal data that is processed for management purposes, such as planning, is exempt from the right of access to the extent that it would be likely to prejudice the business or other activity of the organisation (DPA, Sch 7, para 5).

Example

Senior management of a hospital is planning a reorganisation. This is likely to require some employees to be made redundant. Before the plans are revealed an employee makes a subject access request. In responding, the hospital does not have to reveal its plans to make him redundant if doing so would be likely to affect the operation of the hospital.

NEGOTIATIONS

11.99 Personal data that consists of a record of the data controller's intentions in the conduct of negotiations with an individual is exempt from the right of access to the extent that it would be likely to prejudice the negotiations with him/her (DPA, Sch 7, para 7).

Example

An individual makes a claim to his insurance company for compensation for personal injuries due to an accident. The insurance company disputes the claim. An internal document sets out the company's position and states the maximum amount it is prepared to pay. If the individual makes a subject access request to the company, it would not be required to disclose this document because it would be likely to prejudice the negotiations.

JOURNALISM, LITERATURE AND ART

11.100 This exemption protects freedom of expression in journalism, art and literature. In order for the exemption to apply:

- the data must be processed only for these purposes;
- it must be processed with a view to publication;
- the data controller must have a reasonable belief that the publication is in the public interest; and
- the data controller must have a reasonable belief that compliance with the DPA would be incompatible with the purpose(s) of journalism, art or literature.[18]

11.101 The new Regulation also provides for 'derogations or exemptions' under this heading in order to reconcile freedom of expression and information with the right to protection of personal data:

> 'This should apply in particular to processing of personal data in the audiovisual field and in news archives and press libraries. Therefore, Member States should adopt legislative measures which should lay down exemptions and derogations which are necessary for the purpose of balancing these fundamental rights.'[19]

DOMESTIC PURPOSES

11.102 This exemption applies to personal data that is processed by a data controller who is an individual solely for the purposes of their personal, family or household affairs (DPA, s 36). For example, an individual keeps the names and dates of birth of his/her friends and relatives on a computer database in order to remember their birthdays. The new Regulation also provides for this exemption: processing of data by an individual in the course of a 'purely personal or household activity' is excluded (Art 2(2)(c)). Accordingly, if someone is selling an item of furniture or a household appliance but not in the course of a business, he/she is not processing personal data for purposes of the Regulation.

---

[18] DPA 1998, s 32.
[19] Recital 153.

11.103 Exemptions under the DPA also apply to the following:

- data processing for the purposes of national security (s 28) and by the armed forces (Sch 7, para 2);
- personal data that is processed only for research, statistical or historical purposes, provided it is not disclosed to third parties and no individual can be identified from the results (s 33);
- personal data relating to an individual's physical or mental health, provided that subject access would be likely to cause serious harm to the physical or mental health of him/her or someone else (s 30);
- personal data that consists of educational records or personal data obtained in the course of social work by a public body or a voluntary organisation funded by the public (s 30);
- personal data relating to human fertilisation and embryology, adoption records and reports, statements of a child's special educational needs and parental order records and reports (s 30);
- personal data that is processed in connection with a corporate finance service involving price-sensitive information (Sch 7, para 6);
- examination marks and personal data contained in examination scripts (Sch 7, para 9);
- personal data processed for the purposes of making public appointments or conferring honours (Sch 7, para 3); and
- right against self-incrimination – disclosure of personal data that might incriminate the controller in respect of certain offences, eg perjury (Sch 7, para 11).

11.104 Instead of prescribing these or other exemptions, the new Regulation leaves it to the Member States to provide for exemptions from the data protection principles or for specific categories of data (Arts 85–91, discussed in Chapter 13. It remains to be seen whether the UK will leave the current exemptions to stand.

CHAPTER 12

DATA PROCESSING AND SECURITY

INTRODUCTION

12.1 This chapter discusses both the DPA and the new Regulation as they govern the processing of personal data. As discussed at **10.26** et seq above, the processing of personal data includes any operation performed on the data, whether automated or not, including collection, recording, storage, disclosure, alteration and deletion of the data. Both the DPA and the new Regulation apply to data processing either on a computer system or in manual files that consist of a filing system or a relevant filing system as defined.

12.2 Certain processing operations are excluded, and so are outside the scope of data protection. For example, processing of data by an individual in the course of his/her personal, family or household affairs (DPA, s 36) or in the course of a purely personal or household activity is excluded, even if it involves a profit or gain (Art 2(2)(c) of the Regulation). Recital 18 of the Regulation provides that purely personal or household activities include 'correspondence and the holding of addresses, or social networking and on-line activity undertaken within the context of such activities' but provided these have no connection to a professional or commercial activity. Likewise, the Regulation does not apply to a public body that processes data 'for the purposes of prevention, investigation, detection or prosecution of criminal offences, the execution of criminal penalties or the safeguarding against and the prevention of threats to public security' (Art 2.2(d)). This obviously includes the police and HM Revenue & Customs and any other bodies that investigate or prosecute criminal offences.

12.3 Principle 1 of the data protection principles discussed at **11.2** et seq above requires that personal data must be processed 'lawfully, fairly and in a transparent manner'. Many of the conditions that must be met to comply with this principle relate to the purpose(s) for which the controller intends to use the data. The conditions for processing also take account of the nature of the personal data in question: they are more exacting when the information is sensitive personal data, such as an individual's health or criminal record. Fairness may be seen as the starting point in determining what approach to take. The ICO has guided that if the controller is satisfied that what it proposes to do is fair it is likely to identify a condition for processing that fits its purpose(s) and therefore meets the requirement.

FAIR & LAWFUL PROCESSING

12.4   There are a number of ways in which the processing of personal data may be lawful:

- the processing is done with the data subject's 'unambiguous consent' for one or more specific purposes; or
- it is necessary to perform a contract with the data subject or for him/her to enter into the contract; or
- it is necessary for the controller to comply with a legal obligation; or
- it is necessary to protect the 'vital interests' of the data subject, i e a matter of life and death, or of another person; or
- it is necessary in the public interest or the exercise of a public duty by the controller; or
- it is necessary for purposes of the legitimate interests of the controller or a third party 'except where such interests are overridden by the interests or fundamental rights and freedoms of the data subject which require protection of personal data, in particular where the data subject is a child'.[1]

The last of these ways in which the processing may be lawful, i e the legitimate interests of the controller, do not apply to processing carried out by a public authority in the performance of its duties (Art 6(1)). Presumably this is because public authorities are assumed to have legitimate interests in doing what they do and that they so in accordance with the interests and 'fundamental rights and freedoms of the data subject'.

12.5   Schedule 2 to the DPA 1998 sets out similar conditions for fair and lawful processing. Processing of personal data for archiving purposes in the public interest or for historical, statistical or scientific research will also be lawful if it complies with the requirements of the new Regulation (Art 83).

Data subject's consent

12.6   The first condition for processing is that the individual concerned has consented to his/her personal data being obtained and used in the manner and for the specified purpose(s). The controller should satisfy itself that in every case an adequate consent has been given. The 1995 Directive defines an individual's consent as 'any freely given specific and informed indication of his wishes by which the data subject signifies his agreement to personal data relating to him being processed'. Accordingly, there must be some active communication between the parties in order for the individual to signify his/her agreement. Consent must also be appropriate to the age and capacity of the individual and to the particular circumstances of the case, eg where the relationship with a customer or client has ended. For example, if the

---

[1]   Article 6.1(a)–(f).

organisation intends to continue to hold an individual's personal data after the relationship ends, his/her consent should be obtained. Even when consent has been obtained, it may not last forever. The individual may withdraw his/her consent, depending on the nature of the consent and the circumstances in which the data controller is holding or using the data. The ICO has guided that a controller should not rely exclusively on consent to legitimate its processing: the overriding principle is that the controller should treat data subjects fairly.

12.7 Even before a controller starts processing personal data, it must fully inform the data subject so that he/she can decide whether to consent or not. This is to ensure that the processing is lawful, fair and done in a transparent manner (see 'Right to information and access' at **14.6** et seq below).

12.8 The new Regulation stresses the importance of consent as a basis for the lawful processing of personal data:

> 'Consent should be given by a clear affirmative action establishing a freely-given specific, informed and unambiguous indication of the data subject's agreement to the processing of personal data relating to him or her, such as by a written statement, including by electronic means, or an oral statement. This could include ticking a box when visiting an Internet website, choosing technical settings for information society services or by any other statement or conduct which clearly indicates in this context the data subject's acceptance of the proposed processing of his or her personal data. Silence, pre-ticked boxes or inactivity should not therefore constitute consent. Consent should cover all processing activities carried out for the same purpose or purposes. When the processing has multiple purposes, consent should be granted for all of them. If the data subject's consent is to be given following a request by electronic means, the request must be clear, concise and not unnecessarily disruptive to the use of the service for which it is provided.'[2]

12.9 What are the 'information society services' referred to above? These are defined as services 'normally provided for remuneration at a distance, by means of electronic equipment for the processing (including digital compression) and storage of data, at the individual request of a recipient of the service' (Electronic Commerce (EC Directive) Regulations 2002). These services include the operation of websites and all forms of electronic commerce, including buying and selling online. The 2002 Regulations provide that these services may or may not be paid for by those who receive them, and so they include online information, advertisements and services provided by search engines such as Google.

12.10 The Regulation provides some guidance for controllers as to how the consent may be obtained:

> 'Where processing is based on the data subject's consent, the controller should be able to demonstrate that the data subject has given the consent to the processing operation. In particular in the context of a written declaration on another matter, safeguards should ensure that the data subject is aware that and the extent to

---

2   Recital 32.

which consent is given. In line with Council Directive 93/13/EEC, a declaration of consent pre-formulated by the controller should be provided in an intelligible and easily accessible form, using clear and plain language and it should not contain unfair terms. For consent to be informed, the data subject should be aware at least of the identity of the controller and the purposes of the processing for which the personal data are intended; consent should not be regarded as freely-given if the data subject has no genuine and free choice and is unable to refuse or withdraw consent without detriment.'[3]

12.11 Accordingly, the onus is on the controller, in the event of a dispute, to show that the data subject consented to the processing (Art 7(1)). If this consent is contained, as is usually the case, in a standard form along with other matters such as permission to contact the person at certain times, 'the request for consent shallt be presented in a manner which is clearly distinguishable from the other matters in an intelligible and easily accessible form, using clear and plain language' (Art 7(2)). The data subject has the right to withdraw consent at any time – 'It shall be as easy to withdraw consent as to give it (Art 7(3)). Any processing carried on before withdrawal is not affected. He/she must be kept fully informed at all times of the right to do so and of the consequences. This may include the end of the relationship with a service provider or supplier.

12.12 How can it be established that consent is freely-given? What the Regulation describes as 'utmost account' must be taken of whether, for example, the performance of a contract depends on consent for the processing of data that is not necessary (Art 7(4)).

12.13 The respective positions of the parties involved may be relevant to the question whether consent is freely given. Consent will not be a valid ground for the processing if there is a 'clear imbalance' between the data subject and the controller, and this imbalance makes it unlikely that consent was freely given in the circumstances (Recital 43). Consent will also be regarded as not freely given if the processing consists of separate and distinct operations, each of which should require a specific consent. Likewise if the performance of a contract is stated to be dependent on the data subject's consent, where this is not so.

12.14 Accordingly, the default cannot be that the data subject has consented, in the absence of some indication by him/her. However, if consent is withdrawn the controller may discontinue the relevant service if it depends on processing of the data concerned. A supplier cannot continue to supply goods and services to a customer who has withdrawn consent to use of his/her name and address. It is unclear how a controller is to determine whether the original intended purpose of the processing has concluded so that the controller will have to engage with the data subject again for a 're-affirmation' of his/her consent. The controller's data protection procedures should provide for ongoing review of personal data it holds to ensure that it is only held for a specific purpose(s). These procedures should form part of the controller's data protection framework – see **15.19** et seq below.

---

[3]   Recital 42.

12.15 The data subject's consent, or lack of it, is perhaps the reason most often used to argue that processing is lawful or unlawful, as the case may be. Data consents are written into terms and conditions of products and services of all kinds. The Regulation defines consent as 'freely-given, specific, informed and unambiguous indication of the data subject's wishes by which he or she ,by a statement or by a clear affirmative action, signifies agreement to the processing of personal data relating to him or her' (Art 4(11)). In order for someone to consent, he/she obviously must know that his/her personal data is being processed, and why. This is the controller's responsibility. It is not the responsibility of the data subject to find out. The consent must also be explicit, which rules out implied consent. However, it may be either by statement, ie in writing, or by action, which suggests that even if there is nothing in writing from the data subject he/she may have consented to the processing by behaving in such a way as to show that he/she knew about it and agreed to it. For example, a customer of a bank that routinely carries out a property valuation as standard practice before giving a mortgage loan will be taken to have consented to the valuation if this was drawn to his/her attention. In particular, the customer will be regarded as having consented to the processing of any personal data required for this purpose if he/she proceeds with the loan transaction. This may be so even if the loan agreement does not contain a clause to that effect.

Case study

In April 2009 the Data Protection Commissioner (DPC) in Ireland received a complaint that a recruitment agency had shared a person's curriculum vitae (CV) with another agency. The two agencies were part of the same group of companies but were separate legal entities. The individual concerned had not been told that his CV might be shared between two different companies, and so had not consented to it. The DPC commented: 'It is important for any data controller to make individuals fully aware at the outset as to how their personal data will be processed and to whom it may be disclosed. As a general rule personal data may not be shared between two legal entities without the consent of the individual about whom the data relates.'

Performance of a contract

12.16 Processing will be lawful if it is necessary to perform a contract 'to which the data subject is party or in order to take steps at the request of the data subject prior to entering into a contract' (Art 6(1)(b)). This is data processing that either party or both parties need(s) to be done in order to perform their obligations under the contract. For example, a supplier of goods for delivery will obviously need the customer's address.

Compliance with a legal obligation

12.17 The processing may be necessary for the controller to comply with a legal obligation (Art 6(1)(c)). The obligation here is not contractual but arises from a legal or regulatory provision that applies to the controller. If, for example, a retailer is under investigation for price fixing or some other matter, and has to disclose to the relevant authorities personal data about customers or employees, this is being done to comply with a legal obligation, and so is lawful even without consent of the data subjects involved. Likewise, a financial institution as a 'designated person' under anti-money laundering legislation, is required to keep customer records, including personal data, for a minimum period from the date of account closing or completion of a particular transaction, as the case may be. This is a legal obligation that does not require the customer's consent.

Case study

The Data Protection Commissioner in Ireland confirmed in September 2015 that it was in order for the Department of Justice to publish the names and addresses of all those who had received Irish citizenship. This was on the basis of a provision in the Irish Nationality and Citizenship Act 1956, as amended, which requires the official publication of every notice of issue of a certificate of naturalisation. The Migrant Rights Centre Ireland had expressed concerns that the practice exposed individuals to a risk of fraud.

12.18 The Regulation makes special provision for the processing of personal data for compliance with a legal obligation in allowing Member States to introduce laws to specify how the requirement is to apply in practice (Recital 10). This allows Member States some flexibility in deciding how to apply the requirement:

> 'Regarding the processing of personal data for compliance with a legal obligation … Member States should be allowed to maintain or introduce national provisions to further specify the applicaton of the rules of this Regulation … The Regulation also provides a margin of manoeuvre for Member States to specify its rules including for the processing of sensitive data. To this extent, this Regulation does not exclude Member State law that sets out the circumstances for specific processing situations, including determining more precisely the conditions under which processing of personal data is lawful.'

Vital interests of the data subject

12.19 The processing will be lawful if it is necessary to protect an interest essential to the data subject's life or that of another person.

> 'Some types of processing may serve both important grounds of public interest and the vital interests of the data subject as, for instance when processing is necessary

for humanitarian purposes, including for monitoring epidemic and their spread or in situations of humanitarian emergencies, in particular in situations of natural and man-made disasters.'[4]

12.20 Accordingly, the processing will be lawful if it is necessary to protect the 'vital interests' of the data subject (Art 6(1)(d)). The new Regulation does not define what these interests are. As the main objective of the Regulation is to guarantee the fundamental right to privacy, the data subject's vital interests obviously include the privacy of his/her personal data. However, a data subject has a range of interests to be protected, eg health and medical needs to be addressed with or without a specific consent. It may be that he/she is not in a position to give consent for medical reasons to a particular medical procedure necessary to preserve health or indeed life. He/she may be unconscious or otherwise incapacitated. Accordingly, in these circumstances all data processing required for the procedure may be carried out in the absence of consent.

Public interest/public duty

12.21 The processing may be necessary 'for the performance of a task carried out in the public interest or in the exercise of official authority vested in the controller' (Art 6(1)(e)). If the controller is a public body, eg a government department or a local authority, it is permitted to process personal data for the purpose of performing the tasks, or exercising the duties, assigned to it. For example, a local authority responsible for the electoral register will process names and addresses of all those entitled to vote. The authority is permitted to do so, provided, of course, that as a controller it adopts all necessary safeguards to protect the data. The new Regulation recognises that some kinds of processing may serve both the public interest and the vital interests of a data subject, and will therefore be lawful on both grounds (Recital 46).

12.22 As in the case of compliance with a legal obligation, the new Regulation makes special provision for the processing of personal data in the exercise of official authority vested in the controller in allowing Member States to introduce laws to specify how the requirement is to apply in practice (Recital 10). This allows Member States some flexibility in deciding how to apply the requirement.

Legitimate interests

12.23 The processing will be lawful if it is necessary for purposes of the 'legitimate interests' of the controller (Art 6(1)(f)) or a third party to whom the data is disclosed, ie a processor or other third party to whom it is disclosed with the data subject's consent or to comply with a legal obligation. This is subject to the overriding interests or 'fundamental rights and freedoms of the data subject' that require protection. This basis for lawful processing does not

---

[4]   Recital 46.

apply to public authorities in the exercise of their duties, presumably on the grounds that public authorities have duties to perform rather than interests to be protected.

12.24 The new Regulation makes clear the scope of legitimate interests as basis for lawful processing of personal data:

> 'The legitimate interests of a controller including of a controller to which the data may be disclosed or of a third party may provide a legal basis for processing, provided that the interests or the fundamental rights and freedoms of the data subject are not overriding, taking into consideration the reasonable expectations of data subjects based on the relationship with the controller. Such legitimate interest could exist for example where there is a relevant and appropriate relationship between the data subject and the controller in situations such as where the data subject is a client or in the service of the controller. At any rate the existence of a legitimate interest would need careful assessment including whether a data subject can reasonably expect at the time and in the context of the collection of the data that processing for that purpose may take place. The interests and fundamental rights of the data subject could in particular override the interests of the data controller where personal data are processed in circumstances where data subjects do not reasonably expect further processing.... The processing of personal data strictly necessary for the purposes of preventing fraud also constitutes a legitimate interest of the data controller concerned. The processing of personal data for direct marketing purposes may be regarded as carried out for a legitimate interest.[5]

12.25 A controller can only rely on this basis for data processing if it is 'necessary', ie directly related to its legitimate business interests. For example, an accounting firm or a law firm is allowed to keep personal records of their clients in order to send out invoices for fees or, if necessary, issue legal proceedings in default of payment. However, it may not retain these records after the relationship has ended merely in order to send the client some marketing material in the future, in the absence of the client's consent.

Example

Cash Grab Limited is unable to locate a customer who has stopped making loan repayments. The company hires a debt collection agency to find the customer and collect the debt. It discloses the customer's personal data to the agency for this purpose. This is done for the purposes of the finance company's legitimate interests – to collect the debt. However, the controller's legitimate interests must be balanced against the interests of the individual(s) concerned. The processing must be fair and lawful and must comply with all the data protection principles.

12.26 The new Regulation recognises that legitimate interests also include network and information security (Recital 49).

---

[5]   Recital 47.

Marketing & profiling

12.27 The DPA defines direct marketing as 'the communication (by whatever means) of any advertising or marketing material which is directed to particular individuals' (s 11). Accordingly, direct marketing refers to any communication to an individual to promote a product or service. More and more companies are marketing their products and services directly to prospective customers, whether by post, email, fax or phone (mobile and landline). The right to object to processing for direct marketing purposes is one of the rights derived from Principle 6 of the data protection principles discussed at **1.22** above and **11.65** et seq above. (This is the principle that personal data must be processed in accordance with the rights of data subjects.)

12.28 The Privacy and Electronic Communications (EC Directive) Regulations 2003 (PECR), as amended in 2004, 2011 and 2015, define electronic mail as 'any text, voice, sound, or image message sent over a public electronic communications network which can be stored in the network or in the recipient's terminal equipment until it is collected by the recipient and includes messages sent using a short message service'. Email, text and picture messages are all considered to be electronic mail for this purpose. Marketing transmitted in WAP (wireless application protocol) messages is also considered to be electronic mail. WAP Push allows a sender to send a specially formatted SMS (short message service) to a handset that allows the recipient to access and view content stored online.

12.29 An organisation cannot transmit unsolicited marketing material by electronic mail to an individual subscriber unless he/she has previously notified the sender that he/she consents, for the time being, to receiving the communication. This implies that he/she has the option to withdraw that consent at a later stage. The ICO has stated that it will take enforcement action against organisations that persistently fail to comply with opt-out requests from individual subscribers.

12.30 An exception to this rule is often referred to as the 'soft opt in'. This means that electronic mail for marketing purposes may be sent to an individual subscriber where:

- the sender has obtained the contact details of the recipient in the course of a sale or negotiations for the sale of a product or service to him/her; and
- the direct marketing material being sent relates only to similar products and services provided by the sender; and
- the recipient was given a free and simple means of refusing the use of their contact details for marketing purposes when those details were initially collected and, if he/she did not refuse the use of those details, at the time of each subsequent communication.

12.31 If these conditions are met, the sender does not need prior consent to send marketing by electronic mail to individual subscribers. Accordingly, if the conditions are not met, marketing material may not be sent by electronic mail to individual subscribers without their prior consent.

12.32 Is there any difference between an 'individual subscriber' and the 'recipient' of marketing material by electronic mail? The relevant EU Directive provides that unsolicited marketing should not be sent by electronic mail to an 'individual subscriber' unless he/she has given consent. However, the PECR refer to the 'recipient's' consent. The ICO has guided that 'recipient' means the intended recipient. If a household member has an individual email address, then the consent of that individual is required unless the soft opt-in criteria are satisfied. If a household has a collective email address, eg familyname@domainname.com, the consent of someone whom the sender reasonably believes can speak on behalf of the family is sufficient, unless the soft opt-in conditions are satisfied.

12.33 Accordingly, the PECR provide that a data subject's consent is required if his/her personal data, ie name, address, email address, phone number, is to be used for marketing purposes. However, email may be used to send an unsolicited communication for the purpose of direct marketing to an individual if the email address reasonably appears to be an email address used mainly by the recipient for their 'commercial or official activity' and the communication relates solely to that activity. This is provided that the recipient has not informed the sender that he/she does not consent to receipt of the communication.

12.34 Unaddressed post, eg brochures or leaflets, and post addressed to 'The Occupant' or 'The Householder', do not involve the use of personal data but if a controller can identify an individual from his/her address in conjunction with other data, this may constitute personal data that is protected by law. In order to use personal data for marketing by post, the controller must inform the intended recipients that it plans to use their data for this purpose, and give them an opportunity to object to receiving this material. This should be done at the time the data is obtained from the data subject(s). Likewise, if the controller obtained the data from a third party source such as a public register, it must give the intended recipient(s) the opportunity to object to receipt of the material.

Case study

The ICO received many complaints about a company called First Financial who sent unsolicited communications for the purposes of direct marketing. Between 1 February 2013 and 31 March 2013, First Financial sent 4,031 unsolicited direct marketing texts to mobile phone subscribers who had not consented to receive them. The company was fined £175,000 and the ICO commented:

'The texts were an invasion of privacy ... The texts were designed to appear as if they were from a friend and were deceptive ... The texts were about ➥

loans when the recipient had never had a loan, credit card or other kind of credit, had never had cash flow problems and did not need a loan/was ineligible for one; … the issue of unsolicited texts is a matter of considerable and widespread public concern. [First Financial] knew or ought to have known that there was a risk that the contravention would occur and that it would be of a kind likely to cause substantial damage or substantial distress … It cannot be said to be a "one-off" contravention, as might be the case where there were systems in place but they momentarily failed. The sheer volume of complaints amounts to evidence that there were no systems in place.'

Case study

In November 2012 the ICO imposed penalties of £440,000 on the owners of a marketing company, Tetrus Telecoms, who had sent millions of text message over a three-year period. These were sent without the consent of recipients and without identifying the sender. In the course its investigation, the ICO raided the company's premises and the home of one of its owners.

12.35 Where personal data is held for direct marketing, the data subject can request the controller not to process the data for that purpose or to stop processing if it has already started (DPA, s 11(1)). A court may order the controller to comply with the request. The new Regulation provides for a specific right to object by data subjects to the processing of personal data for direct marketing:

'Where personal data are processed for direct marketing purposes, the data subject shall have the right to object at any time to the processing of personal data concerning him or her for such marketing, which includes profiling to the extent that it is related to such direct marketing.'[6]

12.36 Accordingly, the data subject must be informed at the outset of any communications that he/she has the right to object. If he/she exercises that right, the data cannot be processed for these purposes (Art 21(3)). The right to object is discussed further at **14.30** et seq below. (See **Appendix 7** for a *Direct Marketing Checklist*.)

12.37 Companies need to know as much as possible about their customers and prospective customers in order to provide them with suitable products and services. In particular, companies who operate in advertising or social media seek to profile their audience and tailor their message to suit. However, the new Regulation sets limits on the extent to which companies can create a personal profile of an individual. *Profiling* is defined as 'any form of automated processing of personal data intended to evaluate certain personal aspects relating to a natural person or to analyse or predict aspects concerning that

---

[6]   Article 21(2).

natural person's performance at work, economic situation, location, health, personal preferences, interests, reliability, behaviour, location or movements' (Art 4(4)). This is processing designed to paint a picture of a customer or prospective customer for marketing purposes. The Regulation is concerned with decisions made by a controller based solely on automated processing, including profiling, that produce 'legal effects' concerning the data subject or significantly affect him or her (Art 22(1)). The Regulation prohibits any profiling that does not include appropriate measures to safeguard the rights of the data subject, including his/her right to be consulted, and is not:

- necessary to enter into or perform a contract with the data subject;
- expressly authorised by law; or
- done with the data subject's explicit consent, and appropriate safeguards. This consent can be withdrawn at any time. In the event of a dispute, the onus is on the controller to show that the data subject consented to the profiling.[7]

12.38 Profiling is commonly carried out through the use of data analytics or 'data mining' by companies that hold large amounts of information about the behaviour of their customers or prospective customers. This is sometimes known as 'Big Data'. Companies will analyse this data to make key decisions about their products and services, including branding, packaging and pricing. For example, retailers who distribute loyalty cards to customers in order to gather information about their purchasing patterns will use this data to market their products and services. The new Regulation allows profiling only in certain circumstances to protect customers from improper or unlawful use of this data.

12.39 A further prohibition applies to profiling that has the effect of discriminating against individuals on the basis of *special categories* of personal data. These are data relating to an individual's criminal record, health, race, politics, religion, sex life or trade union membership (Art 9(1)). A controller cannot attempt to profile data subjects using these categories of data unless appropriate measures are put in place to safeguard the rights of the data subject and the processing is either done with his/her consent or the processing is necessary for reasons of 'substantial' public interest (Art 22(4)).

12.40 The special categories of personal data referred to above are the same as 'sensitive personal data' as defined by the DPA – see **10.24** et seq above. It may happen that a company carries out profiling, not on the basis of sensitive personal data, but uses profiling to create or imply this data. For example, a postal address is not sensitive personal data (although it can be personal if linked to an individual) but taken together with data that someone regularly goes to that address and data about activities that take place there, the address may be enough to disclose information about his/her medical condition or sex life or other sensitive personal data, depending on the activities involved. This profiling is prohibited if it does not safeguard the individual's data protection

---

[7]   Article 22(2)(a)–(c) .

rights and discriminates against him/her because it generates sensitive personal data even if it does not include such data in the profiling operation itself, ie the address, travel to that address and activities carried on there, which separately may not amount to sensitive personal data.

'APPROPRIATE MEASURES'

12.41 The data protection regime imposes strict obligations on controllers and processors as to the security of processing of personal data. As discussed at **11.77** above, one of the basic principles is that the data must be kept safe and secure. Principle 7 refers to 'appropriate technical and organisational measures' and 'measures to provide 'appropriate security. These must be put in place to safeguard against unauthorised alteration, disclosure or destruction of the data:

> 'Taking into account the state of the art and the costs of implementation and the nature, scope, context and purposes of processing as well as the risk of varying likelihood and severity for the rights, and freedoms of individuals, the controller and the processor shall implement appropriate technical and organisational measures, to ensure a level of security appropriate to the risk, including inter alia, as appropriate:
>
> (a)   the pseudonymisation and encryption of personal data;
> (b)   the ability to ensure the ongoing confidentiality, integrity, availability and resilience of systems and services;
> (c)   the ability to restore the availability and access to data in a timely manner in the event of a physical or technical incident;
> (d)   a process for regularly testing, assessing and evaluating the effectiveness of technical and organisational measures for ensuring the security of the processing.'[8]

12.42 Adherence to approved codes of conduct or an approved certification mechanism provided for by Art 39 will demonstrate compliance with these requirements (Art 40(3)). Controllers and processors must take steps to ensure that anyone acting under their authority will not process the relevant data except on the controller's instructions unless required to do so by law (Art 40(3)). They should also be aware that the legal standard for the protection of personal data, ie the standard imposed by the data protection regime, is higher than, and additional to, any legal obligation as to confidentiality arising from a contract. Accordingly, an organisation may enter into a contract with an employee or a supplier that provides for confidentiality, but over and above this contractual obligation the organisation will have data protection obligations that arise from the DPA and the new Regulation. The controller must take all reasonable steps to ensure that employees and others are aware of these measures and comply with them.

12.43 Accordingly, controllers and processors must implement 'appropriate technical and organisational measures' to ensure compliance with the new

---

[8]   Article 32(1).

Regulation. In particular, as regards security, the Regulation requires that controllers and processors implement these measures and procedures to ensure a level of security appropriate to the risks involved in the processing itself and the nature of the data itself (Art 32(3)). Accordingly, the more sensitive the data involved, the higher the level of security required to protect it. This requires an analysis of the data itself and of the risks involved in processing it. This analysis should form the basis of an Information Security Policy to be adopted by the controller/processor. An Information Security Policy is one of those policies required by the new Regulation to demonstrate compliance with the relevant requirements. (For a sample Information Security Policy, see FP 13.2.)

12.44   The draft EU Network and Information Security Directive (NISD) will apply to companies and organisations in critical areas such as energy, transport, financial services, food supply, internet service providers and health. These organisations must implement specified security measures to ensure a level of protection appropriate to the risk presented. They must also notify the competent authorities of any incident having a significant impact on the security of the core services they provide. The NISD was expected to be finalised by end of 2015 and will be implemented in all Member States within two years from that date.

12.45   The results of the UK Government's Information Security Breaches Survey 2015 are instructive. They show that security breaches are on the increase. In 2015 90% of large organisations suffered a security breach as compared to 81% in 2014. The cost of dealing with them also increased, with an average cost of between £1.46 million and £3.14 million in 2015 compared to between £600,000 and £1.15 million in 2014. While many attacks came from outside the organisation (69%) an even greater number originated from within (75%), with a significant number of these due to human error (50%).

Case Studies:

The multinational media company Sony Inc. announced in October 2015 that it had agreed terms with its employees who were affected by the hacking of their personal data in 2014 in relation to the film *The Interview*. Sony agreed to pay up to $2.5 million in total to staff for 'unreimbursed losses from identity theft or misuse' and up to $2 million for 'preventative measures' that staff had taken to prevent identity theft. The US payments company, Target, suffered a 'cyber attack' on its point of sale systems in 2013, and the card details of 40 million customers were stolen. The company saw a 46% drop in its profits for Q4 2013 and estimated the cost of the attack at $148 million.

12.46   Personal data of employees is often a cause of concern to employers. In particular, the extent to which an employer may carry out surveillance of employees' electronic communications raises a number of concerns for the organisation. The EU's Article 29 Working Party on Data Protection produced a report on the subject in 2001. (The Article 29 Working Party is a body comprised of representatives of EU data protection authorities.) The report recommended that any surveillance should be transparent, necessary, fair, proportionate and done for a specific purpose, eg to protect the legitimate interests of the organisation. The report also recommended that an employer should ask itself whether the proposed surveillance could be done by other, less obtrusive means. A minimalist approach should be followed, ie the minimum necessary to achieve the objective. The strategy should be prevention of wrongdoing in order to protect the organisation while respecting the privacy of employees (*Opinion 8/2001 on the processing of personal data in the employment context* (2001)).

Example

A manufacturing company regularly sends its sales representatives on sales missions to foreign countries. They travel with laptops and other mobile devices that contain personal data relating to their employment. Provided these devices remain under the control of employees, and the company has effective procedures to deal with data security, there is adequate protection of the data.

12.47 The International Labour Organisation Code of Practice on Protection of Workers Personal Data 1997 recommends that:

- employees should be informed in advance of reasons, time schedule, methods and techniques used and the personal data collected;
- the monitoring must minimise the intrusion on the privacy of employees;
- secret monitoring must be in conformity with legislation or on foot of suspicion of criminal activity or serious wrongdoing; and
- continuous monitoring should only occur if required for health and safety or protection of property.

Case study

In November 2013 the French data protection authority CNIL issued a warning to a company that operated shopping centres regarding its use of surveillance equipment. The cameras were installed at various locations including locker rooms, medical offices and break rooms, as well as locations where there was toilet access. They allowed the employees to be monitored continuously throughout the working day. The CNIL stated that the presence of 240 cameras, which monitored the company's 230 employees, was both excessive and disproportionate to the purpose for which the cameras were installed:

- the cameras were used to control the employees' work schedule;
- the employees were not informed that the surveillance equipment had been installed; and →

> • the employer failed to ensure confidentiality and security of the
> personal data, since the videos were easily accessible.

12.48 The sample Information Security Policy at Appendix 2 [FP 13.2] provides for the right of the organisation to monitor use of its computer and communications systems, including email. Employees should be made aware that email is an essential communications tool but carries risks. Employees should not download any software from the Internet without approval, and access to certain websites should be restricted. Social networking should not be allowed without approval. Employees should receive clear guidance on the use of passwords, the need to keep them confidential and to change them at regular intervals. Remote access to the organisation's computer system should be subject to specific requirements as to secure login. Finally, employees should only be allowed to use their own electronic device for work purposes if appropriate security requirements are complied with. The Employment Practices Code published by the ICO provides further guidance for employers.

OUTSOURCING

12.49 Outsourcing has become an industry in its own right as companies seek to concentrate on their core profit-making operations and leave other operations to a third party. The new Regulation recognises that a controller may outsource, ie engage a third party to perform, a particular task or function that is not central to the company's operations or does not contribute to profits. This may be the payroll function or some other function that the company does not need to perform itself. In the case of payroll, for example, this will involve transfer to a third party of personal data relating to employees. The third party will then become a data processor acting on behalf of the data controller – see 'Key definitions' at **10.24** et seq above. The data protection regime requires that a formal contract is put in place for this purpose, together with appropriate security standards.

Example

An electricity provider decides to outsource part of its customer services function to a third party who operates a call centre for that purpose. Staff at the call centre have access to the provider's customer database in order to handle calls from customers. However, they can only use information about customers for a specific purpose. There are strict contractual arrangements between the provider and the company that operates the call centre, and staff are trained to handle customer calls in accordance in accordance with these arrangements. Accordingly, the electricity provider is the controller and the company is the processor.

12.50 The new Regulation makes specific provision for the processing of personal data by a processor on behalf of a data controller. The processing must be carried on in pursuance of a contract between processor and controller. The contract should set the subject-matter, nature and purposes of the processing, the types of personal data and the categories of data subjects, and the rights and duties of the controller (Art 28(3)). It must oblige the processor to act only in accordance with the controller's instructions (Art 28(3)(a)) and in compliance with the same obligations that bind the controller, in particular 'appropriate technical and organisational measures' to protect the data against unauthorised access to, or unauthorised alteration, disclosure or destruction.

12.51 What are these 'technical and organisational measures' that must be implemented by the processor? As discussed above, they must form part of a binding contract between controller and processor (Art 28(3)).

> 'The responsibility and liability of the controller for any processing of personal data carried out by the controller or on the controller's behalf should be established. In particular, the controller should be obliged to implement appropriate and effective measures and be able to demonstrate the compliance of processing activities with this Regulation, including the effectiveness of the measures. Those measures should take into account the nature, scope, context and purposes of the processing and the risk for the rights and freedoms of natural persons.'[9]

12.52 The contract must oblige the processor to:

- act only on the controller's instructions, unless otherwise required by law – in that event the processor must so inform the controller prior to the processing unless prohibited 'on important grounds of public interest';
- take all measures required to ensure security of the data;
- comply with the conditions for engaging another processor, including the prior agreement of the controller;
- as far as possible, assist the controller to protect the rights of data subjects, notify data security breaches to them and to the supervisory authority, ie the ICO; complete a data privacy impact assessment and engage in prior consultation with the ICO as required by Art 36;
- return or delete the data, at the controller's option, on termination of the processing unless otherwise required by law; and
- provide 'all information necessary' to enable the controller to demonstrate compliance with these obligations and allow on-site audits by the controller.[10]

12.53 The processor must inform the controller immediately if it believes that any instruction is in breach of the new Regulation or any EU law or Member State law (Art 28(3)).

12.54 Accordingly, a controller should take great care in selecting a processor to work on its behalf. The controller remains responsible for compliance with the new Regulation. The Regulation is quite specific about the requirements:

---

[9] Recital 74.
[10] Article 28.3(a)–(h).

'To ensure compliance with the requirements of this Regulation in respect of the processing to be carried out by the processor on behalf of the controller, when entrusting a processor with processing activities, the controller should use only processors providing sufficient guarantees, in particular in terms of expert knowledge, reliability and resources, to implement technical and organisational measures which will meet the requirements of this Regulation, including for the security of processing. The adherence of the processor to an approved code of conduct or an approved certification mechanism may be used as an element to demonstrate compliance with the obligations of the controller. The carrying-out of processing by a processor should be governed by a contract or other legal act under Union or Member State law, binding the processor to the controller, setting out the subject-matter and duration of the processing, the nature and purposes of the processing, the type of personal data and categories of data subjects, taking into account the specific tasks and responsibilities of the processor in the context of the processing to be carried out and the risk to the rights and freedoms of the data subject ...'[11]

(See *Outsourcing: A Guide for Small and Medium-Sized Businesses* at Appendix 5.)

12.55 As stated above, a processor can only process personal data on the instructions of the controller, unless required to do otherwise by law (Art 28(3)(a)). If the processor acts contrary to those instructions, or effectively becomes the 'determining party', ie determines the purpose and means of the processing, it will be regarded as a *joint controller* and will share all the obligations imposed on the controller. The processor cannot engage another processor without the controller's agreement (Art 28(2)).

12.56 Accordingly, the new Regulation provides specifically for a situation where the controller processes personal data jointly with other parties. All parties concerned will be regarded as joint controllers if they jointly determine the purposes and means of the processing (Art 26(1)) and they must decide among themselves how they are to comply with the new Regulation with regard to the data:

'The arrangement shall duly reflect the joint controllers' respective effective roles and relationships vis-à-vis the data subjects, and the essence of the arrangement shall be made available to the data subject.' (Art 26(2))

Example

The local council and the police jointly operate a network of CCTV cameras around the town centre. They decide together how the network operates and what the images captured on camera are used for. The council and the police are joint controllers as defined by the Regulation. They both have responsibilities as controller in relation to the personal data processed in operating the network.

12.57 Joint controllership is only possible where a special legal basis provides for processing the data jointly for a common purpose: a database jointly run by

---

[11]   Recital 81.

several credit institutions on their defaulting customers is a common example. When someone applies for credit from a bank that is one of the joint controllers, the bank checks the database to help it make an informed decision about the individual's creditworthiness.

12.58 A joint controllership arrangement will include how data subjects can exercise their rights, eg access to the data, right to object, right to be forgotten. However, regardless of the arrangement between them, the data subject can exercise his/her rights against either any of them. In that event all joint controllers will be liable to the data subject.

12.59 Likewise, if the processor engages another processor, ie a sub-processor, to carry out specific activities on behalf of the controller, the relevant obligations must be set out in a contract (Art 28(4)). The contract must provide for the same obligations as provided for in the contract between controller and processor. The processor will remain liable to the controller for the performance of the relevant activities by the sub-processor.

12.60 The Regulation provides for 'standard contractual clauses' to be laid down by the European Commission or adopted by the ICO to be used by controllers and processors, and sub-processors if applicable (Art 28(7) and (8)). These are similar to the standard clauses prescribed for the transfer of personal data outside the EU as discussed further below.

12.61 The Article 29 Working Party has provided useful guidance on contractual safeguards in the relationship between controller and processor ('Opinion 05/2012 on Cloud Computing'). The opinion focuses on the core security objectives of availability, confidentiality and integrity. For example, as regards availability it emphasis the risk arising from the potential loss of connectivity and failures of network infrastructure or hardware. It advises that appropriate diligence should be applied to check there are adequate mechanisms to deal with these risks.

DATA TRANSFER OUTSIDE EU

12.62 As discussed at **11.87** et seq above, the DPA provides for a specific principle (Principle 8) that seeks to protect personal data transferred outside the EU: 'Personal data shall not be transferred to a country or territory outside the European Economic Area unless that country or territory ensures an adequate level of protection for the rights and freedoms of data subjects in relation to the processing of personal data.'[12]

12.63 The European Economic Area (EEA) comprises the EU Member States in addition to Liechtenstein, Norway and Iceland. There is no equivalent

---

[12] DPA 1998, Sch 1, Part 1.

statement of principle in the new Regulation but it provides for transfer of data to countries and territories outside the EU.

12.64 The new Regulation provides for the cross-border transfer of personal data, and in particular transfer of personal data to countries/territories and organisations outside the EU:

> 'Flows of personal data to and from countries outside the Union and international organisations are necessary for the expansion of international trade and international co-operation. The increase in such flows has raised new challenges and concerns with regard to the protection of personal data. However, when personal data are transferred from the Union to controllers, processors or other recipients in third countries or to international organisations, the level of protection of natural persons ensured in the Union by this Regulation should not be undermined, including in cases of outward transfers of personal data from the third country or international organisation to controllers or processors in the same or another third country or international organisation. In any event, transfers to third countries and international organisations may only be carried out in full compliance with this Regulation. A transfer may only take place if, subject to the other provisions of this Regulation, the conditions laid down in Chapter V are complied with by the controller or processor.'[13]

12.65 Accordingly, personal data can be transferred outside the EU provided the country or organisation concerned ensures that 'an adequate level of protection' applies to the data (Art 45(1)). No specific authorisation is required. The Regulation seeks to ensure that data is not transferred outside the EU without adequate protection, equivalent to the protection afforded to data within the Union.

Example

An insurance broker uses a company outside the EU for data entry in relation to customer. The broker sends handwritten notes to the company for entry into a computer system for managing customer accounts. This amounts to a transfer of data outside the EU even though the information is not part of a relevant filing system or held on a computer in the UK. Accordingly, the transfer must comply with the requirements of the new Regulation.

12.66 Chapter V of the Regulation lays down mandatory obligations for the transfer of data outside the EU:

> 'Any transfer of personal data which are undergoing pro*cessing or are intended for processing after transfer to a third country or to an international* organisation may only take place if, subject to the other provisions of this Regulation, the conditions laid down in this Chapter are complied with by the controller and processor, including for onward transfers of personal data from the third country or an international organization. All provisions in this Chapter shall be applied in order to ensure that the level of protection of individuals guaranteed by this Regulation is not undermined.' (Art 44)

---

[13]   Recital 101.

12.67 The European Commission is the institution that decides whether a non-EU country or international organisation is able to provide an adequate level of data protection. In deciding whether the country or organisation concerned can provide the necessary level of protection, the Commission will take the following factors into account:

- the rule of law, respect for human rights and fundamental freedoms, relevant legislation, data protection rules and security measures, 'effective and enforceable data subject rights, and effective administrative and judicial redress';

- an effective and independent supervisory authority, or an authority to which the organisation is subject, as the case may be, with responsibility for enforcing compliance with data protection rules, including adequate sanctioning powers; and

- the international commitments that country or organisation has entered into, in particular relating to data protection.[14]

12.68 The new Regulation empowers the Commission to adopt what are called 'delegated acts', ie delegated to it by the Council and European Parliament to decide that a third country, or territory within that country, or the international organisation, provides the necessary level of protection or does not provide it, as the case may be (Art 45(3) and (5)). (Article 92 confers on the Commission the power to adopt these delegated acts for 'an indeterminate period of time' unless revoked at any time by the European Parliament or by the Council.)

12.69 If the Commission decides in favour of a country or organisation outside the EU, personal data may be transferred without any specific authorisation. If the Commission has made no decision, the data cannot be transferred unless the appropriate safeguards are put in place. In that event the controller or processor, as the case may be, must commit to putting these safeguards in place to protect the data to be transferred outside the EU:

> 'In any case, where the Commission has taken no decision on the adequate level of data protection in a third country, the controller or processor should make use of solutions that provide data subjects with enforceable and effective rights as regards processing of their data in the Union once this data has been transferred so that they will continue to benefit from fundamental rights and safeguards.'[15]

12.70 These safeguards may take the form of any of the following:

- 'legally binding and enforceable instruments' between public authorities;
- binding corporate rules;
- standard contract clauses adopted by the Commission or the ICO or both;

---

[14] Article 45(2)(a)–(c).
[15] Recital 114.

- an approved code of conduct with contractual commitments by the controller or processor to apply the appropriate safeguards to protect the data;

- an approved certification mechanism with contractual commitments by the controller or processor to apply the appropriate safeguards to protect the data;

- a contract between the controller or processor, as the case may be, in the EU and the country or international organisation concerned, subject to authorisation from the supervisory authority, ie the ICO;

- administrative arrangements between public authorities 'which include enforceable and effective data subject rights'.[16]

Binding corporate rules

12.71   One of the appropriate safeguards are *binding corporate rules* (Art 47). These are rules within a group of companies that commit the organisation to specific standards in relation to the transfer of data outside the EU. The rules must bind all members of the group. This option is available to multinational companies that transfer personal data outside the EU but within a group of companies. The rules can take the form of a written statement or formal agreement on the corporate governance of the group. They must 'expressly confer enforceable rights on data subjects' (Art 47(1)(b)) and must also specify the following at a minimum:

- the structure and contact details of the group, if applicable, and those of its members;

- 'the data transfers or set of transfers', data or categories of data transferred, the processing and its purpose(s), the category of data subjects affected, and the country or countries that may receive the data;

- 'legally binding nature, both internally and externally' of the relevant rules;

- application of the data protection principles, including purpose limitation, data minimisation, limited storage periods, data quality, data protection by design and by default, legal basis for the processing, processing of special categories of data, measures to ensure data security, and requirements for any onward transfer to parties not bound by the binding corporate rules;

- the rights of data subjects, including the right not to be subject to decisions based solely on automated processing, including profiling, and the right to make a complaint and, where appropriate, obtain redress and compensation;

- acceptance by the controller or processor of liability for any breach of the binding corporate rules by any member of the group established outside

---

[16]   Article 46(2)(a)–(f) and Article 46(3)(a) and (b).

the EU, if applicable, unless the controller or processor shows that the member concerned is not responsible for the breach;

- how information about the rules is to be provided to data subjects;
- the tasks of the data protection officer or any other party in monitoring compliance with the corporate rules within the company or group, as well as training and complaint handling;
- procedures for handling complaints;
- mechanisms for verifying compliance with the corporate rules, including data protection audits and methods to ensure any corrective actions necessary to protect the rights of data subjects;
- mechanisms for reporting to the ICO any changes to the corporate rules;
- mechanisms for co-operating with the ICO, including reporting the results of verification tests;
- mechanisms for reporting to the ICO any legal requirements affecting a member of the group outside the EU that may affect the safeguards provided by the corporate rules; and
- appropriate training for personnel with access to the data.[17]

Standard contract clauses

12.72   The appropriate safeguards to be put in place may consist of 'standard contract clauses', also called model clauses, to be used in contracts between the sender and recipient of the data concerned. These are contract clauses, also called 'model clauses', adopted by the ICO with the approval of the European Commission (Art 46(2)(d)) or clauses agreed between the controller/processor and the party receiving the data outside the EU (Art 46(3)(a)). Whether binding corporate rules or contract clauses are used, no further authorisation is required for transfer of the data. However, in the case of contract clauses agreed between the parties involved in the transfer these must be submitted to the ICO for approval (as distinct from clauses adopted by the ICO with the approval of the Commission).

12.73   There are several types of contract that may be put in place to ensure an adequate level of protection of personal data to be transferred outside the EU. These include contracts based on the model clauses, approved by the European Commission or the ICO, and other contracts drawn up by the data controller after a risk assessment and that includes clauses agreed between the parties and approved by the ICO.

12.74   The European Commission has approved four sets of standard contract clauses, or model clauses, for use in contracts for transfer of data so as to provide an adequate level of protection. A controller that uses these model clauses in the contract will not have to complete its own risk assessment of the transfer. Two of the sets of clauses relate to transferring personal data from one

---

[17]   Article 47(2)(a)–(n).

organisation to another that will then use it for its own purposes as a controller, ie controller to controller. The other two sets of clauses are for transferring personal data to a processor acting under a controller's instructions, such as a company that provides IT services, ie controller to processor. (There is no set of clauses for data transfers from processor to processor.) The ICO has authorised the use of these model clauses in relevant contracts.

(1) *Controller to controller*: set of model clauses for transfers from data controllers in the EEA to data controllers outside the EEA (Commission Decision 2004/915/EC).

(2) *Controller to processor*: set of model clauses for transfers from data controllers in the EEA to data processors outside the EEA (Commission Decision 2010/87/EU).

12.75 The model clauses impose obligations on both the sender, or exporter, and the recipient, or importer, of the data to ensure that the transfer arrangements protect the rights and freedoms of the data subjects. The clauses may not be amended but may be incorporated into other contracts such as a data processing service agreement, or additional clauses may be added to them, provided that nothing changes the effect of any of the model clauses.

12.76 Alternatively, the controller may decide to use its own form of contracts to ensure adequacy for a particular transfer. These contracts may address a particular weakness the controller is aware of, or indeed form the entire basis for the protection of individuals' rights in the process of transfer of the data concerned. However, these contracts must be approved by the ICO. If the controller uses contract clauses that differ from the model clauses, it risks challenge to the adequacy of the contract's level of protection. It must be able to justify the use of alternative contract clauses on objective grounds that are documented clearly. Accordingly, the controller may use an internal code of conduct, similar to binding corporate rules, to transfer information from the UK without an authorisation, provided it has conducted a risk assessment, and is satisfied that the code provides the level of required safeguards. However, if the controller uses an unauthorised code of conduct it risks challenge to the adequacy of the level of protection afforded by the code.

DEROGATIONS IF NO COMMISSION DECISION & NO SAFEGUARDS

12.77 What if the European Commission has made no decision, ie a decision on the adequacy of data protection in the non-EU country or organisation, and there are no 'appropriate safeguards' in place, whether by way of binding corporate rules or any of the other mechanisms specified in the new Regulation? In that event the transfer can only take place if:

•   the data subject(s) has/have explicitly consented to the proposed transfer, having been informed that it may involve risks for him/her due to the absence of a Commission decision and appropriate safeguards. This consent must be given clearly and freely and may be withdrawn at any time. The ICO has guided that consent is unlikely to provide a long-term solution to repeated transfers or a transfer due to a corporate restructure;

- the transfer is necessary to perform a contract between the data subject and the controller or to implement 'pre-contractual measures taken at the data subject's request';

- the transfer is necessary to conclude, ie enter into, or perform a contract in the interests of the data subject between the controller and a third party. For example, the customer of a UK credit card issuer uses his card in the US – it may be necessary for the card issuer to transfer the customer's personal data to the US to validate the card and/or pay for the relevant goods or services;

- the transfer is necessary for 'important reasons of public interest' that are recognised in law; this is most likely to be relevant in the prevention and detection of crime. The public interest here is that of the UK and not the country or territory to which the personal data is to be transferred;

- the transfer is necessary to exercise or defend a legal claim, ie in connection with any legal proceedings, current or pending, or to obtain legal advice or to enforce legal rights. For example, a US company is sued by an employee of its UK subsidiary – relevant employee information may be transferred to the US company as it is required for the defence;

- the transfer is necessary to protect the 'vital interests' of the data subject or another person if he/she is incapable of giving consent due to incapacity. This relates to matters of life and death. For example, a hospital in the UK may transfer relevant medical records to another country where someone has collapsed and his/her medical history is necessary to determine the appropriate treatment;

- the transfer is made from a public register, but not the entire register or an entire category of personal data contained in it, provided the transfer is done in accordance with law; a controller may transfer part of the personal data on a public register, provided the recipient complies with any restrictions on access to, or use of, the information. For example, a professional body such as the General Medical Council may transfer extracts from its register of doctors to respond to enquiries from outside the UK, but it may not transfer the entire register; or

- the transfer is necessary for the 'compelling' legitimate interests of the controller that are not overridden by the interests or rights and freedoms of the data subject, provided the transfer is not frequent or concerns only a limited number of data subjects and the controller has implemented appropriate safeguards that are documented. In that event the controller must inform the ICO of the transfer and also inform the data subject.[18]

12.78 A public authority in the exercise of its powers is exempt from the requirement to obtain the consent of data subjects affected, or the requirements

---

[18] Article 49(1)(a)–(g).

that the proposed transfer is necessary for performance of a contract or implementation of pre-contractual measures or for the legitimate interests of the controller (Art 49(3)). The new Regulation provides that EU law or the law of a Member State may restrict the transfer of specific categories of data outside the EU 'for important reasons of public interest', if the Commission has made no decision (Art 49(5)).

UNAUTHORISED TRANSFER

12.79 What if a court or similar body in a country outside the EU orders a controller or processor to transfer data and no other ground exists for the proposed transfer? The order is not valid in the absence of an international agreement with the country concerned, according to the Regulation:

> 'Any judgment of a court or tribunal and any decision of an administrative authority of a third country requiring a controller or processor to transfer or disclose personal data may only be recognised or enforceable in any manner if based on an international agreement, such as a mutual legal assistance treaty, in force between the requesting third country and the Union or a Member State, without prejudice to other grounds for transfer...' (Art 48)

SAFE HARBOR

12.80 The United States operates a voluntary scheme called *Safe Harbor* introduced in 2000 for organisations that process personal data to undertake to comply with certain standards of data protection. On the basis of this undertaking, the relevant organisation is 'Safe Harbor certified' by the US Department of Commerce, and this certification was recognised by the European Commission as valid basis for the transfer of data to the US. This scheme was availed of by many US companies operating in Europe to transfer personal data of their customers. However, it was reported in October 2013 that hundreds of US companies that handle personal data of EU citizens had made false claims about their Safe Harbor certifications. Christopher Connolly, a director at an Australian consulting firm, told a meeting of the European Parliament's Civil Liberties Committee that one out of every seven Safe Harbor claims of certification are invalid. The firm's research found over 200 false claims in 2008, which had increased to 427 in September 2013.

12.81 The Data Protection Commissioner (DPC) in Ireland announced in July 2013 that he would investigate allegations that personal data of Facebook users in Ireland had been passed on to the US National Security Agency. This followed an official complaint from a privacy rights group called Europe v Facebook. The Commissioner also received queries about the security of online data following revelations by the whistleblower and former National Security Agency worker, Edward Snowden, about the alleged activities of US intelligence agencies.

12.82 In November 2013 the European Commission set out the actions that need to be taken in order to restore trust in data flows between the EU and the US. The Commission's strategy paper called for action in these areas:

- adoption of the new Regulation to establish a strong legislative framework;
- recommendations to improve the Safe Harbor scheme in the US; and
- opportunities for individuals to obtain access to, and rectification or erasure of, their data, or administrative or judicial redress.

12.83 The DPC in his annual report for 2013 expressed serious concerns about access to personal data by intelligence agencies in Europe and the US:

> '2013 was the year of Edward Snowden … who revealed the extent of access by US and European intelligence agencies to personal data held by major internet and telecommunications companies. The revelations provoked a long-overdue debate on the proper balance in a democratic society between the protection of personal data and the obligation on governments to take measures against those who would use these services to further criminal objectives. The disclosures have already led to commitments by the US Administration to rein in the activities of US intelligence services. They have also led to a re-examination of data flows between the EU and the USA under the "Safe Harbour" agreement.'[19]

12.84 These concerns about Safe Harbor and the transfer of personal data to the US were confirmed by the European Court of Justice in a landmark decision in October 2015. The court decided in the case of *Maximillian Schrems v Data Protection Commissioner* (Court of Justice of the European Union, Case C-362/14) that the Safe Harbor scheme is invalid. The case concerned the operations of Facebook in Ireland that had led Mr Schrems to make a complaint to the DPC who had dismissed his complaint. The court observed that the scheme only applies to US companies that sign up to it and not public authorities in the US. National security and other considerations prevail over the rules of Safe Harbor, and US companies are bound to disregard these rules in the event of a conflict. Accordingly, the scheme enables the US authorities to interfere with the fundamental rights of individuals to the privacy of their personal data. Furthermore, the court observed that the scheme does not provide for the rights of data subjects to take legal action for access to their data or to obtain correction or deletion of their data if required. Individuals are therefore denied the 'fundamental right to effective judicial protection'. The court ordered the DPC to examine Mr Schrems' complaint again. Accordingly, the DPC must decide whether transfer of personal data to the US should be suspended in view of the court's ruling. At the time of writing, it had not made a decision.

12.85 The ICO has guided that every company that transfers, or plans to transfer, personal data to the US needs to ensure it is done in accordance with law, in view of the *Schrems* case: 'The [*Schrems*] judgment means that

---

[19]   *The Twenty-Fifth Annual Report of the Data Protection Commissioner 2013* (May 2014), p 4.

businesses that use Safe Harbor will need to review how they ensure that data transferred to the US is transferred in line with the law. We recognise that it will take them some time for them to do this.'[20]

12.86 In February 2016 the US and EU announced they had agreed to put in place a new arrangement for the transfer of personal data between them. This agreement replaces the Safe Harbor scheme that was declared invalid by the European Court of Justice in the *Schrems* case. The US government agrees not to carry 'indiscriminate mass surveillance' of personal data relating to EU citizens if their data is sent to the US. The new agreement is called the *EU-US Privacy Shield* and companies in the US that process personal data will be monitored to ensure they apply data protection standards similar to those that apply in in the EU. Data subjects may complain to an ombudsman if they believe that a complaint about the use of their personal data by a US organisation has not been handled properly. The US Commerce Secretary Penny Pritzker described the agreement as 'a major achievement for privacy and for businesses on both sides of the Atlantic'. However, it remains to be seen whether the new agreement provides a greater degree of data protection than did Safe Harbor, and in particular whether it survives a legal challenge if one is made.

'CYBERSECURITY'

12.87 In December 2015 the EU Member States agreed to a new Directive that will set minimum cybersecurity standards across Europe. Digital service providers must notify the relevant supervisory authority – the ICO in the UK – of any security breach or incident that has a 'substantial impact' on the provision of an online marketplace, online search engine or cloud computing service. The ICO will have the power to obtain information from service providers in order to assess the security of their network and information systems.

12.88 The Directive leaves it open to Member States to provide for appropriate penalties for breach. As in the case of penalties for breach of the General Data Protection Regulation, penalties must be 'effective, proportionate and dissuasive' (see Chapter 16).

---

[20] Deputy Commissioner David Smith, 6 October 2015.

CHAPTER 13

SPECIAL CATEGORIES OF DATA

SENSITIVE PERSONAL DATA

13.1 The DPA and the new Regulation oblige the controller to obtain explicit written consent from a data subject in order to process any sensitive personal data relating to him/her, in addition to the conditions that apply to personal data in general. Sensitive personal data is data relating to a person's racial or ethnic origin, political opinions or religious or philosophical beliefs, physical or mental health, sex life, or trade union membership (DPA, s 2; Regulation Art 9(1)). The DPA also includes data relating to criminal convictions and the alleged commission of an offence, and the Regulation includes genetic data as defined – see **10.24** et seq above. Accordingly, in addition to any other consent obtained by the controller to process personal data in general, the controller must obtain a specific and explicit consent to process these categories of personal data. The inclusion of genetic data will oblige companies in the medical and pharmaceutical sectors to review their business practices in this regard.

13.2 Both the DPA and the new Regulation sets out the circumstances in which the various categories of sensitive, or 'special categories' of, personal data may be processed:

> 'Derogating from the prohibition on processing special categories of personal data should also be allowed when provided for in Union or Member State law, and subject to suitable safeguards, so as to protect personal data and other fundamental rights, where it is in the public interest to do so, , in particular processing data in the field of employment law, social security and social protection law including pensions and for health security, monitoring and alert purposes, the prevention or control of communicable diseases and other serious threats to health. Such a derogation may be made for health purposes, including public health and the management of health-care services, especially in order to ensure the quality and cost-effectiveness of the procedures used for settling claims for benefits and services in the health insurance system, or for archiving in the public interest, scientific or historical research purposes or statistical purposes. A derogation should also allow processing of such personal data where necessary for the establishment, exercise, defence of legal claims, whether in court proceedings or in an administrative or out-of-court procedure.'[1]

---

[1] Recital 52.

13.3 Accordingly, if processing sensitive personal data, the controller must satisfy at least one of the following requirements:

- the data subject has given his/her explicit consent;
- the processing is necessary for the controller to exercise or perform any legal right or obligation conferred or imposed by law on the controller in connection with employment, social security and social protection, or is necessary for collective agreements relating to employment that provide 'appropriate safeguards' for the rights of data subjects;
- the processing is necessary to protect the 'vital interests' of the data subject or another person where he/she cannot give consent for medical or legal reasons;
- the processing is carried out by a not-for-profit organisation that engages in political, philosophical, religious or trade union activities, and carries out these activities with appropriate safeguards for the data, and the data relates only to members or former members of the organisation or 'persons who have regular contact with it', and does not involve disclosure of the data outside the organisation without consent;
- the data has been 'manifestly made public' by the data subject;
- the processing is necessary for the exercise or defence of legal claims or for operations of the courts of law;
- the processing is necessary for 'preventive or occupational medicine' or medical treatment or public health purposes subject to the appropriate safeguards;
- the processing is necessary for reasons of 'public interest' in the areas of public health with safeguards for the fundamental rights and interests of the data subject, in particular professional secrecy; and
- the processing is necessary for archiving purposes in the public interest or the purposes of historical, statistical or scientific research subject to the appropriate safeguards.[2]

13.4 The Regulation allows Member States to decide to introduce or maintain, as the case may be, 'further conditions' for the processing of genetic data, biometric data or health data (Art 9(4)).

13.5 Neither the DPA nor the new Regulation specifies the form of consent but, as discussed above, in the case of sensitive personal data it must be *explicit*. This means that a data subject must be aware of and understand the purposes for which his/her data is being processed. Explicit consent need not require a data subject to sign a form in every case. Consent can be understood to be explicit where a person provides personal data of his/her own free will after the purpose(s) of processing the data has/have been clearly explained. Thus a clear explanation on a form, a website page, or a phone call by properly trained staff might be sufficient to obtain consent. Where a person may be unable to

---

[2] Article 9(2)(a)–(j).

appreciate the nature of consent, by reason of their age or their physical or mental incapacity, the ICO has guided that a parent, grandparent, uncle, aunt, brother, sister or guardian may give consent on his/her behalf. These are the only circumstances in which a third party may give consent on behalf of a data subject.

13.6 An explicit request for goods or services may be considered to be explicit consent. For example, if an airline passenger when booking a flight requires that the airline provide a wheelchair and kosher food, the airline is allowed to use this data even if the passenger did not sign a consent to the use of data that reveals information about his health and religious beliefs.

IDENTIFICATION NUMBER

13.7 The Regulation leaves it to the Member States to provide for the processing of a national identification number or any other identifier of general application:

> 'Member States may further determine the specific conditions for the processing of a national identification number or any other identifier of general application. In this case the national identification number or any other identifier of general application shall be used only under appropriate safeguards for the rights and freedoms of the data subject pursuant to this Regulation.'[3]

FREEDOM OF EXPRESSION

13.8 Likewise, the new Regulation allows Member States to provide for exemptions or derogations from many of its requirements for artists, writers and journalists in processing personal data solely for purposes of their work:

> 'Member States shall by law reconcile the right to the protection of personal data pursuant to this Regulation with the right to freedom of expression and information, including the processing of personal data for journalistic purposes and the purposes of academic, artistic or literary expression.'[4]

13.9 Specifically, these exemptions or derogations may relate to the general principles of data protection as discussed at **11.93** et seq above, responsibilities of controller and processor, data subject's rights, transfer of personal data outside the EU and the provisions of the Regulation that deal with co-operation between supervisory authorities and consistency of application. It remains to be seen whether the UK will allow for an exemption or derogation for these purposes.

---

[3]   Article 87.
[4]   Article 85(1).

DATA HELD BY A PUBLIC BODY

13.10 A public body is permitted by the new Regulation (Art 80a) to disclose personal data in response to a request for access to public information under the appropriate legislation of a Member State, in the UK the Freedom of Information Act 2000, or legislation of the EU itself. Accordingly, a request made under the Freedom of Information Act may result in the public disclosure of personal data. This is designed to achieve a balance between access and privacy:

> 'This Regulation allows the principle of public access to official documents to be taken into account when applying this Regulation. Public access to official documents may be considered to be in the public interest. Personal data in documents held by a public authority or public body should be able to be publicly disclosed by that authority or body if the disclosure is provided for by Union law or Member State law to which the public authority or public body is subject. Such laws should reconcile public access to official documents and the reuse of public sector information with the right to the protection of personal data and may therefore provide for the necessary reconciliation with the right to the protection of personal data pursuant to this Regulation.'[5]

13.11 Personal data held by a private organisation in order to perform a task carried out in the public interest may also be disclosed in response to a request for access 'in order to reconcile public access to official documents with the right to the protection of personal data pursuant to this Regulation' (Art 86). This will arise in the case of a private company engaged by a public authority to provide a service to the public on its behalf.

MEDICAL DATA

13.12 The new Regulation makes special provision for medical or health data. It defines personal data concerning health very widely and includes:

> '[D]ata pertaining to the health status of a data subject which reveal information relating to the past, current or future physical or mental health of the data subject. This includes information about the natural person collected in the course of the registration of the individual for, or the provision of, health care services as referred to in Directive 2011/24/EU of the European Parliament and of the Council to that individual; a number, symbol or particular assigned to a natural person to uniquely identify the natural person for health purposes; information derived from the testing or examination of a body part or bodily substance, including from genetic data and biological samples; and any information on for example a disease, disability, disease risk, medical history, clinical treatment, or the physiological or biomedical state of the data subject independent of its source, for example from a physician or other health professional, a hospital, a medical device or an in vitro diagnostic test.'[6]

---

[5]   Recital 154.
[6]   Recital 35.

13.13 The Regulation makes provision for 'special categories of personal data' to be processed for health-related purposes only where necessary to achieve those purposes. These include:

> '[T]he management of health or social care services and systems including the processing by the management and central national health authorities of such data for the purpose of quality control, management information and the general national and local supervision of the health or social care system, and ensuring continuity of health or social care and cross-border healthcare or health security, monitoring and alert purposes, or for archiving purposes in the public interest, scientific or historical research purposes or statistical purposes based on Union or Member State law which has to meet an objective of public interest ... as well as for studies conducted in the public interest in the area of public health.'[7]

13.14 These special categories of personal data may be processed for reasons of public interest without consent of the data subject. However, this is subject to 'suitable and specific measures so as to protect the rights and freedoms of natural persons' (Recital 54). The Regulation also makes it clear that this data cannot be processed for any other purpose by third parties such as employers, insurance companies and banks (Recital 54).

EMPLOYMENT & SOCIAL WELFARE

13.15 Data relating to employees is highly sensitive and the new Regulation recognises that it may need protection in different ways in different countries. The Regulation allows Member States to adopt their own rules for the processing of personal data relating to employees (Art 88(1)). This includes data relating to recruitment, performance, management, health and safety, and termination of employment.

> 'Member States may by law or by collective agreements provide for more specific rules to ensure the protection of the rights and freedoms, in respect of the processing of employees' personal data in the employment context, in particular for the purpose of the recruitment, the performance of the contract of employment, including discharge of obligations laid down by law or by collective agreements, management, planning and organisation of work, equality and diversity in the workplace, health and safety at work, protection of employer's or customer's property, and for the purposes of the exercise and enjoyment, on an individual or collective basis of rights and benefits related to employment and for the purpose of the termination of the employment relationship.'[8]

13.16 Accordingly, the new Regulation provides that employers and employees may agree collectively as to specific rules for the use of personal data for work purposes.

---

[7] Recital 53.
[8] Article 88(1).

HISTORICAL, STATISTICAL & SCIENTIFIC RESEARCH

13.17 The new Regulation recognises that personal data that is processed for these purposes may also be subject to other laws, whether of a Member State or the EU itself, that must be complied with. These laws may provide for exemptions and derogations in certain circumstances. It is obviously in the public interest to encourage research into medical and scientific matters, and accordingly the Regulation envisages the processing of data in this regard free of at least some of the restrictions that apply to processing for other purposes. One of these restrictions is against further processing without the data subject's consent. What does 'further processing' mean? This is processing additional to, and separate from, the original processing, ie for the original purpose(s) for which the data was obtained. If the further processing is for the purposes of scientific research or archiving, Member States may allow this to be done without consent provided the 'appropriate conditions and safeguards' are in place (Recital 156).

13.18 The new Regulation also recognises that it may not be possible to identify the purpose of data processing as being for scientific purposes at the time the data is obtained. In that event, consent of the data subject may be an issue. Therefore it provides that:

> '[D]ata subjects should be allowed to give their consent to certain areas of scientific research when in keeping with recognised ethical standards for scientific research. Data subjects should always have the opportunity to give their consent only to certain areas of research or parts of research projects to the extent allowed by the intended purpose.'[9]

13.19 Accordingly, the controller does not have to facilitate the provision of consent for part only of the research if this would involve 'disproportionate efforts' on its part. For a controller to avail of this exemption, it needs to show the considerable efforts involved in separating the various parts of the relevant research and that these may be regarded as out of proportion to any risks caused to the data subject(s).

13.20 Personal data may only be processed for archiving purposes in the public interest scientific or historical research purposes or statistical purposes if the processing is subject to 'appropriate safeguards, in accordance with this Regulation, for the rights and freedoms of the data subject' (Art 89(1)) The required safeguards may include pseudonymisation. Data is 'pseudonymised' if it does not identify the data subject but refers to him/her by another name or in some other way. For example, data relating to Joe Bloggs that does not identify him or refer to him in any way but aggregates his data with others is said to be anonymised. Data that does not identify him but refers to him as Customer 123 is said to be pseudonymised, on the basis that the data refers to him but does not identify him. The Regulation recognises the practice of pseudonymisation as a legitimate form of processing, whether for research purposes or otherwise.

---

[9]   Recital 33.

This is provided that the controller has taken the necessary technical and organisational measures and ensures that 'additional information for attributing the personal data to a specific data subject is kept separately' (Recital 29)). A controller is therefore required to have procedures in place to identify the pseudonymised data apart from the relevant additional information. Data is 'anonymised' if it does not identify a data subject, either on its own or in conjunction with other data. (Techniques of anonymisation and pseudonymisation are discussed at **10.29** et seq above.)

ARCHIVE SERVICES

13.21 The Regulation also makes special provision for 'archiving purposes in the public interest' (Art 89(1)). These are purposes to collect or provide archives of historical, statistical or scientific information to the public, ie the results of research for these purposes. Member States will make relevant provisions for the operation of these services. As in the case of processing for purposes of historical, statistical or scientific research, processing for archive purposes is subject to 'appropriate safeguards for the rights and freedoms of the data subject'. The Regulation recognizes the general public interest in preserving archive and historical records and allowing public access to them (Recital 156). The Regulation also allows Member States to make specific rules to allow processing of personal data for statistical purposes subject to 'appropriate measures to safeguard the rights and freedoms of the data subject and for ensuring statistical confidentiality':

> 'The statistical purpose implies that the result of processing for statistical purposes is not personal data, but aggregate data, and that this result or the data are not used in support of measures or decisions regarding any particular natural person.' (Recital 162)

OBLIGATIONS OF SECRECY

13.22 The Regulation provides that Member States may adopt special rules for the protection of people whose data is held by members of professions that are subject to obligations of secrecy, eg accountants, doctors and solicitors. These rules may limit the power of the ICO to access a controller's or processor's systems for processing personal data:

> 'As regards the powers of the supervisory authorities to obtain from the controller or processor access to personal data and access to their premises, Member States may adopt by law, within the limits of this Regulation, specific rules in order to safeguard the professional or other equivalent secrecy obligations, in so far as necessary to reconcile the right to the protection of personal data with an obligation of professional secrecy. This is without prejudice to existing Member States obligations to adopt rules on professional secrecy where required by Union law.'[10]

---

[10] Recital 164.

13.23 Accordingly, Art 90(1) of the Regulation provides that rules adopted by Member States may cover the exercise of the rights of data subjects and for investigations by the ICO into the activities of a controller/processor that is subject to an obligation of secrecy under the laws of a Member State or the EU or equivalent obligations of secrecy. These rules should be 'necessary and proportionate' to strike a balance between professional secrecy and the protection of personal data. In this way the rights of data subjects may be limited where secrecy applies. Article 90(1) also provides that these rules will only apply to personal data obtained from the data subject in the course of an activity subject to the obligation of secrecy, ie in the course of business. Any other activity will not be covered, and so the rights of data subjects in relation to any activity not related to the controller's business will not be limited by any rules to be adopted by a Member State in this regard.

PERSONAL DATA BREACHES

13.24 The DPA provides for a wide range of offences, including:

- processing without registration with the ICO (s 21(1));
- failure to make information available to data subjects (s 24(1)); and
- breach of enforcement notice or information notice (s 47(1) and (2)).

13.25 These offences are in addition to specific offences for direct marketing and electronic communications under the relevant regulations and other offences relating to special categories of data, eg children. Directors and employees of a controller may also be guilty of an offence in addition to the company or entity that is the data controller. However, apart from these specific offences the greatest cause of concern for controllers is the risk of a personal data breach.

13.26 It is often when a breach of data security has occurred that a controller/processor finds out whether its data protection policies and procedures are effective or not. The fact that a breach has occurred may mean that the organisation has not implemented the appropriate procedures. In particular, it soon discovers whether it has effective systems to safeguard the data, and robust procedures to report any breach to the relevant authorities and, if required, to the data subject(s) affected. What does a breach consist of? A personal data breach is defined by the new Regulation as: 'a breach of security leading to the accidental or unlawful destruction, loss, alteration, unauthorised disclosure of, or access to, personal data transmitted, stored or otherwise processed.'[11]

13.27 The controller's data protection officer (DPO) is responsible to monitor any personal data breaches by the controller. The role of the DPO is discussed at **15.30** et seq below.

---

[11]   Article 4(12).

13.28   What are the risks that arise from a lack of preparedness?

- detection – the breach might not be detected soon enough or at all;
- classification – the nature of the breach might not be properly classified;
- evidence – critical evidence might not be preserved; and
- root cause – the cause might not be understood leading to the risk of recurrence.

Case study

The DPC in Ireland was called upon to investigate a major security breach at Loyaltybuild, a database marketing company in Ennis, County Clare, in October 2013. Personal data relating to 1.5 million individuals was put at risk, including 376,000 individuals whose credit card details were compromised. The DPC obtained a full list from Loyaltybuild of all their client companies whose customers were affected, and instructed Loyaltybuild to contact these companies immediately to inform them of the breach. The DPC also contacted the companies and instructed them to inform their customers of the breach. The focus of the DPC investigation was to discover the extent and nature of the personal data involved in the breach and to ensure that affected individuals have been duly notified. In view of the international extent of the data involved, the DPC notified supervisory authorities in other EU Member States.

13.29   The Regulation makes it clear the need for immediate action in the event of a personal data breach. In certain circumstances this includes notification to the authorities:

> 'A personal data breach may, if not addressed in an adequate and timely manner, result in physical, material or non-material damage to natural persons such as loss of control over their personal data or limitation of their rights, discrimination, identity theft or fraud, financial loss, unauthorised reversal of pseudonymisation, damage to the reputation, loss of confidentiality of personal data protected by professional secrecy or any other significant economic or social disadvantage to the individual concerned. Therefore, as soon as the controller becomes aware that a personal data breach has occurred, the controller should without undue delay and, where feasible, not later than 72 hours after having become aware of it, notify the personal data breach to the competent supervisory authority unless the controller is able to demonstrate, in accordance with the accountability principle, that the personal data breach is unlikely to result in a risk for the rights and freedoms of natural persons. Where such notification cannot be achieved within 72 hours, the reasons for the delay should accompany the notification and information may be provided in phases without undue further delay.'[12]

13.30   Accordingly, a data controller must notify the supervisory authority, the ICO, without undue delay of any personal data breach likely to cause 'a risk for

---

[12]   Recital 85.

the rights and freedoms of natural persons' (Art 33(1)). Examples are provided by Recital 85above. Notification must be made within 72 hours of becoming aware of it. If this is not done the controller must explain why. The notification must include the following:

- nature of the breach, including, where possible and appropriate, the approximate categories and number of data subjects affected and approximate number of data records involved;
- identity and contact details of the controller's DPO and any other relevant contact point;
- likely consequences of the breach if known at that time, and otherwise without due further delay;
- measures taken or to be taken by the controller to deal with the breach if known at that time, and otherwise without undue further delay; and
- if appropriate, measures to mitigate the possible adverse effects of the breach if known at that time, and otherwise without undue further delay.[13]

(See *Data Protection Breach Notification Form* at Appendix 3.)

13.31   The controller must document any personal data breach so as to enable the supervisory authority to verify compliance with these requirements (Art 33(5)).

13.32   The new Regulation makes specific provision for communicating a personal data breach to data subjects affected by it:

> 'The controller should communicate to the data subject a personal data breach, without undue delay, where that personal data breach is likely to result in a high risk to the rights and freedoms of the natural person, in order to allow him or her to take the necessary precautions. The communication should describe the nature of the personal data breach as well as recommendations for the natural person concerned to mitigate potential adverse effects. Such communications to data subjects should be made as soon as reasonably feasible and in close co-operation with the supervisory authority, respecting guidance provided by it or other relevant authorities such as law enforcement authorities. For example, the need to mitigate an immediate risk of damage would call for a prompt communication with data subjects whereas the need to implement appropriate measures against continuing or similar data breaches may justify more time for communication.' (Recital 86)

13.33   Similar to the requirement to notify the ICO, the controller must inform the data subject(s) affected without undue delay if the breach is likely to 'result in a high risk to the rights and freedoms of individuals' (Art 34(1)). The relevant communication must describe the breach in 'clear and plain language' (Art 34(2)) and include the following (Art 34(2)):

---

[13]   Article 33(3)(a)–(d).

- identity and contact details of the controller's DPO and any other relevant contact point;
- measures taken or to be taken by the controller to deal with the breach if known at that time, and otherwise without undue further delay; and
- if appropriate, measures to mitigate the possible adverse effects of the breach if known at that time, and otherwise without undue further delay.

13.34 Communication of the breach is not required if it would require a 'disproportionate effort' due to the number of data subjects affected – in that event the controller should make a public communication of some kind, eg a newspaper notice (Art 34(3)(c)).

TELECOMMUNICATIONS & INTERNET

13.35 Telecommunications companies and internet service providers are the subject of a specific regulation, the Privacy and Electronic Communications (EC Directive) Regulations 2003, SI 2003/2426 (PECR 2003), as amended. The PECR 2003 lay down new rules that require telecommunications and internet companies to notify breaches of personal data security to the ICO. A breach of security is defined as: '[A] breach of security leading to the accidental or unlawful destruction, loss, alteration, unauthorised disclosure of, or access to, personal data transmitted, stored or otherwise processed in connection with the provision of a public electronic communications service.'

13.36 The provider must make a notification to the ICO of the discovery or detection of a personal data breach 'without undue delay' (PECR 2003, reg 5A(2)). This means no later than 24 hours where feasible (European Commission Regulation 2013, Art 2(2)). 'Detection' means that 'the provider has acquired sufficient awareness that a security incident has occurred that led to personal data being compromised, in order to make a meaningful notification as required under this Regulation'. If they cannot provide full details at that time, further details should be provided within 3 days of the initial notification. If the company still cannot provide full details at that time, it must explain to the ICO why these details are not available.

13.37 The information that must be provided to the ICO is as follows:

- name of the telecommunications company or internet service provider;
- identity and contact details of the company's data protection officer or other contact where more information can be obtained;
- whether the information concerns a first or second notification;
- initial information on the personal data breach (for completion in later notifications, where applicable);
- date and time of incident, if known, and of detection;
- circumstances of the personal data breach, eg loss, theft, copying;

- nature and content of the personal data concerned;
- technical and organisational measures applied (or to be applied) by the provider to the personal data concerned;
- relevant use of other providers (where applicable);
- summary of the incident that caused the personal data breach, including the physical location of the breach and the storage media involved;
- number of subscribers or individuals concerned;
- potential consequences and potential adverse effects of the breach on subscribers or individuals;
- technical and organisational measures taken by the provider to mitigate potential adverse effects of the breach;
- additional notification to any other subscribers or individuals affected, including content, means of communication, number of subscribers or individuals notified; and
- any personal data breach involving subscribers or individuals in any other Member State, and additional notification of other competent authorities in any such State.

(European Commission Regulation 2013, Annex 1)

13.38 If the personal data breach is likely to 'adversely affect' the personal data or privacy of a subscriber or individual, the PECR 2003 as amended obliges the provider to also notify the subscriber or individual concerned 'without undue delay' (reg 5A(3)), subject to certain exceptions. The question whether the breach is likely to affect an individual in this way should be assessed by taking account of the following:

- nature and content of the personal data, in particular where the data concerns financial information, special categories of data (race, politics, religion, health, sex life, trade union membership), as well as location data, internet log files, web browsing histories, email data, and itemised call lists;
- likely consequences of the breach for the subscriber or individual concerned, in particular where it could result in 'identity theft or fraud, physical harm, psychological distress, humiliation or damage to reputation'; and
- circumstances of the breach, in particular where the data has been stolen or the provider knows that the data is in the possession of an unauthorised third party.[14]

13.39 The notification to the subscriber or individual concerned must be made without undue delay after detection of the personal data breach. This is

---

[14] *Notification of PECR security breaches* (ICO, Version: 2.2), paras 34, 35.

regardless of the notification required to be made to the ICO. It should be made in 'clear and easily accessible language'. The information that must be provided is as follows:

- name of the telecommunications or internet provider;
- identity and contact details of the DPO or other contact where more information can be obtained;
- summary of the incident that caused the breach;
- estimated date of the incident;
- nature and content of the personal data concerned;
- likely consequences of the breach for the subscriber or individual concerned;
- circumstances of the breach;
- measures taken by the provider to address the breach; and
- measures recommended by the provider to mitigate possible adverse effects.[15]

13.40 In 'exceptional circumstances', where notification to the subscriber or individual could put at risk a full investigation of the breach, the provider can delay the notification until a date agreed with the ICO. The means of communication used must ensure that the notification is promptly received and appropriately secured. If the telecommunications or internet provider is unable to identify all individuals who are likely to be adversely affected by the breach without undue delay, it may notify them through advertisements in national or regional media within that timeframe. The advertisement must contain the same information, albeit in a different form. However, the provider must continue to make efforts to identify the individuals concerned and to notify them individually.

13.41 If the personal data breach is likely to 'adversely affect' the personal data or privacy of a subscriber or individual, the PECR obliges the provider to notify the subscriber or individual concerned. However, the provider is not obliged to do so if it has implemented 'appropriate technological protection measures' to the satisfaction of the ICO, and that those measures were applied to the data involved in the breach. The measures are regarded as appropriate if they render the data unintelligible to any person who is not authorised to access it. For this purpose 'unintelligible' means that the data:

- has been securely encrypted with a 'standardised algorithm', the key used to decrypt the data has not been compromised in any security breach, and the key used to decrypt the data has been generated so that it cannot be ascertained by available technological means by any person who is not authorised to access the key; or

---

[15] European Commission Regulation 2013.

- has been replaced by 'its hashed value calculated with a standardised cryptographic keyed hash function', the key used to hash the data has not been compromised in any security breach, and the key used to hash the data has been generated in a way that it cannot be ascertained by available technological means by any person who is not authorised to access the key.

Case study

In November 2013 the Data Protection Authority of the Netherlands decided that Google Inc. had violated data protection laws by combining personal data sourced from its various services, including the Gmail email service and the Google internet search engine. The authority stated: 'Google spins an invisible web of our personal data, without consent. That is forbidden by law'. This decision reflects concerns across Europe about the volume of personal data that is held in foreign jurisdictions in so-called 'cloud' storage services, where the data is stored remotely via the Internet instead of on-site. In this way individuals have little or no control over their personal data. Privacy campaigners have also pointed to documents leaked by the 'whistleblower' and former US National Security Agency worker, Edward Snowden, that suggest access by US intelligence services to personal data stored in US-based cloud services.

CHAPTER 14

RIGHTS OF THE DATA SUBJECT

INTRODUCTION

14.1 Data protection is above all about the rights of data subjects. The obligations and requirements of the data protection regime have one objective: to ensure the privacy of information about individuals in going about their lives. These individuals may be customers or employees of a company or indeed suppliers of goods and services to it. All of them have rights that must be protected. The rights of data subjects underlie the principles of data processing that were discussed at **11.2** et seq above and the specific requirements for processing discussed at **12.4** et seq above. This section describes the rights of data subjects under the DPA and the new General Data Protection Regulation.

14.2 The very first recital to the Regulation makes a clear statement of the position: 'The protection of natural persons in relation to the processing of personal data is a fundamental right ... everyone has the right to the protection of personal data concerning him or her.'

14.3 The data subject has specific rights in relation to his/her data that the Regulation seeks to protect at the level of policy of the controller and also in relation to the controller's procedures, to ensure that he/she can exercise these rights. Data protection policies and procedures are among the 'appropriate measures' discussed at **12.41** et seq above. (See Appendix 1 [FP 13.1] for a sample Data Protection Policy and Appendix 2 [FP 13.2] for a sample Information Security Policy.)

14.4 Below the level of policy, a controller must put the appropriate 'modalities' or procedures in place:

'Modalities should be provided for facilitating the exercise of the data subject's rights under this Regulation, including mechanisms to request and, if applicable obtain, free of charge, in particular access to and rectification or erasure of personal data and the exercise of the right to object. The controller should also provide means for requests to be made electronically, especially where personal data are processed by electronic means ... The controller should be obliged to respond to requests from the data subject without undue delay and at the latest within one month and to give reasons where the controller does not intend to comply with any such request.[1]

14.5 Accordingly, the controller must put in place procedures to ensure that the required information is provided to anyone whose personal data is being processed. And to provide it within one month, ie calendar month.

RIGHT TO INFORMATION & ACCESS

14.6 The new Regulation makes it clear that transparency is key to the provision of information to data subjects. The controller's procedures to provide information must reflect this key requirement:

> 'The principles of fair and transparent processing require that the data subject be informed of the existence of the processing operations and its purpose. The controller should provide the data subject with any further information necessary to ensure fair and transparent processing taking into account the specific circumstances and context in which the personal data are processed.'[2]

14.7 This requirement of transparency is a specific obligation of the data controller, who must take 'appropriate measures to provide any information … relating to the processing of personal data to the data subject in a concise, transparent, intelligible and easily accessible form, using clear and plain language'.[3]

14.8 The information may be given verbally or in writing. If verbally, the controller must take particular care as to the identity of the data subject: identity is harder to establish on a telephone call than in writing. Transparency extends to the purpose(s) of the processing. Where the controller intends to process the data for some purpose(s) other than that/those for which it was obtained, ie 'further processing', the controller should so inform the data subject (Recital 61 and Art 14(4). All of these requirements oblige the controller to provide a clear and comprehensive information notice to data subjects.

Data obtained from data subject

14.9 The controller must also provide data subjects with the following information free of charge at the time the data is obtained from them:

- identity and contact details of the controller and its representatives, if any, and the controller's data protection officer (DPO), if any;
- purposes and 'legal basis' of the processing;

---

[1]   Recital 59.
[2]   Recital 60.
[3]   Article 12(1).

- the legitimate interests of the controller if the processing is based on those interests;
- where applicable, recipient(s) of the data;
- that the controller intends to transfer the data to a country or international organisation outside the EU, if applicable, and whether the European Commission has decided whether the country or organisation provides adequate safeguards or details of these safeguards, as the case may be;
- right of the data subject to obtain the data; right of access to, and correction or deletion of, the data; right to object to the processing; and right to data portability;
- right to complain to the ICO;
- that the data subject can withdraw his/her consent to the processing at any time;
- whether the data subject is required to comply with a statutory or contractual obligation and whether he/she is required to provide it, and of the possible consequences of his/her failure to do so;
- how long the data will be stored or, if not possible to determine the period of time, how the period is determined; and
- the existence of any automated decision making, including profiling, and 'meaningful' information about the logic involved and 'the significance and the envisaged consequences of such processing for the data subject'.[4]

14.10 Where the controller intends to 'further process' the data, ie separately and further to the original processing, it must inform him/her of the purpose of this (Art 14(4)). If the data subject already has any of the above information, it does not need to be provided to him/her again (Art 14(5)).

Data *not* obtained from data subject

14.11 If the data was not obtained from the data subject, the information listed below must be provided within a 'reasonable period' afterwards but at the latest within 1 month, having regard to the circumstances (Art 14(3)(a)).

- identity and contact details of the controller and its representatives, if any, and the controller's DPO, if any;
- purposes and 'legal basis' of the processing; the categories of personal data involved;
- the legitimate interests of the controller if the processing is based on those interests;
- recipient(s) of the data;
- that the controller intends to transfer the data to a country or international organisation outside the EU, if applicable;

---

[4] Articles 13(1)(a)–(f) and 13(2)(a)–(f).

- right of the data subject to obtain the data; right of access to, and correction or deletion of, the data; and right to object to the processing; and right to data portability;

- that the data subject can withdraw his/her consent to the processing at any time;

- right to complain to the ICO;

- source of the data, unless it originates from 'publicly accessible sources'; and

- the existence of any automated decision making, including profiling, and 'meaningful information' about the logic involved and 'the significance and the envisaged consequences of such processing for the data subject'.[5]

14.12 If the data is to be used for communication with the data subject, the information must be provided at the latest at the time of the first communication. If it is envisaged that the data will be disclosed to another party, the information must be provided at time of disclosure.

14.13 Where the controller intends to 'further' process the data, ie separately and further to the original processing, it must inform him/her of the purpose of this (Art 14(4)).

14.14 In certain circumstances it may not be necessary or even possible to provide information in relation to the processing:

> '[I]t is not necessary to impose the obligation to provide information where the data subject already possesses this information, or where the recording or disclosure of the data is expressly laid down by law, or where the provision of information to the data subject proves impossible or would involve a disproportionate effort. The latter could in particular be the case where processing is carried out for archiving purposes in the public interest, scientific or historical research purposes or statistical purposes. In that regard, the number of data subjects, the age of the data, and any appropriate safeguards adopted may be taken into consideration.'[6]

14.15 Accordingly, the Regulation provides for a number of exceptions to the data controller's obligation to provide the required information. First, as already discussed, the data subject may already have the information. Secondly, to provide the information may be impossible or require a 'disproportionate effort by the controller'; if this exception is to apply the controller must take 'all appropriate measures to protect the data subject's rights and freedoms and legitimate interests'. Thirdly, obtaining or disclosure of the data may be subject to laws of the EU or the Member State concerned that provide appropriate measures to protect the data subject's legitimate interests. Finally, the data may be regarded as confidential or subject to an obligation of professional secrecy under the laws of the EU or the Member State concerned (Art 14(5)).

---

[5]   Arts 14(1)(a)–(f) and 14(2)(a)–(g).
[6]   Recital 62.

14.16 All of these requirements to provide information assume that the data controller has the information to provide. The new Regulation obliges the controller to keep proper records: 'Each controller and, if any, the controller's representative, shall maintain a record of processing activities under its responsibility' (Art 30(1)). This record must include the following information:

- name and contact details of the controller and any joint controller, representative and data protection officer, if any;
- purpose(s) of the processing, including the legitimate interests of the controller if the processing is based on those interests;
- categories of data subjects and the personal data relating to them;
- category/ies of recipient(s) or intended recipient(s) of the data, including any in countries outside the EU;
- if applicable, the categories of transfer of personal data to countries or organisations outside the EU, and details of appropriate safeguards if required;
- if possible, the anticipated timeframe for erasure of categories of personal data; and
- if possible, technical and organisational measures to secure the data.[7]

14.17 These requirements for record-keeping do not apply in the case of an organisation with less than 250 employees unless the processing: (a) is likely to cause a risk to the rights and freedoms of data subjects, (b) is not occasional; or (c) includes special categories of data or processing of data relating to criminal convictions and offences (Art 30(5)). This is processing that is likely to cause discrimination, identity theft or fraud, unauthorised reversal of pseudonymisation, financial loss, reputational damage, breach of confidentiality or any other social or economic disadvantage to the data subject(s) involved. Accordingly, regardless of the size of the organisation, these requirements apply in the case of processing that is 'high risk' as defined.

14.18 The new Regulation has similar requirements for *data processors*. They are obliged to keep records that include the following information (Art 30(2)):

- name and contact details of the processor and of each controller on whose behalf it is acting and of the controller's representative, if any;
- name and contact details of the processor's data protection officer, if any
- categories of processing carried out on behalf of each controller it acts for;
- if applicable, the categories of transfer of personal data to countries or organisations outside the EU, and details of appropriate safeguards if required;
- if possible, the anticipated timeframe for erasure of categories of personal data; and

---

[7] Article 30(1)(a)–(g).

- if possible, the technical and organisational measures to secure the data.[8]

14.19 Likewise these requirements for record-keeping do not apply in the case of a company or organisation with less than 250 employees unless the processing is 'high risk' (Art 30(5)).

14.20 The right of access to personal data is perhaps the most important right of a data subject. It can be exercised at any time and without the necessity of any breach of data protection requirements by the controller. According to the ICO's Annual Report for 2014, concerns about subject access rights are the most common concerns raised with the ICO: 46% of the 14,200 concerns raised in 2014 had to do with subject access. The 1995 Directive (Art 12) and the DPA (s 7) provide for the right of access at reasonable intervals and without excessive cost or delay. Likewise, in his annual report for 2013 the DPC in Ireland reported that more than half of the complaints received by his office during the year related to difficulties experienced by individuals in trying to access their personal data. The DPC commented that poor customer service lay behind many of the requests for access to data:

> 'The purpose behind the making of access requests to data controllers in many cases is often a customer service issue which has been badly handled by the data controllers concerned in the first instance. Time and again we find in our investigations customers or clients who believe they have been treated badly in their dealings with a company or entity and who, despite their best efforts, are unable to find adequate redress in pursuing the matter from a customer service perspective. Having failed on that front, they resort to submitting access requests to obtain a copy of all personal data held on them by the data controller concerned. For the data controller's part, the issue moves internally from the customer service department to the data compliance department and a significant amount of time and resources may be expended on processing the access request.'[9]

14.21 The new Regulation recognises the central importance of the right of access for data subjects:

> 'A data subject should have the right of access to data which have been collected concerning him or her, and to exercise that right easily and at reasonable intervals, in order to be aware of and verify, the lawfulness of the processing. This includes the right for data subjects to have access to data concerning their health, for example the data in their medical records containing such information as diagnoses, examination results, assessments by treating physicians and any treatment or interventions provided. Every data subject should therefore have the right to know and obtain communication in particular with regard to the purposes for which the data are processed, where possible the period for which the personal data are processed, the recipients of the personal data, the logic involved in any automatic personal data processing and , at least when based on profiling, the consequences of such processing. This right should not adversely affect the rights and freedoms of others, including trade secrets or intellectual property and in

---

[8]   Art 30(2)(a)–(d).
[9]   *The Twenty-Fifth Annual Report of the Data Protection Commissioner 2013* (May 2014).

particular the copyright protecting the software. However, the result of those considerations should not be a refusal to provide all information to the data subject. Where the controller processes a large quantity of information concerning the data subject, the controller should be able to request that before the information is delivered, the data subject specify the information or processing activities to which the request relates.'[10]

14.22 The data subject has the right to receive confirmation from the controller 'whether or not personal data relating to him or her are being processed, and ... access to the data' (Art 15)(1)). This must be done in 'clear and plain language'. He/she also has the right to know if the controller carries on profiling. If so, the following information about the processing and/or profiling must be provided free of charge:

• purpose(s) of the processing;

• categories of the data concerned;

• party/ies to whom the data has been or may be disclosed, ie recipient(s);

• length of time the data will be kept or how this period is determined;

• right of the data subject to have his/her data corrected or deleted or to object to the processing or to have it restricted;

• right of the data subject to complain to the ICO;

• 'any available information' about the source of the data if not provided by the data subject;

• 'meaningful information' about the logic involved in any automated processing, including profiling, and the significance and 'envisaged consequences' of such processing for the data subject.[11]

14.23 The controller must provide a copy of the data being processed on request and a 'reasonable fee' may be charged for any further copies (Art 15(3)). This information, and a copy of the data if requested, must be provided to the data subject 'without undue delay' and at the latest within 1 month of receipt of the request. This may be extended for a further 2 months depending on the complexity of the request; in that event the controller must inform the data subject data of the delay within one month of receipt and that he/she may complain to the 'supervisory authority', ie the ICO (Art 12(4)).

14.24 The data must obviously be in an intelligible form, ie in a form that can be understood by the average person. (It may or may not be understood by the individual who has made the request but that is not the controller's responsibility provided the data is intelligible.)

Example

A company responds to a request for personal data. The data includes notes of meetings and other events attended by particular employees, and is in the form of

---

[10]   Recital 63.
[11]   Article 15(1)(a)–(h).

codes that stand for attendance at these events. For example, 'P' beside an employee's name indicates that he or she was present while 'A' indicates that he or she was absent. While these letters might be understood to refer to presence or absence, it cannot be assumed without an explanation of the various codes.

14.25 In responding to a request, the controller must make sure that the person making the request is the person to whom the personal data relates, ie the data subject:

'The controller should use all reasonable measures to verify the identity of a data subject who requests access, in particular in the context of online services and online identifiers. A controller should not retain personal data for the sole purpose of being able to react to potential requests.'[12]

14.26 If the controller has reasonable doubts about a person's identity, it may require further information (Art 12(6)). In any event the data subject may use a pseudonym to authenticate himself/herself as the person making the request, ie by providing proof that he/she is the data subject. This means that he/she is not technically required to providing identification if the request can be validated by way of a pseudonym, eg Customer 123, provided that the controller is satisfied on reasonable grounds that he/she is the data subject. While this approach is consistent with other provisions of the new Regulation to protect the identity of data subjects, it presents obvious difficulties for controllers in making sure that they respond to requests for access only to people entitled to make them. Recital 64 also makes clear that personal data cannot be retained just in case the data subject makes a request at some time in the future. This would be in breach of the principles that data may only be retained in relation to the purpose(s) for which it was obtained and only for as long as required for that/those purpose(s). The data protection principles are discussed in Chapter 11.

14.27 There are a number of exceptions to the right of access where the data has not been provided by the data subject. The data need not be provided if to do so would disclose personal data of other data subjects or confidential data of the controller or would breach any intellectual property rights involved in the processing (Art 14(5)). If the data subject makes a request for confirmation as to the data and/or a copy of it, following a previous request, the controller is not obliged to comply with the request unless, in its opinion, a reasonable period of time has passed since the previous request. As regards what is 'reasonable', the ICO has guided that this will depend on the nature of the data, the purpose for which it is processed and the frequency with which the data is changed. The new Regulation provides that repeated requests may be ignored in certain circumstances:

'Where requests from a data subject are manifestly unfounded or excessive, in particular because of their repetitive character, the controller may either (a) charge a reasonable fee taking into account the administrative costs of providing the

---

[12] Recital 64.

information or communication or taking the action requested; (b) refuse to act on the request. The controller shall bear the burden of demonstrating the manifestly unfounded or excessive character of the request.'[13]

RIGHT AGAINST ENFORCED ACCESS

14.28 A data subject cannot be forced to make a request to access his/her personal data in order to disclose it to a third party. This may arise, for example, where a job applicant is asked to request a copy of his/her data from the police or other public authority for the information of the prospective employer. The DPA provides that in these circumstances the prospective employer cannot oblige the applicant to provide the data concerned (s 56(1)). Likewise a provider of goods or services cannot insist that the recipient provide data of this kind as a condition for providing the relevant goods and services (s 56(2)). In the case of medical records, an individual cannot be obliged to provide information relating to his/her physical or mental health (s 57).

14.29 The new Regulation makes no provision for this right.

RIGHTS TO COMPLAIN & OBJECT

14.30 A data subject has the right to make a complaint to the supervisory authority of his/her Member State – in the UK the ICO – if he/she believes there has been a breach of the new Regulation in the processing of their personal data (Art 77(1)). This is in addition to any other remedy that may be available to him/her. The Regulation sets out the right of a data subject to complain and how it should be handled:

> 'Every data subject should have the right to lodge a complaint with a single supervisory authority, in particular in the Member State of his or her habitual residence, and have the right to an effective judicial remedy in accordance with Article 47 of the Charter [of Fundamental Rights] if the data subject considers that his or her rights under this Regulation are infringed or where the supervisory authority does not act on a complaint, partially or wholly rejects or dismisses a complaint or does not act where such action is necessary to protect the rights of the data subject.... The supervisory authority should inform the data subject of the progress and the outcome of the complaint within a reasonable period. If the case requires further investigation or coordination with another supervisory authority, intermediate information should be given to the data subject ....'[14]

14.31 The data subject can make the complaint to the authority where he/she lives or works or where the alleged breach occurred (Art 77(1)). Accordingly, he/she has a wide choice of venues for the complaint. The authority must keep him/her informed of progress and the outcome of the complaint, including the possibility of a judicial remedy in accordance with Art 78.

---

[13] Article 12(5).
[14] Recital 141.

14.32   The DPA provides data subjects with a specific right to object to certain processing likely to cause damage or distress (s 10(1)). An individual can at any time request the controller to stop processing within a reasonable time or not to start processing, as the case may be. This may be for a specified purpose(s) or in a specified manner. He/she may not object if the processing referred to is necessary:

- for the performance of, or entry into, a contract; or
- for compliance with a legal obligation of the data controller; or
- to protect the 'vital interests' of the individual concerned;
- for the controller to perform a task carried out in the public interest or in the exercise of official authority; or
- for the purpose of the legitimate interests of the controller, unless those interests are overridden by the interest of the data subject in relation to his/her fundamental rights and freedoms.[15]

Example

A customer of a mobile phone company writes to the company to ask it to remove her details from its customer database. This amounts to an objection to processing for data protection purposes. The basis for the objection is that the use of her data for credit referencing purposes is causing her distress and recently led to a bank refusal to provide her with a credit card. In this case the company is not obliged to stop processing the data as credit referencing is necessary to perform the contract the customer signed for the use of her phone. The company should explain to her why it does not have to comply with the objection.

14.33   In the event of a request to stop processing, the controller must inform the data subject within 21 days of the request that it has complied with the request or is in the course of doing so. Alternatively, if the controller believes the request is unjustified it must give reasons and the extent, if any, to which it intends to comply with the request (DPA, s 10(3)). A court may order the data controller to comply with the request. Where personal data is held for direct marketing, the data subject can request the controller not to process the data for that purpose or to stop processing if it has already started (DPA, s 11(1)). Likewise a court may order the controller to comply with this request.

14.34   The new Regulation provides for a wider right to object than that provided for by the DPA. The right also applies to controllers acting in the exercise of an official authority, ie public bodies, or acting in the public interest:

'Where personal data might lawfully be processed because processing is necessary for the performance of a task carried out in the public interest or in the exercise of official authority vested in the controller or on the grounds of the legitimate interests of a controller or a third party, a data subject should, nevertheless, be entitled to object to the processing of any personal data relating to his or her

---

[15]   DPA 1998, Sch 2, para 3.

particular situation. It should be for the controller to demonstrate that their compelling legitimate interest overrides the interests or the fundamental rights and freedoms of the data subject.'[16]

14.35 Accordingly, the data subject has the right to object in these circumstances. The controller must stop the processing unless it can show 'compelling legitimate grounds' that override the interests of the data subject or are necessary for the exercise or defence of legal claims (Art 21(1)). This suggests a heavy burden of proof on a controller to show that it can disregard an objection by an aggrieved data subject.

14.36 The Regulation provides for a specific right to object by data subjects to the processing of personal data for direct marketing:

> 'Where personal data are processed for direct marketing purposes, the data subject shall have the right to object at any time to the processing of personal data concerning him or her for such marketing, which includes profiling to the extent that it is related to such direct marketing.'[17]

14.37 Accordingly, the data subject must be informed at the outset of any communications that he/she has the right to object either in general or in particular to direct marketing. If he/she objects to direct marketing, the data cannot be processed for these purposes (Art 21(3)).

14.38 Of course an individual can change his/her mind about whether to receive marketing material or not, and the controller needs to take care to ensure that any change of mind is obtained in an appropriate manner and recorded.

Example

A fitness centre sends a regular newsletter to members by post. Some of them object to the use of their data in this way and the fitness centre duly notes their objection. It now wants to send the newsletter, with expanded content, by email and needs to establish whether the objections already made still apply. The centre cannot assume that the individuals concerned have changed their mind. An appropriate way to check the current state of play is to mention to members in the normal course of business that the newsletter is now available by email. This provides an opportunity to members to change their marketing preferences as part of a message they would receive in any event. However, it is not appropriate to contact the members concerned to sell the idea to them.

14.39 The data subject must be informed of his/her right to object at the time of the first communication by the controller with him/her (Art 21(4)). The information must be presented 'clearly and separately from any other information'. As regards the use of information society services, ie online services, the data subject may object by 'automated means using technical

---

[16] Recital 69.
[17] Article 21(2).

Data Protection

specifications (Art 21(5)). The Regulation also provides for the right to object to processing for historical, statistical or scientific purposes: 'Where personal data are processed for scientific and historical research purposes or statistical purposes pursuant to Art 83(1), the data subject on grounds relating to his or her particular situation, shall have the right to object to processing of personal data concerning him or her, unless the processing is necessary for the performance of a task carried out for reasons of public interest.'[18]

14.40 The data subject has a right not to be subjected to automated decision-making. This refers to decisions made about individuals by computer systems and other automated systems. Similar to the new Regulation, the DPA provides that an individual can require that no significant decision about him/her should be based solely on automated processing of his/her personal data (s 12(1)). Examples of this kind of processing include credit applications, employment applications, employment performance, etc. This right does not apply to processing of data that is:

• obtained in the course of entering into or performing the contract;
• required by law; or
• required for a decision to grant a request of the data subject, or steps have been taken to safeguard the legitimate interests of the data subject (s 10).

14.41 The new Regulation provides for similar restrictions in the case of automated decision-making that 'produces legal effects ... or significantly affects him/her':

'The data subject should have the right not to be subject to a decision which may include a measure, evaluating personal aspects relating to him/her which is based solely on automated processing, which produces legal effects concerning him or her or similarly significantly affects him or her, such as automatic refusal of an on-line credit application or e-recruiting practices without any human intervention. Such processing includes "profiling" that consists of any form of automated processing of personal data evaluating the personal aspects relating to a natural person, in particular to analyse or predict aspects concerning the data subject's performance at work, economic situation, health, personal preferences or interests, reliability or behaviour, location or movements, where it produces legal effects concerning him or her or significantly affects him or her ....'[19]

14.42 Accordingly, an individual can give notice to the controller that he/she does not want their personal data used for automated decision-making, or to reconsider a decision already made by automated means. There are two conditions: first, the decision has to be made solely by these means, with no human intervention; and second, the decision must have a legal or significant effect on the individual concerned.

---

[18] Article 21(6).
[19] Recital 71.

Example

A company issues a formal warning to an employee who consistently turns up late for work. The company's automatic clock-in system keeps a record of all employees' attendance and has detected the late-comer. The HR Department decided to issue a warning on account of the number of times the employee had arrived late. Although the warning was automatically generated by the system, the decision to issue it required human intervention and so was not made solely by automated means. If the employee's pay was linked to productivity by a monitoring system, this would obviously have a significant effect on him if his late-coming affected his productivity. Assuming no human intervention, he could object to the automated processing of his data for this purpose.

14.43 However, the right of the data subject in this regard does not apply in the case of automated decision-making for purposes of preventing fraud or tax evasion in accordance with laws of the EU or the Member States or ensuring services provided by the controller under a contract with the data subject or where the data subject has given his/her 'explicit' consent (Art 22(2)(c)). But even in these cases the data subject has the right to human intervention in the decision-making process, to express his/her point of view and to receive an explanation of any decision made (Art 22(3)). Automated decisions cannot be made on the basis of any the special categories of data unless the data subject has given his/her explicit consent or the processing is in the public interest, and in either case suitable measures to safeguard his/her rights and freedoms and legitimate interests are in place (Art 22(4)).

RECTIFICATION & 'TO BE FORGOTTEN'

14.44 The DPA provides for the data subject's right to rectification of incorrect data and for deletion of the data. A court may order the data controller to rectify or delete personal data and to inform any third party to whom the data has been disclosed of that fact. In that event the controller must rectify or delete the data, as the case may be, and/or inform any relevant third party (s 14).

14.45 The new Regulation also provides for these rights of data subjects:

'A data subject should have the right to have personal data concerning him or her rectified and a "right to be forgotten" where the retention of such data infringes this Regulation or Union or Member State law to which the controller is subject. In particular, a data subject should have the right to have his or personal data erased and no longer processed where the personal data are no longer necessary in relation to the purposes for which they are collected or otherwise processed, where a data subject has withdrawn his or her consent or objects to the processing of personal data concerning him or her, or where the processing of his or her personal data does not otherwise comply with this Regulation. That right is relevant in particular where the data subject has given his or her consent as a child and is fully aware of the risks involved by the processing, and later wants to remove such personal data especially on the internet. The data subject should be able to exercise that right notwithstanding the fact that he or she is no longer a child. However, the further retention of the personal data should be lawful where it is necessary for exercising the right of freedom of expression and information, for compliance with a legal obligation, for the performance of a task carried out in the public interest or in the exercise of official authority vested in the controller, on the grounds of public interest in the area of public health, for archiving purpose in the public interest, scientific or historical research purposes or statistical purposes or for the establishment, exercise or defence of legal claims.'[20]

14.46 Accordingly, the data subject has the right to require the controller to rectify 'without undue delay' any personal data relating to him/her that is inaccurate (Art 16). He/she also has the right to have any incomplete data completed by the controller, including a supplementary statement to be provided by him/her. On receipt of this statement, the controller will hold personal data that is accurate, complete and up to date in accordance with Principle 4 of the data protection principles.

Example

The parents of a seriously ill baby claim that the hospital's records are inaccurate. The baby's health visitor provided some of the data that the parents are disputing. After trying to resolve the matter without success, the couple issue legal proceedings to compel the hospital to amend or rectify its records. The court is satisfied that the records are inaccurate and orders the hospital to correct them. The court also orders that a statement is made by the health visitor to supplement the records held by the hospital.

14.47 Under the Regulation, the controller must erase any personal data without undue delay in any of the following circumstances:

- if the controller no longer requires the data for the original purpose(s) for which it was obtained;
- if the data subject withdraws his/her consent to the processing and there are no other legal grounds for it;
- if the data subject objects to the processing and there are no overriding legitimate grounds for it or the processing is for direct marketing purposes;
- if the processing has not been done lawfully;
- if the data must be erased for compliance with a legal obligation of the controller;
- if the data has been obtained in offering 'information society services'.[21]

14.48 A controller that has disclosed the data to other parties faces the onerous task of contacting them to protect the data subject's right to be forgotten. The Regulation obliges the controller to take reasonable steps to 'inform controllers which are processing the personal data, that the data subject has requested the erasure by such controllers of any links to, or copy or

---

[20]   Recital 65.
[21]   That is, online services. Article 17(1)(a)–(f).

replication of those personal data' (Art 17(2)). In determining the steps to be taken, the controller may take into account the available technology and the cost of implementation.

14.49 The right to erasure does not apply in the following circumstances:

- if the processing is to exercise freedom of expression and information;
- if the processing is to comply with a legal obligation of the controller or to perform a task carried out in the public interest or in the exercise of official authority;
- if the processing is for reasons of public health;
- if the processing is for archiving purposes in the public interest or for scientific or historical research purposes or statistical purposes;
- if the processing is for the exercise or defence of legal claims.[22]

Case study

In an important case in May 2014, the European Court of Justice ruled that the internet search engine Google must amend some of its search results on request if these results show links to outdated, irrelevant information (Case C-131 *Google Spain and Google Inc v Agencia Espanola De Proteccion De Datos Mario Costeja Gonzalez*). Mario Costeja, a lawyer in Spain, had objected that the entry of his name in Google's search engine led to legal notices dating back to 1998 in an online version of a Spanish newspaper that detailed his accumulated debts and the forced sale of his property. Mr Costeja said the debt issues had been resolved and were no longer relevant. The court decided that search engines have control of personal data relating to individuals as they can compile and present links to this data in a systematic way. Individuals have a right to control over their personal data, especially if they are not public figures. If they request that out-of-date or irrelevant information be omitted from search results, the search engine must comply with this request even if the information has already been published.

> 'The operator of a search engine is obliged to remove from the list of results displayed following a search made on the basis of a person's name links to web pages, published by third parties and containing information relating to that person, also in a case where that name or information is not erased beforehand or simultaneously from those web pages, and even, as the case may be, when its publication in itself on those pages is lawful.'

Google was ordered to remove links to pages containing the information from results 'unless there are particular reasons, such as the role played by the data subject in public life, justifying a preponderant interest of the ➡

---

[22] Article 17(3)(a)–(e).

public in having access to the information when such a search is made'. The ruling does not mean the deletion of the data itself, only the Google links to it.

As Google refused to delete these links, Mr Costeja complained to the ICO that Google Inc had failed to comply with the court order. The ICO issued an *enforcement notice* against the company on the basis that it had acted in breach of Principles 1 (fair and lawful processing) and 3 (adequate, relevant and not excessive data) and ordered it to remove the links to the specified websites. (Enforcement notices are discussed at **16.12** below.)

In January 2015 Google was required by the ICO to sign a formal undertaking to provide better information to people about how it collects personal data in the UK after concerns were raised about the company's privacy policy. The ICO determined that the information was too vague when describing how it uses personal data gathered from its web services and products. Google introduced a new privacy policy in March 2012 but the ICO ruled that it did not include sufficient information for service users as to how and why their personal data was being collected. Google undertook to meet the requirements of the DPA and to take steps to ensure that future changes to its privacy policy will also comply. The ICO commented:

> 'Whilst our investigation concluded that this case has not resulted in substantial damage and distress to consumers, it is still important for organisations to properly understand the impact of their actions and the requirement to comply with data protection law. Ensuring that personal data is processed fairly and transparently is a key requirement of the Act ...
>
> This investigation has identified some important learning points not only for Google, but also for all organisations operating online, particularly when they seek to combine and use data across services. It is vital that there is clear and effective information available to enable users to understand the implications of their data being combined. The detailed agreement Google has signed setting out its commitments will ensure that.'

14.50 The right to be forgotten is not about rewriting history. The new Regulation seeks to protect freedom of expression and the freedom of the media, as well as historical and scientific research. It provides exemptions in these cases in order to protect these fundamental rights. This will allow historical and scientific archives to continue operating on the basis of the same principles as today. Equally, personal data may be kept for as long as it is needed to perform a contract or to meet a legal obligation, eg to repay a bank loan. Accordingly, the right to be forgotten is not absolute and does not affect historical research or the freedom of the press.

14.51 The new Regulation recognises the rights of companies to go about their business. If the personal data in question has been made public, eg posted on the Internet, an organisation must make a genuine effort to ensure that third parties know about the data subject's request to delete the data. However, the organisation will not be obliged to wipe out every trace left in search records.

RIGHT TO RESTRICT PROCESSING

14.52   In certain circumstances the data subject has the right to request the controller to restrict the data processing for a period of time. These circumstances are where:

- the data subject contests the accuracy of the data, and the controller is required to verify its accuracy; or
- the processing is unlawful and the data subject objects to erasure of the data and requests its restriction instead; or
- the data is no longer is required by the controller for the relevant purpose(s) but is required for purposes of exercising or defending a legal claim; or
- the data subject has objected to the processing, pending verification of whether the legitimate interests of the controller override those of the data subject.[23]

14.53   Where the processing has been restricted, it can only take place with the data subject's consent, for the exercise or defence of a legal claim, for the protecting the rights of another party or for reasons of 'important public interest' (Art 18(2)). The controller must inform the data subject when the restriction is lifted (Art 18(3)).

DATA PORTABILITY

14.54   The new Regulation aims to make it easier for data subjects to switch from one service provider to another and so requires providers to make the relevant data available in a format that facilitates the transfer. The Regulation provides for the portability of personal data relating to the data subject from one controller to another:

> 'To further strengthen the control over his or her own data where the processing of personal data is carried out by automated means, the data subject should also be allowed to receive the personal data concerning him or her which he or she has provided to a controller in a structured, commonly used, machine-readable and interoperable format and to transmit it to another controller ....'[24]

14.55   This obligation assumes the controller holds the relevant data in the standard format referred to. Indeed, it seems to oblige the controller to do so.

---

[23]   Article 18(1)(a)–(d).
[24]   Recital 68.

Only then is the controller in a position to provide the data as required so that the data subject can transmit same to another controller. There is obvious room for dispute as to what constitutes a 'structured and commonly used and machine-readable format'. While the Regulation provides there is no obligation on controllers to use processing systems that are technically compatible with each other, it recognises the necessity for compatible systems: 'Data controllers should be encouraged to develop interoperable formats that enable data portability.' (Recital 68)

15.56 The Regulation describes the right of data portability as follows:

> 'The data subject shall have the right to receive the personal data concerning him or her, which he or she has provided to a controller, in a structured, commonly used and machine-readable format and have the right to transmit those data to another controller without hindrance from the controller to which the data have been provided ....'[25]

14.57 This right only applies where the data subject provided the data concerned on the basis of his/her consent or for purpose of performing a contract to which the data subject is a party. Accordingly, the data subject cannot insist on the data in a certain format from a controller that processes the data to comply with a legal obligation or to perform a task in the public interest or to exercise an official duty. (Nor does the right of portability apply if the transfer would infringe the intellectual property rights of any party in relation to the processing.) The essential difference between these scenarios and a scenario where the data subject has consented or needs to perform a contract is the voluntary nature of the transaction. A controller who is dealing with a data subject on the basis of his/her consent or performance of a contract freely entered into – and therefore acting in its own interests, typically financial – is in a different position from one who is obliged to process the data for legal or official reasons. It is entirely appropriate that the former should be subject to an obligation of data portability while the latter is not.

RESTRICTIONS

14.58 The new Regulation provides the legal basis for restrictions on the rights of data subjects. These are based on the need to balance the rights and freedoms of individuals with the interests of society:

> 'Restrictions concerning specific principles and concerning the rights of information, access to and rectification and erasure of personal data and on the right to data portability, the right to object, decisions based on profiling, as well as on the communication of a personal data breach to a data subject and on certain related obligations of the controllers may be imposed by Union or Member State law, as far as necessary and proportionate in a democratic society to safeguard public security, including the protection of human life especially in response to natural or man-made disasters, the prevention, investigation and prosecution of

---

[25]   Article 20(1).

criminal offences or the execution of criminal penalties, including the safeguarding against and the prevention of threats to public security, or of breaches of ethics for regulated professions, other important objectives of general public interest of the Union or of a Member State, in particular an important economic or financial interest of the Union or of a Member State, the keeping of public registers kept for reasons of general public interest, further processing of archived personal data to provide specific information related to the political behaviour under former totalitarian state regimes or the protection of the data subject or the rights and freedoms of others, including social protection, public health and humanitarian purposes. Those restrictions should be in accordance with the requirements set out by the Charter [of Fundamental Rights of the European Union] and in the European Convention for the Protection of Human Rights and Fundamental Freedoms.'[26]

14.59 Accordingly, in order to strike a balance between the needs of society and the rights of data subjects, the new Regulation provides for Member States to implement measures that contain specific restrictions that respect 'the essence of the fundamental rights and freedoms' and are necessary and proportionate in order to safeguard:

- national and public security;
- defence;
- prevention, investigation and prosecution of crime;
- 'general public interests' of the EU or a Member State, eg economic or financial interests, public health and social security;
- independence of judicial proceedings;
- prevention, investigation and prosecution of breaches of ethics of regulated professions, eg law, medicine;
- functions connected with the exercise of official authority;
- protection of the data subject or the rights and freedom of others; and
- the enforcement of legal claims.[27]

14.60 Any such restriction must state the purposes of the processing, the categories of personal data, the scope of the restrictions, the controller(s) involved, storage periods for the data, the applicable safeguards for protection of the data, the risks for the rights and freedoms of data subjects and the right of data subjects to be informed about the restriction 'unless this may be prejudicial to the purpose of the restriction' (Art 23.2(a)–(h)).

RIGHT TO COMPENSATION

14.61 The new Regulation recognises the right of data subjects to receive compensation from a controller or processor in the event of 'material or non-material damage as result of an infringement of this Regulation'

---

[26] Recital 73.
[27] Article 23(1)(a)–(j).

(Art 82(1)). In an appropriate case this will reflect the damage suffered by him/her and may include financial loss, ie 'material damage'. ('Non-material damage' may include reputational loss.) Recital 146 sets out the context for assessing the extent of any damage that may be recovered:

> 'The concept of damage should be broadly interpreted in the light of the case-law of the Court of Justice of the European Union in a manner which fully reflects the objectives of this Regulation. This is without prejudice to any claims for damage deriving from the violation of other rules in Union or Member State law.'

Example

A personal data beach occurs at an online mail order company. The bank details of hundreds of customers were made available on the company's website for several hours before the site was taken down. These customers had to make arrangements to stop their bank accounts for this period of time and many of them are worried about the possibility of fraud. A number of customers who suffer financial loss take legal action against the company, and the court awards compensation.

14.62   In March 2015 the Court of Appeal confirmed that damages may also be awarded for non-financial loss. In the case of *Vidal-Hall et al v Google*[28] the court referred to Art 8 of the EU Charter of Fundamental Rights 2000, which guarantees the protection of personal data: 'It would be strange if that fundamental right could be breached with relative impunity by a data controller, save in those rare cases where the data subject had suffered pecuniary loss as a result of the breach.'

Case study

What level of compensation might be awarded for non-financial loss? In February 2015, the High Court in Belfast in the case of *CG v Facebook Ireland Ltd*[29] awarded £20,000 to the plaintiff. He was the victim of a string of abusive emails that arose from the misuse of private information. The court held that Facebook Ireland should have known from the plaintiff's profile, including location data, that he ran a serious risk of violence against him by vigilantes, and therefore should have deleted his private information.

14.63   However, the Regulation distinguishes between the liability of a *controller* and that of a *processor*. The former is liable for any damage caused by non-compliant processing but the latter is only liable 'where it has not complied with obligations of this Regulation specifically directed to processors or where it has acted outside or contrary to lawful instructions of the controller' (Art 82(2)). This seems to narrow the liability of a processor to something done other than on behalf of the controller. Even if the processing itself is non-compliant, a processor will therefore avoid liability if its actions fall

---

[28]   [2014] EWHC 13 (QB).
[29]   [2015] NIQB 11.

within the directions or instructions of the controller. In that event an aggrieved data subject may be forced to establish the extent of the processor's authority in order to fix liability on the processor. The controller or processor, as the case may be, will not be liable if they can show they are not responsible for the damage (Art 82(3)). This seems to reverse the normal burden of proof or at the very least share it with the data subject. Normally the plaintiff in a civil case has to prove his or her case on the balance of probabilities. (The burden of proof in a criminal case is much higher: the prosecution must prove the guilt of the accused person *beyond a reasonable doubt*.) The onus here seems to be on the controller/processor to show they were not responsible for the damage caused rather than on the data subject to show that they were.

14.64 Where two or more controllers/processors are responsible, each of them will be liable for the entire damage, ie joint and several liability (Art 82(4)). In theory, a data subject could recover his/her loss entirely from any one of the parties involved but will be advised to proceed against all of them in order to increase the possibility of holding one of them liable. The Regulation also provides for a right to contribution to be exercised against any of the parties responsible for the damage. If one of the controllers/processors has paid full compensation for the damage they will be entitled to claim payment of any part of the compensation that is attributable to the actions of any of the other parties by way of contribution from that party (Art 82(5)). So if A has paid full compensation for damage caused by A, B and C, A can seek a contribution from B and C to the extent that either party was also responsible.

14.65 Any legal proceedings for compensation as an effective judicial remedy against a controller or processor may be instituted either in the courts of the Member State where the relevant controller/processor has an 'establishment', ie a place of business, or where the data subject has his/her 'habitual residence' (Art 79(2)). The only exception is where the controller or processor is a public authority acting in the exercise of its public powers, which means that a plaintiff in these circumstances must institute legal proceedings in the courts of the Member State of the public authority concerned. The freedom of a data subject to choose where to take legal action is to ensure that he/she has an effective judicial remedy. This is the stated objective of Art 79 of the Regulation. Accordingly, a controller or processor may face legal proceedings in another Member State, which will entail all the difficulties and expense of long-range litigation.

RIGHT TO JUDICIAL REMEDY

14.66 A data subject has the right to an 'effective judicial remedy' against a decision of the ICO that affects him/her (Art 78(1)). This is without prejudice to any other administrative or judicial remedy that may be available. The remedy may take the form of a court order to oblige the ICO to act on a complaint in the absence of a decision or where the authority does not inform him/her of the progress/outcome within three months or any shorter period prescribed by law

(Art 78(2)). The relevant legal proceedings must be issued in the Member State where the authority is established (Art 78(3)). If the case concerns a decision that was the subject of an opinion or a decision of the European Data Protection Board, the authority must forward the opinion or decision, as the case may be, to the court dealing with the case (Art 78(4)).

14.67 A data subject also has the right to an effective judicial remedy against a controller or processor if he/she believes that his/her rights have been infringed as a result of processing that does not comply with the Regulation (Art 79(1)). As in the case of his/her remedy against a decision of the supervisory authority, this right is without prejudice to any other remedy that may be available. He/she may issue the relevant proceedings either in the Member State where the controller or processor has an establishment or where the data subject lives. (If the controller or processor is a public authority, the proceedings must be issued in the Member State where the authority is established.)

14.68 The new Regulation enshrines the remedy of a judicial review of any decision made by the ICO, and any other remedy that may be available from the courts:

> 'Any natural or legal person has the right to bring an action for annulment of decisions of the European Data Protection Board before the Court of Justice of the European Union ... under the conditions provided for in Article 263 TFEU ... Where decisions of the Board are of direct and individual concern to a controller, processor or complainant, the latter may bring an action for annulment against those decisions and they should do so within two months of their publication on the website of the Board in accordance with Article 263 TFEU. Without prejudice to this right under Article 263 TFEU, each natural or legal person should have an effective judicial remedy before the competent national court against a decision of a supervisory authority which produces legal effects concerning that person ....'[30]

14.69 Article 263 of the Treaty on the Functioning of the European Union 2012 (TFEU) referred to above provides that the Court of Justice of the European Union will review the legality of acts done by the Council, the Commission, the European Central Bank and the European Parliament that are intended to have legal effects on any third party. It also provides that an individual or organisation can institute legal proceedings against any such act that is of 'direct and individual concern' to them:

> '[E]ach data subject shall have the right to an effective judicial remedy where he or she considers that his or her rights under this Regulation have been infringed as a result of the processing of his or her personal data in non-compliance with this Regulation.'[31]

14.70 Judicial review is a cornerstone of the rights of the individual against the Crown. It provides the citizen with an opportunity to test any action or decision of a public body that affects him or her, by reference to the courts.

---

[30] Recital 143.
[31] Article 79(1).

14.71 As in the case of complaints on behalf of one or more data subjects, an organisation that acts in the public interest, ie non profit-making, may seek a judicial remedy on their behalf against the ICO or the controller and/or processor (Art 80(1)). The organisation must also be properly constituted under the laws of a Member State.

CHAPTER 15

COMPLIANCE

INTRODUCTION

15.1 The new General Data Protection Regulation makes clear that a controller is required not only to comply but be seen to comply. It must implement 'appropriate technical and organisational measures' and be able to demonstrate compliance with the new Regulation (Art 24(1)). These measures should take into account 'the nature, scope, context, and purposes of the processing as well as the risks of varying likelihood and severity for the rights and freedoms of natural persons'. They may include the implementation of appropriate data protection policies. The measures must be reviewed and updated where necessary. (For a sample Data Protection Policy, see Appendix 1 [FP 13.1.] and for a Sample Information Security Policy see Appendix 2 [FP 13.2.].) The relevant measures must be reviewed and updated where necessary. The data controller may demonstrate compliance by adhering to approved codes of conduct or an approved certification mechanism as discussed at 16.21 et seq below. The 'rights and freedoms of natural persons' will dictate the measures to be taken by the controller:

> 'The protection of the rights and freedoms of natural persons with regard to the processing of personal data requires that appropriate technical and organisational measures be taken to ensure that the requirements of this Regulation are met. In order to be able to demonstrate compliance with this Regulation, the controller should adopt internal policies and implement appropriate measures, which meet in particular the principles of data protection by design and data protection by default. Such measures could consist, inter alia, of minimising the processing of personal data, pseudonymising personal data as soon as possible, transparency with regard to the functions and processing of personal data, enabling the data subject to monitor the data processing, enabling the controller to create and improve security features. When developing, designing, selecting and using applications, services and products that are based on the processing of personal data or process personal data to fulfil their task, producers of the products, services and applications should be encouraged to take into account the right to data protection when developing and designing such products, services and applications and, with due regard to the state of the art, to make sure that controllers and processors are able to fulfil their data protection obligations. The principles of data protection by design and by default should also be taken into consideration in the context of public tenders.'[1]

---

[1] Recital 78.

15.2   Accordingly, it is not sufficient to comply with the new Regulation but the controller must also be able to demonstrate compliance. The Regulation stresses the importance of record-keeping:

> 'In order to demonstrate compliance with this Regulation, the controller or processor should maintain records of processing activities under its responsibility. Each controller and processor should be obliged to co-operate with the supervisory authority and make these records on request available to it, so that it might serve for monitoring those processing operations.'[2]

Case study

An audit trail is important to show that security requirements have been complied with. In *I v Finland*,[3] the European Court of Human Rights decided the state had failed to secure respect for the plaintiff's private life because a hospital had not kept proper control over access to health records or maintain a log of all persons who had access to the plaintiff's medical file.

PRIOR AUTHORISATION & CONSULTATION

15.3   The new Regulation introduces a specific requirement to consult the authorities in certain circumstances, even before any processing starts. The controller must consult with the ICO prior to the processing if a data protection impact assessment required by the new Regulation indicates that a high risk exists 'in the absence of measures taken by the controller to mitigate the risk' (Art 36(1)). This requirement suggests that the ICO must be consulted if the impact assessment shows a high risk, even if the controller has taken the appropriate measures. If the ICO forms the view that the controller has not identified or mitigated the risk adequately or at all, it must so inform the controller within eight weeks and may exercise any of its investigative and enforcement powers under the Regulation (Art 36(2)). The period may be extended for a further six weeks if the processing is particularly complex, and in that event the controller and where applicable the processor must be informed within one month, including the reasons for the delay. Even if the processing is not 'high risk', there may be a need to consult with the ICO before it starts: the Regulation leaves it open to Member States to require prior consultation with, and prior approval from, a supervisory authority in the case of processing in the public interest, including social protection and public health (Art 36(5)).

15.4   When consulting with the ICO, the controller must provide the following information:

---

[2]   Recital 82.
[3]   ECtHR Application No 20511/03, July 2008.

- if applicable, the respective responsibilities of the data controller, any joint controller and any processor that will be involved, eg in processing data for a group of companies;
- the purposes and method of the intended processing;
- the measures and safeguards to protect the rights and freedoms of data subjects;
- contact details for the controller's data protection officer, if any;
- the data protection impact assessment; and
- any other information requested by the ICO.[4]

15.5 The Regulation sets out the rationale for consulting with the 'supervisory authority', ie the ICO:

> 'Where a data protection impact assessment indicates that the processing would, in the absence of safeguards, security measures and mechanisms to mitigate the risk, result in a high risk to the rights and freedoms of natural persons and the controller is of the opinion that the risk cannot be mitigated by reasonable means in terms of available technologies and costs of implementation, the supervisory authority should be consulted, prior to the start of the processing activities. Such high risk is likely to result from certain types of data processing and certain extent and frequency of processing, which may result also in a realisation of damage or interference with the rights and freedoms of the natural person ....'[5]

15.6 The requirement for prior consultation will replace the need for an annual registration with the ICO under ss 18 and 19 of the DPA. What was a recurring obligation under the DPA will be a 'once-off', and even then only in the case of 'high risk' processing. This will reduce the administrative burden of making an annual registration of the data processing activities of the controller/processor as at present. The new Regulation will replace the current registration with 'effective procedures and mechanisms which focus instead on those types of processing operations which are likely to result in a high risk to the rights and freedoms of natural persons by virtue of their nature, scope, context and purposes' (Recital 89). The Regulation gives as examples of these operations those that involve new technology or have not been subject to a data protection impact assessment. In order for the controller/processor to determine whether a consultation is required with their own data protection officer (DPO) and with the ICO, they must risk-assess their processing operations in light of the required impact assessment. If their DPO or the ICO requests it, a consultation must take place regardless of the outcome of any risk assessment. If the ICO believes the processing does not comply with the new Regulation, it will prohibit the processing and make proposals as to how the controller/processor can remedy the breach (Art 36(2)).

---

[4]   Article 36(3).
[5]   Recital 94.

DATA PROTECTION BY DESIGN & BY DEFAULT

15.7 'Data protection by design' is a new concept introduced by the Regulation. It refers to 'appropriate technical and organisational measures' for data protection:

> 'Taking into account the state of the art and the cost of implementation and the nature, scope, context and purposes of processing as well as the risks of varying likelihood and severity for rights and freedoms of natural persons posed by the processing, the controller shall, both at the time of the determination of the means for processing and at the time of the processing itself, implement appropriate technical and organisational measures, such as preudonymisation, which are designed to implement data protection principles, such as data minimisation, in an effective manner, and to integrate the necessary safeguards into the processing in order to meet the requirements of this Regulation and protect the rights of data subjects.'[6]

15.8 An approved certification mechanism, discussed at **16.31** below, may be used by the controller to demonstrate compliance with this requirement.

15.9 'Data protection by default' is also new and requires that a controller must ensure that, by default, only personal data may be processed that is necessary for the purpose(s) of the processing. Likewise access to personal data must be limited to those people who need to have access to it:

> 'The controller shall implement appropriate technical and organisational measures for ensuring that, by default, only personal data which are necessary for each specific purpose of the processing are processed. That obligation applies to the amount of personal data collected, the extent of their processing, the period of their storage and their accessibility. In particular, such measures shall ensure that by default personal data are not made accessible without the individual's intervention to an indefinite number of natural persons.'[7]

15.10 As in the case of data protection by design, an approved certification mechanism discussed at **16.31** below may be used by the controller to demonstrate compliance with this requirement.

15.11 Design and default are new concepts in data protection, introduced by the new Regulation. Under the DPA a data controller is free to decide how it should protect personal data of its customers or other third parties, provided there are adequate safeguards. The Act says nothing about the kind of systems or processes that a controller should have in place. Neither does the new Regulation but it provides there must be 'appropriate technical and organisational measures' in addition to a default position tied to the purpose(s) of the processing. The Regulation introduces these two specific requirements for data protection by default and by design for any system that processes personal data. Whatever about the technical specifications, a controller's (and

---

[6] Article 25(1).
[7] Article 25(2).

processor's) system must be adequate to comply with these new requirements, which must be implemented at all stages in the life cycle of data processing, ie from obtaining at the start to deletion at the end.

RISK ANALYSIS/IMPACT ASSESSMENT

15.12 The new Regulation sets out the specific risks for the 'rights and freedoms of natural persons':

> 'The risks … of varying likelihood and severity, may result from personal data processing which could lead to physical, material or non-material damage. In particular where the processing may give rise to discrimination, identity theft or fraud, financial loss, damage to the reputation, loss of confidentiality of personal data protected by professional secrecy, unauthorised reversal of pseudonymisation, or any other significant economic or social disadvantage; where data subjects might be deprived of their rights and freedoms or from exercising control over their personal data; where personal data are processed which reveal racial or ethnic origin, political opinions, religion or philosophical beliefs, trade-union membership, and the processing of genetic data or data concerning health or data concerning sex life or criminal convictions and offences or related security measures; where personal aspects are evaluated, in particular analysing and prediction of aspects concerning performance at work, economic situation, health, personal preferences or interests, reliability or behaviour, location or movements in order to create or use personal profiles where personal data of vulnerable natural persons, in particular of children, are processed; or where processing involves a large amount of personal data and affects a large number of data subjects.'[8]

15.13 The controller must carry out a data protection impact assessment in the case of 'high risk' processing of personal data (Art 35(1)). This is any processing that involves new technology or has not been subject to an assessment previously or has become necessary due to the passage of time since the initial processing, ie further processing not envisaged at that time.

> 'In such cases, a data protection impact assessment should be carried out by the controller prior to the processing in order to assess the particular likelihood and severity of the high risk, taking into account the nature, scope, context and purposes of the processing and the sources of the risk. That impact assessment should include in particular the envisaged measures, safeguards and mechanisms envisaged for mitigating that risk, ensuring the protection of personal data and demonstrating compliance with this Regulation.'[9]

15.14 The Regulation envisages that 'high risk' would include large-scale processing operations that are likely to make it more difficult for data subjects to exercise their rights. It would also include data processed to make decisions about individuals based on profiling or on sensitive personal data. Video recordings made by CCTV cameras should also be subject to an impact assessment. If the data is protected by professional secrecy, eg personal data

---

8 Recital 75.
9 Recital 90.

processed by a doctor or medical professional, this would not be considered as large-scale and therefore high-risk even if the data relates to a large number or people, and so would not require completion of an impact assessment.

15.15   The impact assessment is required in the following circumstances:

• where a 'systematic and extensive evaluation' is being carried out based on profiling – see 'Key definitions' at **10.24** et seq above – and on the basis of which decisions are made about data subjects that produce legal effects on them or significantly affect them;

• processing on a large scale of special categories of personal data, biometric data – see **10.24** et seq above – or data on criminal convictions and offences on the basis of which decisions are made about individuals 'on a large scale'; and

• monitoring publicly accessible areas 'on a large scale', especially when using optic-electronic devices, ie CCTV cameras.[10]

15.16   The Regulation does not prescribe the form of impact assessment but provides for minimum contents as follows:

• 'systematic' description of the envisaged processing;

• assessment of the necessity and proportionality of the processing operations;

• assessment of the risk involved to the rights and freedoms of individuals; and

• measures envisaged to address the risk involved, 'including safeguards, security measures and mechanisms to ensure the protection of personal data and to demonstrate compliance with this Regulation'.[11]

15.17   As there is no prescribed form of assessment the controller is free to assess the impact on protection of the data on the basis of any industry standards that might apply, provided they meet the relevant requirements.

15.18   The controller must seek the views of data subjects or their representatives on the intended processing 'where appropriate' (Art 35(9)). This is without prejudice to the controller's commercial interests or the security of data but will require a process of prior consultation with the parties involved, eg customers, employees or suppliers. As regards what is 'appropriate', this may include what is possible so that customers or others who are difficult to contact may not need to be consulted.

---

[10]   Article 35(3)(a)–(c).
[11]   Article 35(7)(a)–(d).

DATA PROTECTION FRAMEWORK

15.19 In order to ensure that an organisation complies with its data protection obligations, it is vital to establish a framework or structure for the various elements that make up the compliance effort. Organisations may differ in the way they approach their data protection obligations but they share a common requirement to formalise their approach in a way that ensures compliance and, just as important, demonstrates compliance to a regulator such as the ICO should the need arise. (See *Personal Information Online – Small Business Checklist* at Appendix 4.)

Inventory

15.20 An inventory consists of a cohesive, accurate and up-to-date account of the various processes within the organisation that use personal data, and of the controls that govern use of the data. The inventory will cover:

- business processes, eg manufacturing, customer services, human resources;
- systems, databases and manual processes that support the specified business processes;
- transfers of personal data outside the UK and/or the EU in the case of a multinational company; and
- third parties to whom the data may be transferred for processing, eg outsourcing of payroll.

Policy & governance

15.21 A policy for compliance purposes is a statement of the organisation's business rules relating to the use of personal data. The statement should be in a formal document that is communicated to and understood by everyone in the organisation, or connected with the organisation, who uses personal data as part of their job or in dealing with the organisation. This includes employees, contractors, agents and third parties such as suppliers and even customers. If the organisation has a website, it should include a privacy statement on the site (this is a regulatory requirement). A verbal privacy statement is also required to be made on phone calls to customers for marketing or debt collection.

15.22 Governance refers to a comprehensive set of defined roles and responsibilities, accountabilities, and authorities for the use of personal data by or on behalf of the organisation. A named individual should be accountable for data protection. (This person will be the organisation's data protection officer as required by the new Regulation.) However, everyone in the organisation is responsible to see that he/she complies with the policy and applicable laws, supported by senior management. He/she should be made aware of the importance of compliance and of the consequences of failure to comply. An effective system of governance also provides relevant input from across the organisation to make key decisions about personal data, and accurate and up-to-date management information about data protection risks that have been identified.

Risk management

15.23 Risk management for this purpose refers to the management of data protection risks across the organisation. It addresses the use of technology to process personal data and any transfers of the data outside the UK. It also addresses the extent to which third parties use personal data on behalf of the organisation. In order to manage the risks arising from any of these activities, the organisation should have in place a strategy that defines these risks and sets out how they are managed, ie controlled, tested and reported as appropriate. The strategy itself should be under central control, ie by a manager or director in charge of risk management.

Procedures & controls

15.24 The data protection framework will include formal procedures and controls aligned with the policy and relevant laws and regulations to enforce compliance with them. These procedures and controls will be administrative, technical and physical. Monitoring at process level and organisation-wide is vital to ensure they remain intact and effective.

Information security

15.25 Information security for data protection purposes is concerned with managing the confidentiality, integrity, and availability of personal data and the related technology used to collect, use, retain, and transfer the information. The security infrastructure comprises organisation wide systems, including servers, databases and sites, and portable media and devices, including laptops, USB sticks, tablets, and mobile phones. The infrastructure must deal correctly with all personal data within the organisation, and address the risks involved.

Third party management

15.26 For this purpose third parties are suppliers that share personal data with the organisation due to the goods or services being supplied. Third party risk management consists of documented and robust and processes that protect personal data, including due diligence during the selection process, putting controls in place – both contractually and for the secure transfer of the data – and building confidence that the third parties using the data can use it and protect it to an acceptable standard. The organisation should have in place standard requirements for data protection and security for third parties who process its personal data. For example, standard contractual clauses should be used in contracts with third parties, as discussed at **12.72** et seq above. Regular reporting on compliance with these clauses should be required. The organisation should have the right to satisfy itself, eg by audit, that the third party complies with data protection and security requirements.

Compliance

15.27 The compliance effort should consist of a robust plan to prevent, detect and correct unwanted situations around the use and protection of personal data. It will include a list or inventory of applicable laws and regulations in addition to relevant policies, agreements and other legal commitments to data protection. The plan will also set out how to manage regulatory reporting and risk assessments.

Incident management

15.28 The organisation should have in place a documented incident management process that provides a prompt and effective response to incidents and potential incidents, ie breaches or potential breaches of data protection obligations. The process will set out roles and responsibilities and the steps to be taken to contain an incident and rectify it as appropriate. In this way the process will enable the organisation to provide timely and controlled notifications to stakeholders, customers who have been or may be affected and members of the public as necessary. The process must be tested periodically and validated to ensure it is effective.

Training & awareness

15.29 General and specific training related to the organisation's use and protection of data is essential. This must be supported by an ongoing awareness program and related guidance on data protection matters. Training and awareness should be aimed at all those who handle personal data in the course of their work for and on behalf of the organisation. They should be provided to new hires and existing staff, and updated on a regular basis, at least annually.

DATA PROTECTION OFFICER

15.30 Many organisations have appointed someone to be responsible for all matters to do with data protection. The new Regulation gives a central role to an individual called a data protection officer (DPO). A data controller or processor may appoint a DPO or may be obliged to do so by EU law or the law of a Member State (Art 37(1)). In certain circumstances a DPO *must* be appointed by the controller and processor:

> 'The controller and the processor shall designate a data protection officer in any case where:
>
> (a) the processing is carried out by a public authority or body, except for courts acting in their judicial capacity; or

(b)   the core activities of the controller or the processor consist of processing operations which, by virtue of their nature, their scope and/or their purposes, require regular and systematic monitoring of data subjects on a large scale; or

(c)   the core activities of the controller or the processor consist of processing on a large scale of special categories of data and data relating to criminal convictions and offences ...'[12]

15.31   Among other things, the DPO will be responsible to advise the business of its obligations and monitor its compliance with them. He/she will also be the contact point for any dealings with the ICO (Art 39(1)(e)) and with the public (Art 38(4)).

15.32   The Regulation sets out the basis for this requirement for the appointment of a DPO:

'Where the processing is carried out by a public authority, except for courts or independent judicial authorities when acting in their judicial capacity, or where, in the private sector, processing is controller whose core activities consist of processing operations that require regular and systematic monitoring of the data subjects, a person with expert knowledge of data protection law and practices should assist the controller or processor to monitor internal compliance with this Regulation. In the private sector, the core activities of a controller relate to its primary activities and do not relate to the processing of personal data as ancillary activities. The necessary level of expert knowledge should be determined in particular according to the data processing operations carried out and the protection required for the personal data processed by the controller or the processor. Such data protection officers, whether or not an employee of the controller, should be in a position to perform their duties and tasks in an independent manner.'[13]

15.33   The DPO must be appointed on the basis of his/her 'professional qualities' and, in particular, expert knowledge of data protection law and practices and ability to fulfil the tasks referred to in Article 37. (Art 37(5))

15.34   Accordingly, almost every organisation that processes personal data to a significant extent is within scope of this requirement for a DPO. However, the emphasis is not on size of the organisation but on the extent and relevance of processing carried on. For example, technology companies may be quite small in terms of numbers of employees but they may process an enormous amount of data. All public sector organisations are included, as are private companies and businesses regardless of size whose 'core activity' relates to processing and monitoring of personal data. The only category of data controller/processor that seems to escape the net is a sole trader or small business that does not process personal data as a 'core activity' or at all, eg small retailers and other businesses that process personal data as an ancillary activity, if at all, eg a shop does not usually hold any personal data about its customers. However,

---

[12]   Art 37(1)(a)–(c).
[13]   Recital 97.

professional services firms such as accountants, architects, engineers, estate agents and solicitors would seem to come within this requirement – the nature of their business requires processing and monitoring of their clients' personal data in order to provide services. Likewise, medical professionals are in scope as they process personal data, including sensitive personal data, relating to patients and others as necessary.

15.35 In order to save cost and streamline the DPO's operations, a group of companies may designate a single DPO for all companies within the group 'provided that a data protection officer is easily accessible from each establishment' (Art 37(2)). Similarly, a public authority may designate one DPO for entities within the authority 'taking account of their organisational structure and size'. (Art 37(3))

Appointment of DPO

15.36 As stated above, for someone to be appointed as a DPO, he/she must have the required 'professional qualities' and expert knowledge of data protection law and practices (Art 37(5)). The level of knowledge required will depend on the activities or business of the controller/processor. So it is not necessary that a DPO holds formal qualifications but he/she must obviously be someone of ability and integrity. The onus is on the controller/processor to show they have taken steps to satisfy themselves as to the suitability of the person designated. On appointment of someone to act as DPO, the controller must publish his/her contact details and inform the supervisory authority, ie the ICO, of the appointment. (Art 37(7))

15.37 In addition to the qualities and knowledge required for the job, the DPO's duties must be compatible with his/her other duties, if any. There must be no conflict of interests between the various duties assigned to the DPO (Art 38(6)). Best practice is for the controller to document its policy on conflicts of interest in this regard and put appropriate procedures in place to implement the policy.

15.38 The DPO's protection from dismissal except on the specified grounds suggests that gross misconduct or incompetence may be grounds for dismissal, but not a decision by the DPO that the controller/processor disagrees with. The DPO cannot be dismissed for doing something that does not suit the controller/processor. However, it may also be the case that a conflict of interest arises between his/her duties as DPO and their other duties and for whatever reason the conflict cannot be resolved. This is one of the 'conditions' required and so he/she may be dismissed as DPO in that event, ie their appointment may be terminated. Of course, they will remain as an employee if they are employed in another role, unless grounds exist for dismissal in respect of the specific requirements for that role.

15.39 A controller/processor may not be able to identify someone suitable on their staff to be designated as DPO and may not want to recruit someone for that role. The DPO may be appointed on the basis of a service contract (Art 37(6)), ie as an independent contractor rather than an employee. So it is open to a controller/processor to contract with a third party to act as DPO. For good order, and to protect all parties involved, the contract should specify the tasks to be performed and require the third party to comply with all the requirements of the new Regulation.

Role of DPO

15.40   The DPO will be the contact point for the ICO, and for the public. As stated above, the Regulation obliges the controller/processor to publish the DPO's name and contact details (Art 37(7)). This is to enable data subjects to exercise their right to contact him/her 'with regard to all issues related to the processing of [their] personal data and the exercise of their rights under this Regulation' (Art 38(4)). As the point of contact for all data protection matters, the DPO must therefore be contactable directly by third parties. This will require at the very least a direct phone line and email address. In addition to 'professional qualities' and expert knowledge, the DPO should therefore have good communication skills to engage with the ICO and with data subjects to address their concerns.

15.41   The controller/processor must ensure that the DPO is 'properly and in a timely manner' involved in all matters relating to data protection (Art 38(1)). He/she must be supported in performing his/her tasks by having the necessary resources in addition to access to the relevant data and processing operations (Art 38(2)). He/she must be independent in the exercise of their tasks and take no instruction as to how to exercise them (Art 38(3)). Specifically, he/she cannot be penalised in any way for performing these tasks. He/she must report directly to the 'highest management level' of the controller/processor. By making the DPO independent in this way, the Regulation establishes a unique position for someone who is employed by the data controller/processor and entitled to a salary and other benefits but not subject to any instruction from their employer, at least as regards the exercise of their duties as DPO. In view of his/her protected status, the controller should take great care in making the appointment.

15.42   As stated above, the controller must provide the necessary resources to support the DPO in his/her duties (Art 38(2)). This includes the necessary resources to allow the DPO to maintain his/her expert knowledge. This is clear in the case of a DPO employed by the controller but less so if he/she performs the role as an independent contractor. If the latter, does the controller/processor have an obligation to ensure that the DPO has a suitable office and systems? To comply with any obligation in this regard, the contract for provision of the service should provide for confirmation by the DPO that he/she has all the resources needed to do the job.

Duties of DPO

15.43 The new Regulation specifies the minimum duties or 'tasks' to be performed by the DPO:

- to inform and advise the controller/processor, and their employees, of their obligations under the Regulation and other applicable laws and regulations;
- to monitor compliance with the Regulation and other applicable laws and regulations and with the relevant policies of the controller/processor; this includes assignment of responsibilities, awareness and training, and related audits;
- to advise on the data protection impact assessment and monitor its performance, if requested; and
- to liaise with the ICO as required.[14]

15.44 At the very least he/she must perform the tasks set out above, in addition to any other duties specified in his/her contract of employment or service contract, as the case may be. The role of DPO may or may not the individual's only role within the organisation, provided any other role does not conflict with it.

15.45 The Regulation obliges the DPO to provide a general advisory service to the data controller/processor and to monitor its compliance with the various requirements of the Regulation (Art 39(1)). He/she must 'raise awareness', inform and advise of all relevant obligations on a continuing basis, in particular regarding 'technical and organisational measures and procedures' and document this information/advice and what the controller/processor did to comply or otherwise. This is a demanding and wide-ranging role that requires expertise and the capacity to keep up to date with changes in regulation and in practice. The obligation to record the data controller's response to the DPO's advice brings into play a monitoring role for the DPO in addition to a general advisory one. The DPO must follow-up his/her advice and check to see if it was followed or not. This will require processes and procedures to be put in place to monitor compliance, including assignment of roles and responsibilities, staff training, and relevant audits (Art 39(1)(b)).

15.46 The new Regulation also requires the DPO to monitor implementation of the data controller's policies on data protection, assuming it has these policies (Art 39(1)(b)). If the controller does not have appropriate data protection policies in place, there is surely a role for the DPO to draft relevant policy documents. The requirement to monitor implementation will necessitate processes and procedures and an infrastructure to ensure compliance with the controller's policies. This seems to entrust the DPO with a quasi-audit role alongside the data controller's internal auditors and/or compliance function. Of course, it may be that the DPO *is* the internal auditor or compliance officer. In

---

[14] Article 39(1)(a)–(e).

addition, there is a role for the DPO in assigning responsibilities to, and training of, relevant staff who are involved in processing of data. Accordingly, the role may involve a management responsibility for certain operations and staff of the controller.

15.47 The DPO is obliged by the new Regulation to advise on and monitor the performance of a 'data protection impact assessment' by the data controller (Art 39(1)(c)). This is an assessment of the impact of processing operations where these present specific risks to data subjects. These operations include computer analysis of a person's financial position or personal behaviour, and personal data relating to children. The DPO is also obliged to monitor the controller's compliance with the requirement to carry out a prior consultation with the DPO himself/herself and/or with the ICO, for which the DPO will be the contact point (Art 39(1)(e)). Finally, in performing all of these tasks the DPO must have 'due regard to the risk associated with the processing operations, taking into account the nature, scope, context and purposes of the processing' (Art 39(2)).

CHAPTER 16

ENFORCEMENT

INTRODUCTION

16.1 This chapter sets out the functions and powers of the Information Commissioner's Office ('ICO') and the sanctions it may impose on a party in breach of its data protection obligations. Laws and regulations are only as strong as the measures taken to enforce them. The DPA and the new Regulation will only be effective if they are enforced by the relevant authority against controllers and processors. The ICO is the relevant authority here.

The ICO's stated mission is to 'uphold information rights in the public interest, promoting openness by public bodies and data privacy for individuals'. In terms of data protection, its stated goal is that 'all organisations which collect and use personal information do so responsibly, securely and fairly'. Among its functions is to promote 'good practice' by data controllers and the observance of DPA requirements (s 51(1)). *Good practice* for this purpose means 'desirable having regard to the interests of data subjects and others and includes (but is not limited to) compliance with the requirements of this Act' (s 51(9)). The ICO will also, after consultation with relevant trade associations or data subjects, prepare and promote appropriate codes of practice for guidance (s 51(3)). Trade associations may submit a code of practice to the ICO for approval as to whether the code promotes good practice (s 51(4)). With the consent of a data controller, the ICO can assess any processing of personal data 'for the following of good practice' (s 51(9)). However, the new Regulation will abolish the current requirement under the DPA for controllers and processors to register with the ICO on an annual basis.

ROLE OF THE ICO

16.2 The new Regulation sets out a specific role for the ICO in enforcing the new data protection regime. The ICO 'shall act with complete independence in performing the tasks and exercising the powers entrusted to it' (Art 52(1)). It must be provided with the 'human, technical and financial resources, premises and infrastructure necessary for the effective performance of its tasks and exercise of its powers' (Art 52(4)). In particular, the ICO must be subject to financial control and have its own budget, which does not affect its independence in any way. The member or members of the supervisory authority must be appointed for a period of at least four years (Art 54(1)(d)) – the only exception is the first appointment after the entry into force of the Regulation, which may be made for a shorter period 'where this is necessary to protect the independence of the supervisory authority by means of a staggered appointment procedure' (Art 54(1)(d)). The ICO has only one member, the Commissioner himself/herself, currently Christopher Graham. The Commissioner is subject to 'a duty of professional secrecy both during and after their term of office with regards to any confidential information which has come to their knowledge in the course of the performance of their tasks or exercise of their powers' (Art 54(2)).

Co-operation with the ICO

16.3 Data controllers are obliged to co-operate with the ICO as the supervisory authority. In particular they must provide access to, and information in relation to, personal data so that the Commissioner can perform his duties. They must also provide access to their premises if he/she has reason to believe that processing operations are being carried on in breach of the data protection regime. However, the ICO has confirmed that its current approach of educating and engaging with data controllers where possible prior to any enforcement action will continue after the introduction of the new Regulation.

16.4 As an alternative to a compulsory audit, data controllers can request the ICO at any time to audit their compliance with data protection requirements. An audit provides an assessment of whether the organisation is following good practice and plays a key role to help the organisation to understand and comply with its obligations. The audit looks at whether there are effective policies and procedures in place, and whether they are followed, and includes recommendations from the ICO on how to improve. The organisation benefits from the knowledge and experience of the audit team. It represents an ideal opportunity for staff to discuss relevant issues with the members of the team, at no cost to the organisation. A typical audit will look at:

- data protection governance, and the structures, policies and procedures to ensure compliance;
- the processes for managing electronic and manual records containing personal data;
- the processes for responding to any request for personal data, including requests by individuals for copies of their data as well as those made by third parties, and sharing agreements;
- the technical and organisational measures in place to ensure that there is adequate security over personal data held in manual or electronic form; and
- the provision and monitoring of staff data protection training and the awareness of data protection.

16.5 Following agreement with the data controller for a scope of work, which is formally documented in a letter of engagement, the ICO will:

- carry out an off-site check of policies and procedures;
- carry out an on-site review of the procedures in practice;
- provide a report that outlines good practice and any areas of improvement with practical recommendations to help the organisation to address these where appropriate;
- write an executive summary that may be published on the ICO's website, with the data controller's consent; and
- carry out a follow up review approximately six months after the audit.

16.6 Following completion of the audit, the ICO provides a comprehensive report along with an executive summary. The audit report allows the data controller to respond to its observations and recommendations.

16.7 The ICO can also make an advisory visit on request by a data controller. The aim of an advisory visit is to give practical advice to organisations on how to improve data protection practice. It normally involves a one-day visit from the ICO and a short follow-up report.

16.8 The ICO may also consult with interested parties and those affected by data protection rules. In January 2016 the ICO organised a workshop on the new Regulation, attended by representatives of central and local government, public bodies, and private companies and organisations. The workshop discussed subjects of particular concern to all, including those listed below:

- Scope and principles of the Regulation – requirement for a legal basis of the processing, and the interpretation of *pseudonymisation* (see Chapter 10) and *profiling* (see Chapter 11);
- Transparency and individuals' rights – new requirements for processing information notices to data subjects, in particular the need to ensure these are comprehensive and up to date; and practical implications of the rights to erasure of data, data portability, and to be informed of and object to automated decision-making (see Chapter 14);
- Consent – consistency of approach by the ICO to different sectors, in particular reliance on consent as the basis for fair and lawful processing (see Chapter 12);
- Breach notification – practical implications of duty to notify (see Chapter 12), in particular whether the ICO will apply a threshold based on severity and impact of a breach, and notification of a near-miss;
- Accountability – division of responsibility as between data controller and data processor, in particular for existing contracts (see 'Outsourcing' in Chapter 12); expectations for record-keeping and records management (see Chapter 15) in relation to rights to erasure of data and data portability; and
- International issues – recognition that multinational companies may process data for different purposes in different countries; location of the company's 'main establishment' (see 'Key definitions' in Chapter 10).

The ICO undertook to provide practical guidance for organisations to help them comply, eg the Privacy Notices Code of Practice – see www.ico.org.uk. However, the ICO also stated that its pragmatic approach to interpretation of data protection rules may yield to the need for consistency across the EU Member States.

Duties of the ICO

16.9   The ICO is charged by the new Regulation with the following duties or 'tasks':

- to monitor and enforce the application of the Regulation;
- promote public awareness and understanding of the risks, rules, safeguards and rights in relation to the processing of personal data. 'Activities addressed specifically to children shall receive specific attention';
- advise government and other institutions and bodies about measures relating to the protection of individuals' rights and freedoms;
- promote the awareness of controllers and processors as to their obligations;
- on request, provide information to any data subject about his/her rights and if necessary co-operate with supervisory authorities in other Member States for this purpose;
- deal with and investigate complaints made by a data subject or organisation acting on his/her behalf, in accordance with Art 80;
- conduct investigations, inspections and audits, whether on foot of complaints or information received from another supervisory authority or other public authority or on its own initiative;
- to share information and co-operate with supervisory authorities in other Member States in order to ensure consistency;
- monitor relevant developments, in particular 'information and communication technologies and commercial practices';
- adopt standard contractual clauses for use in binding contracts between controllers and processors in accordance with Arts 28(8) and 46(2)(d) for the processing of personal data;
- identify the processing operations that require a data protection impact assessment in accordance with Art 3(4);
- advise on processing operations referred to it in the course of prior consultation in accordance with Art 36(2);
- encourage the drawing up of codes of conduct in accordance with Art 40 and give an opinion on draft codes of conduct submitted to it in accordance with Art 40(5);
- promote the establishment of data protection certification mechanisms, seals and marks and approve the criteria for certification in accordance with Art 42(5);

- if applicable, conduct a periodic review of certifications issued in accordance with Art 42(7);

- publish the criteria for accrediting a monitoring body in respect of codes of conduct in accordance with Art 41 and a certification body in accordance with Art 43, and conduct the accreditations;

- authorise contractual clauses for use in binding contracts relating to the transfer of personal data to countries and organisations outside the EU, in accordance with Art 46(3);

- approve binding corporate rules in accordance with Art 47;

- take part in the activities of the European Data Protection Board;

- keep records of breaches of this Regulation and of measures taken; and

- 'fulfil any other tasks related to the protection of personal data'.[1]

16.10 The ICO will be obliged to publish an annual report on its activities (Art 59), as it does at present. The report must be presented to Parliament, the government and any other authorities specified by UK law.

Powers of the ICO

16.11 The ICO may require a data controller to provide it with whatever information is required to carry out its functions, such as information to determine whether the data controller has complied or is complying with the data protection principles (DPA, s 43(1)). The ICO exercises this power by serving a written notice, called an *information notice*, on the organisation concerned. Anyone who receives a notice has the right to appeal against it to a special tribunal. Failure to comply with a notice or knowingly to provide false information is a criminal offence. The only exceptions to compliance with an information notice are (i) where revealing the relevant information would incriminate, and (ii) where the information is privileged from disclosure in legal proceedings.

16.12 The ICO may require a data controller to take appropriate steps to comply with the legislation (DPA, s 40). Such steps could include correcting the data, blocking the data from use for certain purposes, supplementing or deleting the data (DPA, s 40(3)). The ICO exercises this power by serving a written notice, called an *enforcement notice*, on the data controller concerned. This will direct the controller to take certain steps or to refrain from taking certain steps in relation to the processing, eg to rectify, erase or destroy any inaccurate data. The notice will specify the relevant provision(s) of the Act that has/have been or may have been breached. A person who receives an enforcement notice has the right to appeal it to a special tribunal. The recipient of the notice, ie the data controller, may be required to notify third parties to whom the data may have been disclosed. It is an offence to fail or refuse to comply with an enforcement notice.

---

[1] Article 57(1)(a)–(v).

Case study

In February 2015 the ICO issued an enforcement notice to North Tees and Hartlepool NHS Foundation Trust. The Trust was ordered by the ICO to review its data protection policy after a file containing sensitive patient information was found at a bus stop. This was the latest in a series of incidents over the previous year, which resulted in data being lost or disclosed without authorisation. Other incidents included letters, notes and reports containing patient data being sent to the wrong people. The ICO reported as follows:

> 'The Commissioner considered, as he is required to do under section 40(2) of the Act when deciding whether to serve an Enforcement Notice, whether any contravention has caused or is likely to cause any person damage or distress. The Commissioner took the view that the likelihood of distress is self-evident. The individuals whose personal data was put at risk of unauthorised access and further dissemination would be likely to have suffered worry and anxiety on account of the risk that their data would come into the possession of unauthorised individuals. While there is no evidence that damage has been caused there was a significant risk that it could have been.'

Accordingly, the ICO ordered the Trust to carry out the following actions:

'(1)   Review its Data Protection Policy to reflect the specific needs and practicalities associated with each internal department. The review should involve a requirement to redact or minimise the personal data contained in correspondence removed from the office wherever possible, and to use secure electronic solutions for document storage and transmission when available;

(2)   Put an action plan in place and carry out comprehensive quality assurance and spot checks to ensure *all* departments are complying with policies relating to the protection of personal data on an ongoing basis including the Data Protection Policy ...;

(3)   As part of this action plan, implement additional technical or organisational measures to ensure that the [correct procedure] is being strictly adhered to by all staff dealing with patient correspondence, particularly with regard to the checking of addresses and non-overtyping of letters; and

(4)   Establish a data breach management policy to deal specifically with containment and recovery solutions, including requirements around the secure retrieval of recovered information.'

16.13 The ICO may serve what is called an *assessment notice* on a data controller to enable the Commissioner 'to determine whether the controller has complied or is complying with the data protection principles' (DPA, s 41A(1)). Data controllers in scope are government departments, certain public authorities and any other designated persons (DPA, s 41A(2)). Officers of the ICO may enter and examine the premises of a data controller and examine any documents found there to enable the Commissioner to carry out his functions, such as to pursue an investigation (DPA, s 41A(3)). Officers have the power to:

- enter the premises and inspect any data equipment there;
- require the data controller, data processor or staff to assist in obtaining access to data, and to provide any related information;
- inspect and copy any documents or information; and
- require the data controller, data processor or staff to provide information about procedures on complying with the DPA, sources of data, purposes for which personal data are kept, persons to whom the data is disclosed, and data equipment on the premises.

16.14 Similar to an enforcement notice, a data controller has the right of appeal against an assessment notice. It is an offence to obstruct or impede an authorised officer or to fail to comply with any of the requirements set out above.

16.15 The ICO can impose fines or 'monetary penalties' and can bring prosecutions that may result in fines being imposed on data controllers or their directors, managers or other officers. The court may also order the forfeiture or destruction of data connected with the offence (DPA, s 31(2)).

Case study

In April 2015 a personal injuries claims company called Direct Assist was issued with a monetary penalty of €80,000 by the ICO for making direct marketing calls to people without their consent. Between January 2013 and July 2014, the ICO and the Telephone Preference Service (TPS) registered 801 complaints about Direct Assist, which offered access to solicitors for personal injury claims.

THE NEW REGULATION

16.16 The ICO will also have wide-ranging powers as a supervisory authority to ensure compliance with the new Regulation. These include *investigative powers* to:

- order the controller/processor and, where applicable, the controller's or processor's representative to provide any information it requires;
- conduct investigations in the form of data protection audits;
- conduct a review of certifications issued in accordance with Art 42(7);
- notify the controller/processor of an alleged infringement of the Regulation;
- obtain access to all personal data and to all information necessary for the performance of its tasks; and

- obtain access to any premises of the controller/processor, including any data processing equipment, in accordance with law.[2]

16.17 The Regulation also provides for the following *corrective powers* of the ICO:

- issue warnings to the controller/processor that intended processing is likely to infringe the Regulation;
- issue reprimands to the controller/processor where processing has infringed the Regulation;
- order the controller/processor to comply with the data subject's requests to exercise his/her rights under the Regulation;
- order the controller/processor to 'bring processing operations into compliance' with the Regulation, where appropriate, in a specified manner and within a specified time;
- order the controller to communicate a personal data breach to the data subject;
- impose a temporary or permanent 'limitation' of the processing;
- withdraw a certification or order a certification body to withdraw a certification issued pursuant to Arts 42 and 43;
- order the rectification or erasure of personal data or restriction of processing;
- order the suspension of data flows to a recipient outside the EU; and
- impose an administrative fine in accordance with Art 84.[3]

16.18 Finally, the ICO will have the following *authorisation and advisory powers*:

- to advise the controller in accordance with the prior consultation procedure referred to in Art 36;
- to publish opinions for Parliament, the government and other institutions and bodies on any issue related to date protection;
- to authorise the processing if UK law requires prior authorisation in accordance with Art 36(5), ie even if the processing is not 'high risk';
- to publish an opinion and approve draft codes of conduct submitted by associations or organisations in accordance with Art 40(5);
- to accredit certification bodies in accordance with Art 43;
- to issue certifications and approve criteria for certification in accordance with Art 42(5);

---

[2] Article 58(1)(a)–(f).
[3] Article 58(2)(a)–(j).

- to adopt standard data protection clauses in conjunction with the European Commission for the purpose of providing appropriate safeguards for the transfer of personal data outside the EU, in accordance with Arts 28(8) and 46(2)(d);

- to authorise contractual clauses for the purpose of providing appropriate safeguards for the transfer of personal data outside the EU, in accordance with Art 46(3)(a);

- to authorise administrative arrangements between public authorities or bodies for the purpose of providing appropriate safeguards for the transfer of personal data outside the EU, in accordance with Art 46(3)(b); and

- to approve binding corporate rules for the purpose of providing appropriate safeguards for the transfer of personal data outside the EU, in accordance with Art 47.[4]

16.19   The ICO will be subject to 'appropriate safeguards' itself in the exercise of its powers (Art 58(4)). These include the right of judicial review as provided for by law. The new Regulation also provides that the ICO will have the power to notify the courts of any infringement and, where appropriate, to commence or take part in legal proceedings to enforce the Regulation (Art 58(5)).

16.20   The Regulation allows for Member States to provide for additional powers for its supervisory authority (Art 58(6)). Accordingly, the ICO may be given additional powers to enforce the Regulation.

CODES & CERTIFICATION

16.21   The new Regulation leaves it open to industry bodies that represent various categories of controllers to draw up appropriate codes of conduct for approval by the ICO, which is obliged to confirm whether or not the relevant code complies with the Regulation (Art 40(2)). The Regulation provides for codes of conduct to be adopted by professional or trade bodies to facilitate compliance within their sector:

> 'Associations or other bodies representing categories of controllers or processors should be encouraged to draw up codes of conduct within the limits of this Regulation, so as to facilitate the effective application of this Regulation, taking account of the specific characteristics of the processing carried out in certain sectors and the specific needs of micro, small and medium enterprises. In particular, such codes of conduct could calibrate the obligations of controllers and processors, taking into account the risk likely to result from the processing for the rights and freedoms of natural persons.'[5]

16.22   Accordingly, the Regulation envisages codes of conduct to apply to specific sectors involved in data processing. These would provide for:

---

[4]   Article 58(3)(a)–(j).
[5]   Recital 98.

- 'fair and transparent' data processing;
- legitimate interests of controllers;
- exercise of the rights of data subjects;
- collection of data;
- pseudonymisation of personal data;
- information for data subjects;
- requests by data subjects for their persona data;
- information for, and protection of, children, and obtaining consent of parents and guardians;
- transfer of personal data to third countries or international organisations;
- dispute resolution procedures for resolving disputes between controllers and data subjects, without prejudice to their rights to compensation and other effective judicial remedies;
- appropriate safeguards to protect the data and its security; and
- notification of personal data breaches to supervisory authorities such as the ICO and to affected data subjects.[6]

16.23 Any such code must contain a mechanism to enable the appropriate body (not the supervisory authority) to monitor compliance with provisions of the code (Art 40(4)). This is without prejudice to the role of the supervisory authority, the ICO. The essential role of the ICO is to consider applications for the approval of codes of conduct submitted to it:

> 'Associations and other bodies ... which intend to prepare a code of conduct, or to amend or extend an existing code, shall submit the draft code, amendment or extension to the supervisory authority ... The supervisory authority shall give an opinion on whether the draft code, amendment or extension code is in compliance with this Regulation and shall approve that draft, amendment or extension if it finds that it provides sufficient appropriate safeguards.'[7]

16.24 If the draft code of conduct relates to processing operations in more than one Member State, ie not just in the UK, the ICO must submit the draft code to a body called the European Data Protection Board. The Board will give an opinion as to whether the draft code complies with the new Regulation, or, in the case of controllers and processors outside the EU, whether it provides the appropriate safeguards for the transfer of personal data to non-EU countries and organisations (Art 40(8)).

16.25 In addition to a data controller or processor that is subject to the new Regulation, a controller or processor outside the EU may also adhere to a code of conduct approved by a supervisory authority such as the ICO. This may be to provide appropriate safeguards for the transfer of personal data to countries or organisations outside the EU. Adherence to an approved code of conduct

---

[6]   Article 40(2)(a)–(k).
[7]   Article 40(5).

will require 'binding and enforceable commitments, via contractual or other legally binding instruments, to apply those appropriate safeguards including with regard to the rights of data subjects' (Art 40(3)).

16.26 If the European Data Protection Board decides that the draft code of conduct complies with the Regulation or provides the appropriate safeguards for the transfer of personal data outside the EU, as the case may be, it must so inform the European Commission (Art 40(8)). The Commission may decide that an approved code of conduct has general validity within the EU (Art 40(9)).

16.27 As stated above, a body other than the supervisory authority will be responsible to monitor compliance with the relevant code of conduct. This body must have the appropriate level of expertise in relation to the subject-matter of the code and be accredited for this purpose by the supervisory authority (Art 41(1)). It must take 'appropriate action' in cases of infringement of the relevant code, including the exclusion or suspension of the controller or processor from the code (Art 41(4)). Processing carried out by public authorities will not be subject to supervision by the monitoring body (Art 41(6)).

16.28 The new Regulation also envisages 'data protection certification mechanisms' and other means to facilitate compliance:

> 'In order to enhance transparency and compliance with this Regulation, the establishment of certification mechanisms and data protection seals and marks should be encouraged, allowing data subjects to quickly assess the level of data protection of relevant products and services.'[8]

16.29 Accordingly, these mechanisms will allow data subjects to assess the level of data protection provided by controllers and processors (Art 40). They will allow a controller or processor to request the ICO to certify that they comply with their obligations under the Regulation:

> 'The Member States, the supervisory authorities, the [European Data Protection] Board and the Commission shall encourage, in particular at Union level, the establishment of data protection certification mechanisms and of data protection seals and marks for the purpose of demonstrating compliance with this Regulation of processing operations by controllers and processors. The specific needs of micro, small and medium-sized enterprises shall be taken into account.'[9]

16.30 The certification itself must be 'voluntary and available via a process that is transparent' (Art 42(3)). The relevant mechanisms will vary according to the different forms of processing carried on by organisations in different

---

[8]   Recital 100.
[9]   Article 42(1).

industries and professions. They will set out the formal procedure for a data protection 'seal' or 'mark', including the credentials of the organisation that issues it.

16.31 In addition to a controller or processor that is subject to the new Regulation, a controller or processor outside the EU may also adhere to a certification mechanism approved by a certification body, a supervisory authority such as the ICO, or the European Data Protection Board. This may be to provide appropriate safeguards for the transfer of personal data to countries or organisations outside the EU. A certification issued on the basis of criteria approved by the Board may result in a common certification, the European Data Protection Seal (Art 42(5)). Adherence to an approved certification mechanism will require 'binding and enforceable commitments ... to apply those appropriate safeguards including with regard to the rights of data subjects' (Art 42(2)). Certification will last for a period of 3 years and may be renewed provided the relevant requirements continue to be complied with (Art 42(7)). However, it may be withdrawn if these requirements are no longer complied with.

16.32

'The controller or processor that submits its processing to the certification mechanism shall provide the certification body..., or the competent supervisory authority, must provide all information and access to its processing activities which are necessary to conduct the certification procedure' (Art 42(6)).

16.33 The certification body must have 'an appropriate level of expertise in relation to data protection' (Art 43(1)). It must be accredited to carry out its activities by the relevant supervisory authority or in certain circumstances by the European Data Protection Board (Art 43(3)). These circumstances are where the consistency mechanism applies as provided for by the new Regulation. Accreditation will last for a period of five years and may be renewed provided the body continues to meet the accreditation requirements (Art 43(4)).

16.34 The adoption of a Europe-wide seal or mark featured throughout the negotiations for the new Regulation which provides for seals and marks to be adopted by the Commission in accordance with Art 43(9). At present the ICO is working on a seal for use by organisations in the UK, similar to the British Standard Institute's Kitemark symbol. The symbol is displayed on many products and services to demonstrate quality and provide assurances that the highest standards are being delivered. An ICO privacy seal would operate in a similar manner by being awarded to organisations that demonstrate that they are complying with, and indeed surpassing, the legal requirements. The ICO plans to operate the scheme as follows:

'We will endorse third party operators to deliver ICO privacy seal schemes. Once approved, the scheme operators will be responsible for the day-to-day running of the scheme. It is anticipated that the different scheme operators will focus on different sectors, processes, products or areas of compliance. For example, one operator may focus their privacy seal scheme on the collection of personal information by mobile apps, while another operator may run a scheme for organisations providing data protection training services for health service providers. This approach allows our office to draw upon specialist skills from parties already recognised in the field of accreditation and certification. It also gives organisations the opportunity to apply for an ICO privacy seal from an operator whose scheme is specifically tailored to their products or sector. The seal can be used by the organisation for a certain period, likely to be four years, after which time, revalidation is required. The seal can also be removed if the organisation who has been awarded the seal fails to maintain these standards – for example if they suffer a serious data breach.'

REMEDIES & LIABILITIES

16.35 In addition to any criminal sanctions that may be imposed on a controller under the DPA or the new Regulation, whether on foot of a complaint by a data subject or otherwise, the controller may be subject to legal action by him/her in the event of any loss or damage caused by negligence. This will arise from the controller's duty of care to the data subject. A duty of care is implied in all cases where personal data is processed. In the event of a breach of duty of care leading to financial loss (or non-financial loss in certain circumstances), the data subject has the right to claim compensation as discussed at **14.61** above.

16.36 The use of online communications such as the internet and social networking websites may cause loss or damage to individuals referred to in these communications. This could arise from abusive or defamatory material posted on these websites. The owners and operators of these websites may be liable in addition to those responsible for posting the offending material.

16.37 The new Regulation provides that data subject may seek the remedy of judicial review of a decision by the ICO, as discussed at **14.66** above. He/she has the right to an 'effective judicial remedy' against a decision that affects him/her (Art 78(1)). This is without prejudice to any other administrative or judicial remedy that may be available. The remedy may take the form of a court order to oblige the ICO to act on a complaint in the absence of a decision or where the authority does not inform him/her of the progress/outcome within three months or any shorter period prescribed by law (Art 78(2)). Accordingly, the ICO may be ordered to investigate a complaint.

FINES & PENALTIES

16.38 The new Regulation provides for administrative fines and penalties to be imposed in the event of breach. These may be in addition to, or instead of, any other measures taken by the ICO.

'In order to strengthen the enforcement of the rules of this Regulation, penalties and administrative fines should be imposed for any infringement of the Regulation, in addition to, or instead of, appropriate measures imposed by the supervisory authority pursuant to this Regulation. In the case of a minor infringement or if the fine likely to be imposed would constitute a disproportionate burden to a natural person, a reprimand may be issued instead of a fine. Due regard should however be given to the nature, gravity and duration of the infringement, the intentional character of the infringement, actions taken to mitigate the damage suffered, degree of responsibility of any relevant previous infringement, the manner in which the infringement became known to the supervisory authority, compliance with measures ordered against the controller or processor, adherence to a code of conduct and any other aggravating or mitigating factor. The imposition of penalties including administrative fines should be subject to appropriate procedural safeguards in accordance with the general principles of Union law and the Charter [of Fundamental Rights] including effective judicial protection and due process.'[10]

Case study

The monetary and other penalties for breach of data protection laws are considerable. In January 2014 the internet search engine, Google, was found guilty of three serious violations of Spanish data protection law, and was fined €900,000. The violations resulted from Google's collection of personal data across nearly 100 services and products in Spain, without giving details about what data it collects and what it uses the data for, and without obtaining a valid consent from data subjects. Google was fined €300,000 for each of the three violations and ordered to take the 'necessary measures without any delay to comply with the legal requirements'. Google is also under investigation in other countries in Europe as a result of its decision in 2014 to harmonise privacy policies across many of its services.

16.39 The ICO as the supervisory authority in the UK must ensure that an administrative fine arising from a breach of the Regulation is applied in a way that is 'effective, proportionate and dissuasive' (Art 83(1)). Each Member State can decide whether and to what extent administrative fines may be imposed on public authorities and bodies (Art 83(7)). A fine may be in addition to, or instead of, any measure adopted by the ICO on foot of its *corrective powers* under Art 58(2)(a)–(h).

16.40 Accordingly, the ICO will have the power to apply administrative fines in accordance with the new Regulation. A fine may be imposed up to €10 million (£7.4 million approx.) or, in the case of a company/group, 2% of the company/group's total worldwide annual turnover in the preceding financial year, whichever is higher,if the company/group, whether acting as controller or processor, fails to comply with the following provisions:

---

[10]   Recital 148.

- notification of data subject by controller that it cannot identify him/her (Art 11(2));
- data protection by design and by default (Art 25);
- responsibilities of joint controllers (Art 26);
- appointment of processor by controller (Art 28);
- processor acting only on controller's instructions (Art 29);
- records of processing activities (Art 30);
- co-operation with ICO (Art 31);
- security of processing (Art 32);
- notification of personal data breach (Art 33);
- communication of personal data breach to data subject (Art 34);
- data protection impact assessment (Art 35);
- prior consultation with the ICO (Art 36);
- designation of data protection officer (Art 37);
- position of data protection officer (Art 38);
- tasks of data protection officer (Art 39); and
- certification mechanisms and data protection seals and marks (Arts 42 and 43).

(Art 83(4))

16.41   A fine may be imposed up to €20 million (£14.8 million approx.) or, in the case of a company/group, up to 4% of the company/group's total worldwide annual turnover in the preceding financial year, whichever is higher. The fine may be imposed if the company/group, whether acting as controller or processor, fails to comply with any of the following requirements:

- principles of processing, including conditions for consent (Arts 5, 6, 7 and 9);
- rights of data subjects (Arts 12-22);
- transfers of personal data outside the EU (Arts 44-49)
- specific processing situations (Chapter IX); and
- orders by the ICO for limitation or suspension of processing (Arts 58(1) and 58(2)).

(Art 83(5))

16.42   The new Regulation is specific that a breach may be committed either 'intentionally or negligently'. Accordingly, a breach may occur even if the data controller/processor did not intend to do anything wrong. It will be sufficient for the controller/processor to have done something through inadvertence or failure to take care. The ICO will take account of certain factors to determine the amount of any fine:

- nature of the breach, including gravity, duration and number of data subjects affected and the level of damage suffered;
- whether the breach was intentional or negligent;
- how the breach came to the attention of the ICO, in particular whether the controller/ processor, as the case may be, reported it;
- degree of responsibility of the controller/processor having regard to the 'technical and organisational measures' adopted by them;
- any relevant previous breach by the controller/processor;
- degree of co-operation with the ICO to remedy the breach and mitigate the possible adverse effects;
- the categories affected by the breach;
- if applicable, whether the controller/processor has complied with any warning, order for rectification, restriction or erasure of data or data processing, or any order for limitation of processing or for suspension of data transfer outside the EU, made by the ICO arising from the matter;
- adherence to approved codes of conduct or approved certification mechanisms;
- action(s) taken by the controller/processor to mitigate the damage; and
- any other aggravating or mitigating factors in the case, including financial benefits gained or losses avoided, directly or indirectly.[11]

16.43 The Regulation caps the amount of any fine at the fine imposed for the most serious breach in the event of multiple breaches of the Regulation (Art 83(3)).

16.44 In addition to these administrative fines, the new Regulation provides for penalties for more serious breaches. Member States will determine the penalties to be imposed in these cases (Art 84(1)). Presumably these heavier penalties may include fines of greater amounts or even the ultimate sanction – imprisonment – in an appropriate case. They must likewise be 'effective, proportionate and dissuasive'.

Case study

The case for imprisonment as the ultimate sanction was made by the ICO in a prosecution against a bank official who gained illegal access to a customer's account. In September 2011 the official pleaded guilty to using her position at the bank to access the account of the victim of a sex attack. The official's husband had been convicted of carrying out the attack and was sent to jail. She looked up the victim's account to find information about her. In his report on the case the ICO stated: →

---

[11] Article 83(2)(a)–(k).

'It beggars belief that – in an age where our personal information is being stored and accessed by more organisations than ever – the penalties for seriously abusing the system do not include the possibility of a prison sentence, even in the most serious cases. Access to online records is now part and parcel of almost every transaction the citizen makes ... This only makes the risk to privacy greater and the need for security greater still.'

16.45 In an ideal world companies and organisations that handle personal data would not need regulatory sanctions to comply with the law. They would behave as good corporate citizens and comply with their data protection obligations because it is the right thing to do:

'Data is the pollution problem of the information age and protecting privacy is the environment challenge. Almost all computers produce personal information. It stays around, festering. How we deal with it – how we contain it and how we dispose of it – is central to the health of our information economy. Just as we look back today at the early decades of the industrial age and wonder how our ancestors could have ignored pollution in their rush to build an industrial world, our grandchildren will look back at us during these early decades of the information age and judge us on how we addressed the challenge of data collection and misuse.'[12]

---

[12] Bruce Scneier, *Data and Goliath – The Hidden Battles to Collect Your Data and Control Your World*, WW Norton, 2015.

APPENDIX 1

SAMPLE DATA PROTECTION POLICY

1. SCOPE

This Policy applies to XYZ Limited ('XYZ', 'the Company', 'we', 'our', 'us'). XYZ is a financial services provider, with offices in London and Manchester. It operates in the global financial services sector in the UK and Europe, with a focus on retail and commercial banking. The Policy describes (i) the requirements of relevant law and practice to protect personal data in the Company's possession relating to our customers, suppliers, employees and other parties, and (ii) the Company's commitment to ensure compliance with these requirements.

Data is information in a form that can be processed. It may be held in manual or computer records. Personal data is data relating to a living individual who is identified or identifiable from the data either by itself or together with other information.

2. PURPOSE AND OVERVIEW

XYZ is obliged to comply with laws and regulations to protect personal data relating to our customers, employees and other parties. This Policy determines our procedures to ensure compliance in the way we obtain, process, secure and disclose this data in all our operations and systems. These procedures include handling actual or suspected disclosure of personal data to unauthorised third parties, and for responding to Subject Access Requests (SARs) from individuals.

Data protection is a fundamental right of every individual, or data subject. He/she is entitled to expect that any personal data relating to him/her is protected by anyone who holds it. This Policy sets out the Company's commitment to ensure that we do so.

3. RISK DEFINITION

Failure to implement this Policy will lead to non-compliance with the Company's legal and regulatory obligations, exposing the Company to the following risks:

- Regulatory sanction by the Financial Conduct Authority (FCA) or the Information Commissioner's Office (ICO);
- Criminal prosecution by the police, FCA or the ICO;
- Civil action by data subjects;
- Financial loss, including loss of earnings and loss of capital; and
- Reputational damage to the Company and other members of our group of companies.

4. ROLES AND RESPONSIBILITIES

CEO – Policy Owner: responsible to ensure that the Policy is fully implemented by the Company in all its operations.

Head of Compliance – Policy Issuer: responsible for content of the Policy, to communicate the Policy to all Company operations and to update the Policy as required.

5. RISK STRATEGY

Principles

1. Obtainment and retention of personal data only for defined purpose(s) and period of time;
2. Clear identification of personal data in operations and systems, distinct from other records;
3. Agreed approach to disclosure of personal data to customers and third parties, and notification of breach in the event of unauthorised disclosure;
4. Zero tolerance of non-compliance, which may have disciplinary consequences; and
5. Escalation of incidents of non-compliance if required.

Monitoring & Testing

1. Agreed methodology to test compliance with requirements;
2. Ongoing monitoring of SARs in accordance with agreed methodology; and
3. Sample review of records on periodic basis to test compliance.

6. POLICY STATEMENT

XYZ Limited obtains and processes personal data relating to customers and employees, including name, address, age, occupation, bank details and other information provided by the customer/employee.

The Company has a legal and ethical responsibility to safeguard the privacy of our customers, employees and other parties, by protecting all personal data in our possession. We are bound by the Data Protection Act 1998, and other relevant laws and regulations. We are also bound by codes of conduct implemented by the ICO and by industry codes of practice.

In particular, we are committed to complying with the principles of data protection as set out below.

'1. Personal data shall be obtained only for one or more specified and lawful purposes, and shall not be further processed in any manner incompatible with that purpose or those purposes.
2. Personal data shall be accurate and, where necessary, kept up to date.
3. Personal data processed for any purpose or purposes shall not be kept for longer than is necessary for that purpose or those purposes.
4. Personal data shall be processed in accordance with the rights of data subjects under the Data Protection Act 1998.
5. Appropriate technical and organisational measures shall be taken against unauthorised or unlawful processing of personal data and against accidental loss or destruction of, or damage to, personal data.
6. Personal data shall not be transferred to a country or territory outside the European Economic Area unless that country or territory ensures an adequate level of protection for the rights and freedoms of data subjects in relation to the processing of personal data.'

The Company provides suitable training for all employees and relevant contractors who have access to our records and systems. This ensures that all are aware of the legal and ethical requirements and our responsibility to comply with them.

Sensitive Personal Data

The Company obtains explicit written consent from a data subject in order to process any sensitive personal data relating to him/her. This is personal data relating to his/her racial origin, political opinions or religious or other beliefs, physical or mental health, sexual life, criminal convictions or the alleged commission of an offence, or trade union membership.

Transfer of Data outside the EEA

The Company may transfer personal data outside the European Economic Area (EEA) for legitimate business reasons. (The EEA consists of the Member States of the European Union, and Norway, Iceland and Liechtenstein.) In that event we will put adequate safeguards in place to ensure that the recipient of the data complies with UK data protection requirements. If required by law, we will do so in an appropriate contract to commit the data recipient to comply with these requirements.

Third Parties

The Company may use third parties to process personal data on our behalf for business reasons. In that event we will ensure there is an appropriate contract in place to commit the third party to process the data strictly in accordance with our instructions and in accordance with appropriate standards to ensure that the third party complies with its obligations to protect the data in the same way.

The Company may disclose personal data to professional advisors, credit reference agencies and any other parties for business or legal reasons, including a purchaser or prospective purchaser of all or part of its business, under conditions of strict confidentiality.

7. NON-COMPLIANCE AND ESCALATION

XYZ business functions are responsible to identify any matter of non-compliance or potential non-compliance under this Policy through annual self-assessments. Any such matter must be notified to the Policy Issuer immediately upon discovery. Business functions are also responsible to identify any matter of non-compliance or potential non-compliance, as the case may be, that arises in the course of their business and to notify the Policy Issuer immediately.

Following confirmation by the Policy Issuer of the non-compliance, the relevant XYZ business function will prepare an action plan to remedy the matter within a time agreed with the Policy Issuer. The action plan will identify the person(s) responsible for its implementation.

The Policy Issuer will report a summary of all such confirmed matters of non-compliance to the Policy Owner including progress made to resolve them in accordance with the relevant action plan.

8. REVIEW

The Policy is subject to review at least every two years, or more often if required by legal or regulatory developments or business requirements.

Compliance is responsible to ensure that the Policy is consistent with applicable laws and regulations, and for the design and effectiveness of our operational controls. Compliance audits the extent to which the business complies with the Policy on a periodic basis in accordance with the testing plan.

9. EXCLUSIONS AND SPECIAL SITUATIONS

There are no exclusions or special situations where the Policy does not apply.

10. RELATED PROCESSES AND PROCEDURES

The following documents contain related policies, and processes and procedures to implement this Policy:

1. Information Security Policy;
2. Data Protection Procedures; and
3. SAR Procedures.

The Policy may be implemented by other processes and procedures to be documented and read in conjunction with it.

APPENDIX 2

SAMPLE INFORMATION SECURITY POLICY

1. INTRODUCTION

XYZ Limited ('XYZ', 'the Company', 'we', 'our', 'us') is a financial services provider, with offices in London and Manchester. It operates in the global financial services sector in the UK and Europe, with a focus on retail and commercial banking.

Effective security is a team effort involving the participation and support of every employee of the Company who deals with information and/or information systems. It is the responsibility of every user to read and know this Policy, and conduct their activities accordingly.

2. MISSION STATEMENT

The Board and Management of XYZ are committed to preserving the confidentiality, integrity and availability of all the information assets throughout the organisation in order to preserve its competitive edge, cash-flow, profitability, legal, regulatory and contractual compliance, as well as commercial reputation. Information and information security requirements are aligned with organisational goals and this Information Security Policy ('the Policy') is intended to be an enabling mechanism for information sharing, for electronic operations, and for reducing information-related risks to acceptable levels.

The Company's strategic business plan and risk management framework process provide the context for assessing and controlling information-related risks through the establishment and maintenance of appropriate policies, procedures and processes.

The Company is committed to achieving future certification to the SOC-1 (Service Organisation Controls – Level 1) globally-recognised standard.

The Policy is subject to continuous, systematic review and improvement.

3. SCOPE

3.1 Applicability

This Policy applies to XYZ Limited and its employees, as well as any other person or entity, who use, support or supply the business systems, infrastructure or information of the Company. The definition of employee includes employees, contractors and consultants. All employees are expected to comply with the Policy and with the risk management framework process that aids in the implementation of the Policy.

For the purpose of this Policy, information security ('IS') is defined as:

'preserving

This means that management, full-time or part-time staff, contractors, project consultants and any external parties have been (or will be) made aware of their responsibilities defined in their job descriptions or contracts to preserve information security, to report security breaches and to act in accordance with the requirements of this Policy. The consequences of policy violations are described in the Company's disciplinary policy. All staff will receive information security training and specialised staff will receive specialised information security training.

the availability,

This means that information assets should be accessible to authorised users when required and therefore physically secure. The computer network must be resilient and XYZ must be able to both detect and respond rapidly to incidents (such as viruses/malware, inappropriate access, breaches, data leakage, etc) that threaten the continued availability of assets, systems and information. There must be appropriate disaster recovery ('DR') and business continuity plans ('BCP') in place and they must be tested (at least) annually.

confidentiality,

This involves ensuring that information is only accessible to those authorised to access it and, therefore, preventing both deliberate and accidental unauthorised access to that information and systems, including data storage area(s), transactional system(s), network(s), website(s), Intranet(s), Extranet(s), and eCommerce systems.

and integrity

This involves safeguarding the accuracy and completeness of information and processing methods and, therefore, requires preventing deliberate and/or accidental, partial and/or complete, destruction, or unauthorised modification, of either physical assets or electronic data. There must be appropriate contingency, including for data storage area(s), transactional system(s), network(s), website(s), Intranet(s), Extranet(s), eCommerce systems and data back-up plans, and security incident reporting. XYZ must comply with all relevant data-related legislation in those jurisdictions where it operates.

of the physical assets

The physical assets of XYZ, including computer hardware, data cabling, telephone systems, filing systems and physical data files.

and information assets

The information assets include information printed or written on paper, transmitted by post or shown in films, or spoken in conversation, as well as information stored electronically on storage areas, servers, website(s), Extranet(s), Intranet(s), individual desktops/laptops, mobile devices, as well as on CDs/DVDs, back-up media and any other digital or magnetic media, and information transmitted electronically by any means.

of the organisation.'

This includes XYZ and any partners that are part of our integrated network and have signed up to this Policy.

This Policy document describes the Company's IS control requirements and establishes the minimum standards to be complied with by all employees and regulated entities (where applicable).

3.2 Effective Date

The Effective Date of this Policy is [DATE].

3.3 Review Schedule

This Policy is a living document and, therefore, must be reviewed annually to ensure its continuing suitability, adequacy and effectiveness. The Company's IS function has primary responsibility for the review process.

4. ORGANISATION OF INFORMATION SECURITY

4.1 Information Security Program

This Policy implements the Company's Information Security Program.

4.2 Internal Organisation (within XYZ)

4.2.1 *Information Security Coordination*

IS strategic activities will be coordinated through the XYZ Information Security Group (ISG) that consists of the following roles:

- XYZ Information Security Officer (ISO) – primary IS resource;
- XYZ Compliance Officer (CO); and
- XYZ Chief Financial Officer (CFO).

The ISG assists the Company's ISO with the strategic development and implementation of the Information Security Program.

4.2.2 *Allocation of Information Security Responsibilities*

Information security is the responsibility of every XYZ staff member up to and including Executive Committee (EXCO) level. The ISO holds primary responsibility for implementing and maintaining the Company's Information Security Program.

The ISG is responsible for regular (quarterly) reporting of XYZ's security status to EXCO.

4.2.3 *Risk Register*

The Compliance team, in coordination with all XYZ teams, maintains and manages the Risk Register. It is the responsibility of all XYZ teams to regularly review and/or update their particular risk areas, so as to ensure that they remain valid and current.

4.3 External Organisation

Risks emerging from relationships with third parties must be identified and appropriate controls implemented prior to granting access to the Company's systems or data. As such, all third parties must be issued with a due diligence IS questionnaire and satisfactory responses received.

In addition, XYZ reserves the right to audit all third parties that conduct business with and/or have access to data within the organisation.

5. ASSET MANAGEMENT

5.1 Responsibility for Assets

5.1.1 Inventory of Assets

The CFO is responsible for implementing, managing and reviewing (at least annually) the Company's asset inventory.

The asset inventory must identify:

1. Asset name and description;
2. Whether it is physical or logical in nature;
3. Asset owner;
4. Information or data owner;
5. Asset location;
6. Whether the system is managed, or accessed, by a third party;
7. Whether the system is public-facing, eg Internet;
8. Date of last security assessment for in-scope applications;
9. Business criticality, eg SOC-1; and
10. Data classification to the highest level of information processed.

5.1.2 Acceptable Use of Information Assets

XYZ system users are accountable for all activity associated with their user IDs. Users are also responsible for compliance with the requirements of the Acceptable Use of Company Information Sources policy.

Reference: Acceptable Use of Company Information Sources Policy.

5.2 Classification Categories

XYZ must be protected in accordance with the following data classification categories. These categories are defined as follows:

Data Classification

Each member of staff is responsible for classifying and protecting data according to the XYZ Information Security Classification Guidelines Procedure, as well as this Policy, using the following four data classification categories:

Public

Public information is non-sensitive information available for public disclosure, eg website, publicity material. There is little or no risk to XYZ (or its customers) from the disclosure of this type of information.

Internal

XYZ Internal information is information belonging to XYZ and not for disclosure to the general public or external parties, eg internal policies and procedures. The information is generally available to employees and authorised third parties and/or partners. Its release to the general public would cause limited harm to XYZ and/or its customers. Risk to XYZ (and/or its clients) would be considered Medium should this type information be compromised/disclosed/leaked.

Confidential

XYZ Confidential information is information that is sensitive, or confidential, within the organisation and intended for business use only by those with a need-to-know, eg XYZ business plans. Unauthorised disclosure of such information could cause significant harm (eg legal or financial liability; harm to XYZ or its customers' reputation). Risk to XYZ and/or its clients would be considered High should this type of information be compromised/disclosed.

Restricted

XYZ Restricted information is information that is restricted to specified levels of Management within XYZ or to EXCO, eg disciplinary proceeding. Risk to XYZ and/or its clients would be considered Extremely High should this type of information be compromised/disclosed.

6. HUMAN RESOURCE (HR) SECURITY

6.1 Prior to Employment

All staff must accept and acknowledge their information security responsibilities as part of the HR on-boarding process.

6.2 Information Security Awareness, Education and Training

XYZ will have and maintain an Information Security Awareness Program. XYZ employees, who have access to the Company's information/data and/or customer information/data, must receive annual IS training and certify that they understand their IS responsibilities.

Any third party contractors who have access to the Company's information/data and/or customer information/data, should receive regular IS training (conducted by their employer) and certify that they understand there is responsibilities in line with security best-practice. Should this not be the case, at a minimum, all third party contractors are obliged to read this Policy and formally sign-up to its requirements.

6.3 Termination or Change of Employment

6.3.1 Termination and Removal of Access Rights

XYZ managers must submit an off-boarding request before the next business day in the event of an employee termination.

Physical building access, interactive network login account(s) and any remote access rights assigned to the employee in question must be disabled within 24 hours of the off-boarding request being submitted. The employee's account access-/privilege-rights to XYZ systems/applications/data, eg Covered Data, must be completely disabled and/or removed within 30 days of employment termination.

6.3.2 Change of Employment

XYZ managers are responsible for submitting a transfer request when an employee's role significantly changes within the organisation, such as a new business segment, manager and location. When a manager initiates the transfer process, they should explicitly note if current access rights should be retained or revoked.

6.3.3 Return of Company-Owned Assets

XYZ managers are responsible for ensuring that employees return all XYZ assets in their possession at the termination of their employment (or contract), in accordance with the Acceptable Use of Company Information Sources Policy, as well as applicable laws and regulations.

7. PHYSICAL SECURITY

7.1 Working in Secure Areas

XYZ data centres and/or third party hosting facilities must have physical security controls in place that prevent unauthorised individuals from gaining physical access to them, as well as alert to actual and/or potential unauthorised access. These controls include:

- Access to data centre and/or Comms rooms must be via appropriately secured and monitored ingress/egress points.

- Access to data centre facilities must be prior approved and both logged and recorded at all times.

- Access logs to data centre facilities must be reviewed on a semi-annual basis, so as to ensure that only appropriate access is granted.

- Equipment in third party facilities that are shared with other customers must be physically segregated from XYZ equipment, by use of either locked cages or racks.

- ID badges must be issued to individuals before access is granted to such facilities.

7.2 Secure Disposal or Re-use of Equipment

XYZ Covered Data and licensed software must be securely removed/wiped from both computer equipment and removable media prior to disposal or re-use. Secure methods of disposal such as wiping, degaussing or physical destruction are acceptable.

No disposal or destruction shall take place without confirming that the data has reached the end of its legislated retention period and that there is no additional retention period required (such as a litigation hold or preservation notice).

Other technologies, including photocopiers, fax machines and printers, may contain a hard drive or flash memory device that stores XYZ (and/or our customers') data in various forms, such as digital images of documents sent to the device. In the case of leased printer devices, XYZ must ensure that the leasing company (on retrieval of device) performs a secure data-wipe on the flash memory portion of the device.

All secure removal/wiping of XYZ (and/or our customers') data prior to device disposal or re-use must be formally confirmed by the ISO.

8. INFORMATION SECURITY POLICIES

When referring to IS systems they can be broadly broken down to a number of sub-elements, those being the following:

- Infrastructure;
- System and User Software; and
- Data.

The following are the generic policies that apply regardless of the particular element. These should be applied as required to any individual element.

8.1 Granting Access Policy

The following overall policy applies to all logical access to information systems in XYZ. This particular policy is necessary so as to ensure that access to information is granted correctly to properly authorised individuals and for legitimate/valid business purposes. All queries relating to access to information systems should be referred to the ISO.

8.1.1 High Level Policy Details

- Users cannot authorise access for themselves (ie in line with security principle of segregation of duties), all access must be authorised by their Manager, or someone delegated in their stead.

- Requests for access may be sent from the Manager by email, FAX, or paper to the ICT Department.

- All access is granted on a needs basis (in line with security principle of least privilege). This is essential when granting access to personal data in order to comply with the terms of the Data Protection Act 1998.

- All users are set up with a unique username and a password that is valid only for first login. They are prompted to change it to one of their own choosing immediately after they have successfully logged in.

- All users must ensure that they do not allow anyone else access XYZ systems in their name ie under their privileges).

- All accounts will be disabled automatically if unused/inactive for 21 days or more.

- Managers are responsible for informing the ICT Department when a staff member leaves their area, or the organisation.

- Additional rules may apply to requests for privileged (data) access and remote access.

- Physical access to information and information systems will be controlled to prevent theft or negligent, malicious or fraudulent use.

- Appropriate security controls will be applied during application development and hardware/software installation to achieve the necessary level of system protection in line with organisational/regulatory/legislative requirements.

- Business continuity plans (BCPs) are developed and then maintained and tested on an annual basis. This activity is co-ordinated by the Business Continuity Co-ordinator.

8.2 Data Access Control Policy

The data stored within XYZ systems is a key asset to the organisation. Therefore, its confidentiality, integrity and availability is of primary importance. As a rule, all data held by the Company will be considered (at a minimum) Internal. This policy sets out the ICT provisions for access to data within XYZ.

8.2.1 High Level Policy Details

Access Control Management

- Access to all XYZ systems must be controlled by appropriate mechanisms. System or application owners must define the range of available access rights within their respective system and the conditions under which these can be assigned and revoked.

- The method of controlling access to all XYZ systems and applications, together with the levels of authorisations available, must be formally recorded with the documentation kept up-to-date and access rights/ sanctions reviewed both periodically and in line with changes to business requirements.

- Only vetted, approved and designated ICT Department staff may access production program libraries. Amendments must only be made using a combination of technical access controls and robust procedures operated under a dual-control approach.

- Access to Operating System (OS) commands within XYZ infrastructure must be restricted to those persons who are qualified and authorised to perform systems administration/management functions.

- Data stored within XYZ infrastructure must be protected against unauthorised or accidental changes, and may only be deleted with the proper authority.

- For authorised XYZ personnel, appropriate data and information regarding who has access eg ACLs and sanction lists, must be made available as and when required.

- Approved XYZ system login procedures must be strictly observed and users leaving their screen unattended must ensure to lock access to their workstation or log off.

- Vendors will be allowed remote access to the system only when needed and as per strict SLA conditions (including NDA) in line with remote access policy.

- All XYZ personnel are required to protect Covered Data in both digital and physical format that is used or stored at their workspace. This information must not be left in open view after general business hours and must be kept in locked cabinets, where available.

Access Privilege Assignment

- The true identity, username and access privileges to be granted to a user, or vendor, must be verified and documented before the privilege is assigned. This can be performed by the Manager authorising the access request.

- Accounts can only be given to named individuals (or vendor). No generic accounts can be used that cannot be associated with a named individual (for accountability purposes).
- Upon completion of an access request, the user or vendor and their Manager (or XYZ staff member responsible for that vendor) must be contacted and the rights assigned to the user or vendor explicitly stated to ensure that the correct (and appropriate) rights have been assigned.

Authentication

- All systems and applications must identify and verify individual users. All applications must have a form of authentication, either integrated with the OS or dedicated to the application being accessed.
- Where possible, all systems and applications should not store, display or transmit authentication information using clear-text, where access is within the XYZ network. When accessing systems external to the XYZ network, this requirement is mandatory.
- Accounts will be disabled or suspended after 5 unsuccessful logon attempts, where the system has this capability, unless there is a documented business reason for overriding this security measure.
- In the event of usage-inactivity, accounts must be either logged out automatically or locked to prevent system abuse. Where systems are capable of locking sessions upon a period of inactivity, this should be set to lock after a maximum of 10 minutes of inactivity.

User Responsibilities

XYZ Managers are responsible for ensuring that their staff have the correct access rights assigned and that requests to revoke access in the event of a staff member leaving are made in an appropriate, and timely, manner.

All users must comply with the requirements of the password management guidelines.

8.3 Network Access Control Policy

8.3.1 High Level Policy Details

- Only approved Wireless Local Area Networks (WLANs) may be connected to the XYZ corporate local area network (LAN).
- All external networking connections must be made through XYZ managed network infrastructure and must include network security monitoring.
- Computing and network resources provided by XYZ are intended for use only by authorised XYZ employees, contractors and third parties.

- Personal computer hardware cannot be connected to the XYZ corporate network unless in certain exceptional circumstances. If so, the business case for doing so must be prior reviewed and formally approved by ICT Department, in conjunction with the ISO, and only for valid business requirements.

- XYZ corporate networks must provide segregation between internal and external networks.

8.4 Virus/Malware Protection Policy

Anti-malware software must be installed on all servers and workstations before connection is permitted to the XYZ corporate network. Under no circumstances should non-XYZ hardware/devices be allowed to connect to the Company's corporate network (unless under extreme circumstances, with the explicit review, risk assessment and permission of the ISO).

Any unsanctioned interference with the operation of anti-malware software is strictly prohibited.

8.4.1 High Level Policy Details

Malware protection should be implemented at every layer of the technical architecture (in line with the security principle of layering). An incoming/outgoing data stream should be scanned at each layer as it traverses the network. It is considered best practice to deploy different malware protection products at the differing infrastructure layers (in line with the security principle of defence-in-depth).

In line with the security principle prevention is better that cure, the ISO subscribes to automatic malware alert lists and multiple security watchdog distribution lists.

8.5 Third-Party Access to ICT Systems Policy

This policy sets out the responsibilities of third parties where access to XYZ networks or systems is granted to such parties. The definition of third parties covers individuals/organisations who are not employed on a regular basis by XYZ as permanent, temporary or contract staff. Access to XYZ networks or systems by third parties is conditional on formal acceptance (in writing) by such third parties of the conditions below.

8.5.1 High Level Policy Details

- Access is only granted where authorised by the owner (eg Manager) of the system, approved by XYZ ICT Department and is in accordance with the terms of our Data Protection Registration.

- Access is granted only to named individuals within an organisation, and such access is not transferable at any time.
- Any documentation provided by XYZ vis-a-vis the connection, eg IP addresses, hostnames, network architecture diagrams, etc., remain confidential.
- The specific purpose(s) for which remote access to any of XYZ systems or networks is granted is set out in this authorisation. Any deviation from the specific purposes(s) set out herein, without prior authorisation from the Company's ISO, shall be deemed unauthorised access.
- The access granted to the third party is for the stated purpose only as outlined by this authorisation.
- Under no circumstances should data on XYZ systems be copied or disclosed to any other party without the express written prior approval of XYZ.
- Authentication mechanisms remain the property of XYZ, which retains the right to demand return of same at any time. The third party agrees to return these immediately when requested to do so by XYZ.

8.6 Data Transfer Policy

With all data transfer mechanisms (but to a lesser extent with non-secure email), there is an element of initial set-up and configuration involved prior to transfer.

Therefore, at a high level, before attempting to send any data between parties, ensure to determine the type and sensitivity of the data being transferred (ie data classification – see Appendix A), potential risk of compromise and/or leakage and/or disclosure, repercussions thereof (strategic/reputational/financial/legal/regulatory/contractual/etc.) and current control measures in place (where applicable).

Subsequently, ensure to engage with the other party/parties with whom data is being transferred, so as to determine what the most optimal method of transfer is (ie ascertain what each end can support) and configure accordingly.

All data transfers should be recorded within the Data Transfer Risk Registry Matrix document (managed and maintained by Compliance).

8.6.1 High Level Policy Details

- Covered Data that is physically shipped on removable media (including tape, CD, DVD, USB) must be encrypted using corporate-approved encryption technologies, or secured using a secure and/or bonded courier service.
- Covered Data that is electronically transferred outside the XYZ network, ie using methods including, but not limited to, email, FTP, Secure SHell

(SSH), HTTP, etc., must be encrypted using corporate-approved encryption technologies, in accordance with local laws and regulations.

8.7 Monitoring Policy

Logging, log management and monitoring of those records form a core component of any information security approach. Continuous and active monitoring is critical to ensuring the CIA of ICT solutions, as well as the security of the data traversing and stored thereon.

8.7.1 High Level Policy Details

Audit Logging

- Security-relevant events must be logged and reviewed on a periodic basis (no less frequent than quarterly), commensurate with the risk and criticality level of the information resource and user role.
- Logs must be retained in compliance with local and business data retention requirements.
- All monitoring activities must be in compliance with local legal requirements.

Protection of Log Information

- The Company's ICT Department is responsible for the protection and integrity of audit logs and must ensure that log files cannot be deleted or modified. Audit logs must be kept in compliance with local and business data retention requirements.

8.8 Information Systems Acquisition, Development and Maintenance Policy

8.8.1 High Level Policy Details

Application Security Assessment

- Information security requirements must be included in the application Software Development Life Cycle (SDLC) process.
- Any new or planned Internet application must have an application security assessment performed prior to go-live.
- Internet-facing applications are subject to a risk assessment to determine the need for enhanced authentication and/or authorisation controls including multi-factor authentication.

Cryptographic Controls – Usage

- Use of encryption must follow applicable local laws and regulations.

Data Protection in Non-Production Environments

- XYZ Covered Data must be protected in both production and non-production environments, including maintaining an audit trail. Non-production environments using this data must either:
  - Scrub, scramble or sanitise sensitive data (or sensitive data fields), so as to reduce the classification level (see Appendix A), OR
  - Where the above is not possible, implement controls commensurate with the production environment.

Management of System and Network Vulnerabilities

- Security vulnerability assessments must be conducted on a regular periodic basis (recommended at least every 12 months) across the Company's ICT systems and networks to detect information security vulnerabilities.
- Highlighted vulnerabilities and/or system patches must be prioritised by the ISO for remediation commensurate with the risk to XYZ systems, networks and data.

8.9 Information Security Incident Management Policy

This particular policy provides a consistent process for identifying, reporting, investigating and closing information security incidents.

8.9.1 High Level Policy Details

Reporting Information Security Incidents

- Employees must immediately report information security incidents, subject to local law and any legal restrictions on such reporting.
- Security incidents include unauthorised access to, or loss of, Covered Data.
- Information security incidents are to be reported directly to the Company's ISO.
- Some illustrative examples of information security incidents include, but are not limited to, the following:
  - Lost or stolen laptops, hard drives or data storage devices containing XYZ data (or that of their customers);
  - Denial-of-Service (DoS) or Distributed Denial-of-Service (DDoS) attacks against XYZ infrastructure (in all its forms);
  - Improper handling or disposal of Covered Data;
  - Unauthorised changes to applications, configurations, code or data; and
  - Theft of corporate technology, intellectual property or business secrets.

- Spam email messages are not considered security incidents and can simply be deleted or forwarded to the ICT Department (as an attachment) for review.

Business Continuity and Disaster Recovery Management

Overall, when initiated and active, business continuity and disaster recovery environments must have the same information security controls as found in the XYZ production environment.

9. COMPLIANCE

9.1 Compliance with Policy

All XYZ staff are responsible for ensuring compliance with this Policy.

In addition, in line with XYZ's established values and entrepreneurial culture of openness, trust and integrity, we request that staff highlight any areas of change and/or improvement directly with the ISO, so as to enable appropriate and timely response/action.

9.2 Non-Compliance with Policy

In the event of non-compliance with this Policy:

- The ISO must establish an exception and action plan to close the gap. These plans must be documented with a clear timeline for closure and an identified responsible party to oversee implementation of the action plan, OR
- The ISO must grant an exemption from the requirements of this Policy, with the rationale and compensating controls clearly documented, as well as maintained and reviewed annually by the ISO.

Any individual found to have violated this Policy may be subject to disciplinary action, up to and including termination of employment or contract.

10. EXCLUSIONS AND SPECIAL SITUATIONS

If local laws or regulations establish a higher standard than what is provided by this Policy document, XYZ must comply with those laws. If local requirements require a less stringed standard than that established by this Policy, it must be brought to the attention of the ISO who, in consultation with the ISG (and, if required, legal counsel) shall determine which standard should prevail.

Information security risk assessments and measurement processes shall be gradually adopted in the development of XYZ Information Security Program. The ISG is responsible for identifying any areas of potential non-compliance under this Policy through regular (currently annual) self-assessments. Areas of potential non-compliance must be formally highlighted and addressed accordingly on a case-by-case basis.

APPENDIX 3

DATA PROTECTION BREACH NOTIFICATION FORM

This form is to be used when data controllers wish to report a breach of the Data Protection Act to the ICO. It should not take more than 15 minutes to complete.

If you are unsure whether it is appropriate to report an incident, you should read the following guidance before completing the form: Notification of Data Security Breaches to the Information Commissioner's Office.

Please provide as much information as possible and ensure that all mandatory (*) fields are completed. If you don't know the answer, or you are waiting on completion of an internal investigation, please tell us. In addition to completing the form below, we welcome other relevant supporting information, e.g. incident reports.

In the wake of a data protection breach, swift containment and recovery of the situation is vital. Every effort should be taken to minimise the potential impact on affected individuals, and details of the steps taken to achieve this should be included in this form.

1. ORGANISATION DETAILS

(a) *What is the name of your organisation – is it the data controller in respect of this breach?

(b) Please provide the data controller's registration number. Search the online Data Protection Public Register.

(c) *Who should we contact if we require further details concerning the incident? (Name and job title, email address, contact telephone number and postal address.)

2. DETAILS OF THE DATA PROTECTION BREACH

(a) *Please describe the incident in as much detail as possible.

(b) *When did the incident happen?

(c) *How did the incident happen?

(d) If there has been a delay in reporting the incident to the ICO please explain your reasons for this.

(e) What measures did the organisation have in place to prevent an incident of this nature occurring?

(f) Please provide extracts of any policies and procedures considered relevant to this incident, and explain which of these were in existence at the time this incident occurred. Please provide the dates on which they were implemented.

3. PERSONAL DATA PLACED AT RISK

(a) *What personal data has been placed at risk? Please specify if any financial or sensitive personal data has been affected and provide details of the extent.

(b) *How many individuals have been affected?

(c) *Are the affected individuals aware that the incident has occurred?

(d) *What are the potential consequences and adverse effects on those individuals?

(e) Have any affected individuals complained to the organisation about the incident?

4. CONTAINMENT AND RECOVERY

(a) *Has the organisation taken any action to minimise/mitigate the effect on the affected individuals? If so, please provide details.

(b) *Has the data placed at risk now been recovered? If so, please provide details of how and when this occurred.

(c) What steps has your organisation taken to prevent a recurrence of this incident?

5. TRAINING AND GUIDANCE

(a) As the data controller, does the organisation provide its staff with training on the requirements of the Data Protection Act? If so, please provide any extracts relevant to this incident here.

(b) Please confirm if training is mandatory for all staff. Had the staff members involved in this incident received training and if so when?

(c) As the data controller, does the organisation provide any detailed guidance to staff on the handling of personal data in relation to the incident you are reporting? If so, please provide any extracts relevant to this incident here.

6. PREVIOUS CONTACT WITH THE ICO

(a) *Have you reported any previous incidents to the ICO in the last 2 years?

(b) If the answer to the above question is yes, please provide: brief details, the date on which the matter was reported and, where known, the ICO reference number.

7. MISCELLANEOUS

(a) Have you notified any other (overseas) data protection authorities about this incident? If so, please provide details.

(b) Have you informed the Police about this incident? If so, please provide further details and specify the Force concerned.

(c) Have you informed any other regulatory bodies about this incident? If so, please provide details.

(d) Has there been any media coverage of the incident? If so, please provide details of this.

Sending this form

Send your completed form to casework@ico.org.uk with 'DPA breach notification form' in the subject field, or by post to: The Information Commissioner's Office, Wycliffe House, Water Lane, Wilmslow, Cheshire SK9 5AF. Please note that we cannot guarantee security of forms or any attachments sent by email.

What happens next?

When we receive this form, we will contact you within seven calendar days to provide:

• a case reference number; and
• information about our next steps.

If you need any help in completing this form, please contact our helpline on 0303 123 1113 or 01625 545745 (operates 9am to 5pm Monday to Friday).

(Courtesy ICO)

APPENDIX 4

PERSONAL INFORMATION ONLINE SMALL BUSINESS CHECKLIST

This checklist will help small- and medium-sized businesses that operate online to make sure they collect and use information about the people they deal with properly. This checklist applies to information such as customers' names and email addresses, or records of their purchases or enquiries. It also applies to information collected through the use of a 'cookie', for example where this is used to target marketing at people.

Adopting the following good practice points will give you a competitive advantage because people will trust you with their information and will be more willing to provide the information you need to run your business successfully.

- Consider whether you actually need to collect information about people. Don't ask people to log in, register or provide their personal details unless you need them to. It is acceptable to ask for this information once people make an enquiry or decide to do business with you.
- When you collect information about people they should know who you are and what you're going to do with their information. There should be a clear, prominent explanation of this on your website.
- You are under a legal duty to keep customer information secure. Ask your IT supplier to give you advice on encrypting information and make sure staff with access to the information are trained to keep it secure and look after it properly.
- If you use a subcontractor, for example to manage your database, make sure there is a written contract in place that requires them to look after your information properly, including keeping it secure.
- If you are going to use customer information to send them marketing material, eg promotional emails, give them a clear choice over this. You should be aware that different rules under the Privacy and Electronic Communications Regulations 2003 might apply depending on the method you use to send the marketing.
- Your website might show content provided by third parties, for example adverts. Although you may not be legally responsible for this content, your customers may assume you are. Therefore it is good practice to act as a single point of contact for the content displayed on your site. For example, you need to have proper procedures in place where a customer objects to a particular advert.

- Ensure that you only collect the information that you use. If you no longer require the information then stop collecting it and dispose securely of any unnecessary information that you may have collected.

- Remember that people have a right of access to information you hold about them. Make sure your staff recognise a 'subject access request' and know how to deal with it.

- Encourage your customers to check the information you hold about them, for example by giving them online access to their account details. Give them facilities for updating and correcting their records if they are wrong.

For further information on collecting and using personal data online, see the full **Personal information online code of practice.**

https://ico.org.uk/media/for-organisations/documents/1591/personal_
information_online_cop.pdf

For further information and good practice advice regarding data protection in general, see **The Guide to Data Protection.**

https://ico.org.uk/for-organisations/guide-to-data-protection/

Contains public sector information licensed under the Open Government Licence v3.0.

APPENDIX 5

OUTSOURCING

A GUIDE FOR SMALL AND MEDIUM-SIZED BUSINESSES

Data Protection Act

The Data Protection Act 1998 (DPA) is based around eight principles of 'good information handling'. These give people specific rights in relation to their personal information and place certain obligations on those organisations that are responsible for processing it.

An overview of the main provisions of DPA can be found in The Guide to Data Protection. This is part of a series of guidance, which foes into more detail than the Guide to DPA, to help you to fully understand your obligations, as well as promoting good practice.

This guide explains the factors to be considered when choosing to use another organization (whether inside or outside the EEA) to process personal data on your behalf.

Overview

As a data controller you may wish to use another organisation to process personal data on your behalf. If you decide to outsource your data processing to another organisation the DPA imposes certain restrictions and obligations on you in relation to that processing, as set out below.

> An organization that processes personal data is required to handle personal data in accordance with the data protection principles. A data controller may choose to use another organization to process personal data on its behalf – a data processor.
>
> The data controller remains responsible for ensuring its processing complies with the DPA, whether it processes in-house or engages a data processor.
>
> Where a data processor is used the data controller must ensure that suitable security arrangements are in place in order to comply with the seventh data protection principle.
>
> If a data processor is located outside the EEA, the data controller must ensure that any transfer of personal data to the processor complies with the requirements of the eighth data protection principle.

What the DPA says

The seventh Data Protection Principle provides that:

> 'Appropriate technical and organizational measures shall be taken against unauthorized or unlawful processing of personal data and against accidental loss or destruction of, or damage to, personal data.'

Where a data controller chooses to use a data processor, paragraphs 11 & 12 of Schedule 1 of the DPA introduce additional obligations on the data controller as follows:

> '11.
>
> Where processing of personal data is carried out by a data processor on behalf of a data controller, the data controller must in order to comply with the seventh principle:
>
> (a)   choose a data processor providing sufficient guarantees in respect of the technical and organizational security measures governing the processing to be carried out; and
> (b)   take reasonable steps to ensure compliance with those measures.
>
> 12.
>
> Where processing of personal data is carried out by a data processor on behalf of a data controller, the data controller is not to be regarded as complying with the seventh principle unless–
>
> (a)   the processing is carried out under a contract –
>   (i)   which is made or evidenced in writing, and
>   (ii) under which the data processor is to act only on instructions from the data controller, and
> (b)   the contract requires the data processor to comply with obligations equivalent to those imposed on a data controller by the seventh principle.'

The eighth Data Protection Principle provides that:

> 'Personal data shall not be transferred to a country or territory outside the European Economic Area unless that country or territory ensures an adequate level of protection for the rights and freedoms of data subjects in relation to the processing of personal data.'

Security Measures and outsourcing

The seventh Data Protection Principle requires you to take appropriate technical and organisational measures to protect the personal data you process, whether you process it yourself or whether someone else (in the UK or overseas) does it for you.

In deciding what security measures are appropriate, you need to take into account the sort of personal data you are dealing with, the harm that might result from its misuse, the technology that is available to protect the data and the cost of ensuring appropriate security for the data.

If you decide to use another organisation to process personal data for you, you will remain legally responsible for the security of the data and for protecting the rights of the individuals whose data is being processed (the data subjects).

The DPA requires you to ensure that you chose a data processor that you consider will be capable of carrying out the processing in a secure manner. In addition, while they are working for you, you should have in place arrangements (such as regular reports or inspections) to allow you to check that your chosen processor is processing the data in an appropriate manner. Remember, although you may be passing the job of processing to another organisation, you will continue to be responsible to both the Information Commissioner and the data subjects for the security of the data and the protection of the data subjects' rights.

The DPA requires you to have a written contract with your chosen processor. The contract must ensure that the processor:

- may only use and disclose the personal data in accordance with your instructions; and
- must take appropriate security measures to protect the data.

International outsourcing

You may wish to use another business located outside the UK to process personal data on your behalf. If you decide to outsource your data processing to a data processor located outside the European Economic Area (the EEA), the arrangement will involve the transfer of personal data falling within the restriction contained in the Eighth Data Protection Principle.

The eighth Principle prohibits the transfer of personal data from the UK to a country outside the EEA unless that country (the third country) ensures an adequate level of protection for the rights and freedoms of the individuals (data subjects) whose data is being transferred. Therefore, if you transfer personal data, for example, to a call centre based in Asia or a processor based in the USA, you will need to ensure that your data subjects' rights are adequately protected.

If you transfer personal data to a data processor in a third country you will remain subject to the Information Commissioner's powers of enforcement and will continue to be responsible for protecting the data subjects' in relation to the overseas processing of their personal data by your chosen data processor.

Means of ensuring adequate protection for the rights of data subjects in international outsourcing

Model Contract Clauses

One means of ensuring adequate protection is the use of European Commission-approved Model Contract Clauses. The clauses tailored outside the EEA data controller to data processor have been approved by the European Commission and the Information Commissioner as offering adequate safeguards for the protection of the rights and freedoms of data subjects in connection with international transfers of data.

The clauses are in a standard form which may not be amended. They may however be incorporated in their entirety into your data processing service agreement with your overseas data processor. By incorporating the clauses in their entirely you will ensure adequate safeguards for the rights of the data subjects provided that nothing in the rest of the agreement changes the effect of the clauses.

Using model contract terms will satisfy the requirement (in the seventh principle) for a written security contract and will fall within an exception to restriction on international data transfers set out in the eighth Principle. For these reasons model contract clauses are often used in international outsourcing arrangements.

For more information on the model clauses see the ICO Guidance Sending personal data outside the European Economic Area web page and the detailed guidance on model contract clauses.

Other means

You do not necessarily need to use the model contract clauses when entering into an international outsourcing arrangement if you have found an alternative means of complying with, or using an exception to, the eighth Principle. For example, ensuring compliance with the security requirements of the seventh Principle will go some way towards satisfying the adequacy requirements of the eighth Principle (given the continuing contractual relationship between you and your processor and your continuing liability for data protection compliance under the Act).

For further information about compliance with the eighth Principle and exceptions to the eighth Principle see the ICO Guidance Sending personal data outside the European Economic Area web page and the detailed guidance on Assessing adequacy of protection for the rights of data subjects.

International sub-processing arrangements

If you choose to use a UK organisation to process personal data on your behalf, your UK data processor may suggest that it may be advantageous to you both if it subcontracts the processing to an organization located outside the EEA.

As data controller you will remain liable for compliance with the DPA in relation to both the processing and any sub-processing (whether that processing is carried out in the UK or overseas). It is therefore important that you are satisfied that the proposed subcontracting will not materially increase the security risks to the data being processed nor adversely affect the rights of the data subjects.

Where the sub-processing arrangements will result in personal data being transferred outside the EEA, you must also ensure that any proposed transfer of personal data complies with, or falls within an exception to, the eighth principle prohibition on the international transfer of personal data. As data controller you must expressly authorise any international subcontracting. The data processor cannot choose to enter into sub-processing arrangements without your approval.

Non-EEA Processor and non-EEA Sub-processor

If you are outsourcing your data processing to an organisation outside the EEA the Eighth Principle issues will already have been addressed in the initial outsourcing arrangements between you and your overseas processor.

If your overseas processor proposes sub-contracting the processing to another overseas business he cannot do so without your prior approval. Given that you will remain responsible for protecting the rights of the data subjects (whether the processing is carried out by you, your processor or a sub-processor) you will need to ensure that appropriate contractual arrangements are in place to protect your position and seek redress from any party (the processor or sub-processor) that is in breach of its data processing obligations.

This is perhaps most simply achieved by inserting an additional clause into the controller to processor model contract clauses. If you approve the proposed sub-contracting you should also ensure that the controller to processor model contract clauses include additional obligations on the processor to:

- contract with the sub-processor on the same terms (particularly with regard to security arrangements) as set out in the main controller to processor agreement; and
- enforce the terms of the sub-processing contract against the sub-processor should there be any breach of its terms.

Any contract between your processor and the sub-processor should therefore mirror the main contract between you and your processor.

The Commission-Approved Controller to Processor contract clauses allow for the possibility of your non-EEA processor wishing to use a sub-processor. These clauses may therefore provide an appropriate means of addressing your eighth Principle obligations where you are using a non-EEA processor.

UK Processor and non-EEA Sub-processor

Where your contract with your processor envisaged all processing being carried out in the UK, if it later agreed that some sub-processing is to be carried out outside the EEA, you will need to amend your controller/processor service contract. The contract will need to be amended firstly, to authorise the sub-processing and secondly, to address how the eighth Principle is to be complied with in relation to the transfer of personal data to the sub-processor outside the EEA.

You should remember that the model contract clauses only deal with international transfers of personal data from data controllers to either other data controllers or to data processors. The model contract clauses do not cover transfers by data processors in the EEA to sub-processors outside the EEA. Therefore, any proposed sub-processing by your UK processor involving a transfer of data outside the EEA will need to use a means other than the model contract clauses to satisfy, or be exempted from, the requirements of the eighth Principle.

General points on international outsourcing

Before using a non-EEA based data processor you should consider whether there is any particular legislation in place in the country or territory where your chosen processor is located which might adversely affect the rights of the data subjects whose data is to be transferred.

If particular legislation gives rise to concern, as part of your assessment as to the adequacy of the protection available for the rights of the data subjects, you will need to consider any risks the legislation may pose, the likelihood of you or your processor being subject to that legislation and how you will respond if required to do so under that legislation.

Where, in the light of the above considerations, foreign legislation poses unacceptable risks to the rights of data subjects you may not be able to transfer personal details to that country unless you can identify and use an exception to the eighth Principle (such as the model contract clauses). Even if you are able to transfer data in reliance upon such an exception, you should have procedures and measures in place to deal with any requests for information that you or your processor may receive under legislation in the country in which your processor is located.

If you or your data processor receives a request for information from another jurisdiction, you will need to decide whether you are able to comply with the request. If you decide to comply it is good practice to ask for more information from the requesting authority to ensure that the request is specific enough to allow you to be able to identify, retrieve and transfer only that information that is relevant and necessary to comply with the request.

Good practice recommendations

The following good practice recommendations may be helpful if you decide to use an organisation to process data on your behalf:

- Select a reputable organisation offering suitable guarantees as to their ability to ensure the security of personal data.
- Ensure the organisation has appropriate data security measures in place.
- Ensure your processor makes and has made appropriate security checks on its staff.
- Ensure that you are able to transfer personal data to a non- EEA processor in compliance with, or in reliance upon an exception to, the eighth Data Protection Principle.
- Ensure the contract with your processor is enforceable in the UK (and if your processor is located in another jurisdiction, the jurisdiction of the processor).
- Require your processor to report any security breaches or other problems (including requests for personal data from other jurisdictions).
- Have procedures in place to allow you to act appropriately on receipt of security or problem reports from your processor.

Other considerations

Further guidance on international transfer arrangements is available at: https://ico.org.uk//for-organisations/guide-to-data-protection/

- Making your own assessment of the adequacy of the level of protection for the rights of data subjects;
- Using Standard Contractual Terms (Model Contract Clauses); and
- Binding Corporate Rules.

More information

This guidance will be reviewed and considered from time to time in line with new decisions of the Information Commissioner, Tribunals and courts.

It is a guide to our general recommended approach, although individual cases will always be decided on the basis of their particular circumstances.

If you need any more information about this or any other aspect of freedom of information or data protection, please contact us: see our website at www.ico.org.uk.

Contains public sector information licensed under the Open Government Licence v3.0.

APPENDIX 6

A PRACTICAL GUIDE TO IT SECURITY

Under the Data Protection Act, you have responsibilities to protect the personal information that you and your staff collect and use. This includes a requirement to have appropriate security to prevent it being accidentally or deliberately compromised.

Breaches of data protection legislation could lead to your business incurring a fine – up to £500,000 in serious cases. The reputation of your business could also be damaged if inadequate security contributes to high profile incidents of data loss or theft.

This guide gives advice for small businesses on how to keep IT systems safe and secure.

10 PRACTICAL WAYS TO KEEP YOUR IT SYSTEMS SAFE AND SECURE

Keeping your IT systems safe and secure can be a complex task and does require time, resource and specialist knowledge. If you have personal data within your IT system you need to recognise that it may be at risk and take appropriate technical measures to secure it. The measures you put in place should fit the needs of your particular business. They don't necessarily have to be expensive or onerous. They may even be free or already available within the IT systems you currently have.

The following practical steps will help you decide how to manage the security of the personal data you hold.

ASSESS THE THREATS AND RISKS TO YOUR BUSINESS

Before you can establish what level of security is right for your business you will need to review the personal data you hold and assess the risks to that data. You should consider all processes involved that require you to collect, store, use and dispose of personal data.

Consider how valuable, sensitive or confidential the information is and what damage or distress could be caused to individuals if there was a security breach.

With a clear view of the risks you can begin to choose the security measures that are appropriate for your needs. The next step is to begin putting them in place.

GET IN LINE WITH CYBER ESSENTIALS

What is the problem?

There is no single product that will provide a complete guarantee of security for your business.

The recommended approach is to use a set of security controls that complement each other but will require ongoing support in order to maintain an appropriate level of security.

What can I do?

The UK Government's Cyber Essentials Scheme describes the following five key controls for keeping information secure. Obtaining a Cyber Essentials certificate can provide certain security assurances and help protect personal data in your IT systems.

Boundary firewalls and internet gateways

This will be your first line of defence against an intrusion from the internet. A well configured firewall can stop breaches happening before they penetrate deep into your network. An internet gateway can prevent users within your organisation accessing websites or other online services that present a threat or that you do not trust.

Secure configuration

Almost all hardware and software will require some level of set-up and configuration in order to provide the most effective protection. You should remove unused software and services from your devices to reduce the number of potential vulnerabilities. Older versions of some widespread software have well documented security vulnerabilities. If you don't use it, then it is much easier to remove it than try to keep it up-to-date.

Make sure you have changed any default passwords used by software or hardware – these are well known by attackers.

Access control

Restrict access to your system to users and sources you trust. Each user must have and use their own username and password.

Each user should use an account that has permissions appropriate to the job they are carrying out at the time.

You should also only use administrator accounts when strictly necessary (eg for installing known and trusted software).

A brute force password attack is a common method of attack, perhaps even by casual users trying to access your Wi-Fi so you need to enforce strong passwords, limit the number of failed login attempts and enforce regular password changes.

Passwords or other access should be cancelled immediately if a staff member leaves the organisation or is absent for long periods.

Malware protection

You should have anti-virus or anti-malware products regularly scanning your network to prevent or detect threats. You will also need to make sure they are kept up-to-date and that it is switched on and monitoring the files that it should be. You should also make sure you receive and act upon any alerts issued by the malware protection.

Patch management and software updates

Computer equipment and software need regular maintenance to keep it running smoothly and to fix any security vulnerabilities. Security software such as anti-virus and anti-malware needs regular updates in order to continue to provide adequate protection.

Keep your software up-to-date by checking regularly for updates and applying them. Most software can be set to update automatically.

If your system is a few years old, you should review the protection you have in place to make sure that it is still adequate.

SECURE YOUR DATA ON THE MOVE AND IN THE OFFICE

What is the problem?

The physical security of equipment is important to consider as devices containing personal data could be stolen in a break-in or lost whilst away from the office. You should ensure that personal data on your systems is protected against these types of threats.

You can also prevent or limit the severity of data breaches by separating or limiting access between your network components. For example, if you can confine the processing of personal data to a specific section of your network you may be able to reduce the scope of the required security measures.

You also need to ensure that the same level of security is applied to personal data on devices being used away from the office. Many data breaches arise from the theft or loss of a device (eg laptop, mobile phone or USB drive) but you should also consider the security surrounding any data you send by email or post.

Allowing untrusted devices to connect to your network or using work devices on untrusted networks outside your office can also put personal data at risk.

What can I do?

You can increase the physical security of your office including storing your servers in a separate room with added protection. Back-up devices, CDs and USBs should not be left unattended and should be locked away when not in use.

You can ensure that personal data is either not on the device in the first place or that is had been appropriately secured so that it cannot be accessed in the event of loss or theft. Good access control systems and encryption will help here.

Encryption is a means of ensuring that data can only be accessed by authorised users. Typically, a (strong) password is required to 'unlock' the data. You can find more information on choosing the right encryption on our website.

Encryption comes in many different forms and offers protection under different circumstances.

Full disk encryption means that all the data on the computer is encrypted.

- File encryption means that individual files can be encrypted.
- Some software offers password protection to stop people making changes to the data but this may not stop a thief reading the data. Make sure you know exactly what protection you are applying to your data.

Some mobile devices support a remote disable or wipe facility. This allows you to send a signal to a lost or stolen device to locate it and, if necessary, securely delete all data. Your devices will normally need to be pre-registered to use a service like this.

If you permit employees or other users to connect their own devices to your network you will be increasing the range of security risks and these should also be addressed. You can find more information about these risks in the ICO's guidance on Bring Your Own Device (BYOD).

SECURE YOUR DATA IN THE CLOUD

What is the problem?

There are a wide range of online services, many incorporated within today's smartphones and tablets that require users to transfer data to remote computing facilities – commonly known as the cloud.

Processing data in the cloud represents a risk because the personal data for which you are responsible will leave your network and be processed in those systems managed by your cloud provider. You therefore need to assess the security measures that the cloud provider has in place to ensure that they are appropriate.

What can I do?

Make sure you know what data is being stored in the cloud as modern computing devices, especially those targeted at consumers, can have cloud backup or sync services switched on by default.

Consider the use of two factor authentication especially for remote access to your data in the cloud.

You can find more information about the use of cloud services in the ICO's Guidance on the use of cloud computing.

BACK UP YOUR DATA

What is the problem?

If you were to suffer a disaster such as fire, flood or theft you need to be able to get back up and running as quickly as possible. Loss of data is also a breach of the DPA.

Malware can also disrupt the availability of access to your data. Known as 'ransomware' this type of malware can encrypt all your data and only provide you with the means to decrypt the data after payment of a ransom.

What can I do?

You need to have a robust data backup strategy in place to protect against disasters but also malware, such as ransomware.

Back-ups should not be stored in a way that makes them permanently visible to the rest of the network. If they are then they can be encrypted by malware or the files accidentally deleted.

At least one of your back-ups should be off-site.

TRAIN YOUR STAFF

What is the problem?

Your employees may have a limited knowledge of cyber security but they could be your final line of defence against an attack. Accidental disclosure or human error is also a leading cause of breaches of personal data.

This can be caused by simply sending an email to the incorrect recipient or opening an email attachment containing malware.

What can I do?

Employees at all levels need to be aware of what their roles and responsibilities are. Train your staff to recognise threats such as phishing emails and other malware or alerting them to the risks involved in posting information relating to your business activities on social networks.

You should encourage general security awareness within your organisation. A security aware culture is likely to identify security risks.

You should also keep your knowledge of threats up-to-date by reading security bulletins or newsletters from organisations relevant to your business.

KEEP AN EYE OUT FOR PROBLEMS

What is the problem?

Cyber criminals or malware can attack your systems and go unnoticed for a long time. Many people only find out they have been attacked when it is too late even though the warning signs were there.

What can I do?

Check your security software messages, access control logs and other reporting systems you have in place on a regular basis. You should also act on any alerts that are issued by these monitoring services.

Make sure you can check what software or services are running on your network. Make sure you can identify if there is something there which should not be.

Run regular vulnerability scans and penetration tests to scan your systems for known vulnerabilities – make sure you address any vulnerabilities identified.

KNOW WHAT YOU SHOULD BE DOING

What is the problem?

A good policy will enable you to make sure you address the risks in a consistent manner. Well written policies should integrate well with business processes.

Some organisations do not have adequate levels of protection because they are not correctly using the security they already have, and are not always able to spot when there is a problem. You should also consider what actions you should put into place should you suffer a data breach. Good incident management can reduce the damage and distress caused to individuals.

What can I do?

Review what personal data you currently have and the means of protection you have in place.

Make sure you are compliant with any industry guidance or other legal requirements.

Document the controls you have in place and identify where you need to make improvements.

Once any improvements are in place, continue to monitor the controls and make adjustments where necessary.

Consider the risks for each type of personal data you hold and how you would manage a data breach. This way you can reduce the impact if the worst was to happen.

You should also have an acceptable-use policy and training materials for staff so that they know their data protection responsibilities.

MINIMISE YOUR DATA

What is the problem?

The DPA says that personal data should be accurate, up-to-date and kept for no longer than is necessary. Over time you may have collected large amounts of personal data. Some of this data may be out-of-date and inaccurate or no longer useful.

What can I do?

Decide if you still need the data. If you do, make sure it is stored in the right place.

If you have data you need to keep for archive purposes but don't need to access regularly, move it to a more secure location. This will help prevent unauthorised access.

If you have data you really no longer need, you should delete it. This should be in line with your data retention and disposal policies. You might need specialist software or assistance to do this securely.

MAKE SURE YOUR IT CONTRACTOR IS DOING WHAT THEY SHOULD BE

What is the problem?

Many small businesses outsource some or all of their IT requirements to a third party. You should be satisfied that they are treating your data with at least the same level of security as you would.

What can I do?

Ask for a security audit of the systems containing your data. This may help to identify vulnerabilities which need to be addressed.

Review copies of the security assessments of your IT provider.

If appropriate, visit the premises of your IT provider to make sure they are as you would expect.

Check the contracts you have in place. They must be in writing and must require your contractor to act only on your instructions and comply with certain obligations of the DPA.

Don't overlook asset disposal – if you use a contractor to erase data and dispose of or recycle your IT equipment, make sure they do it adequately. You may be held responsible if personal data gathered by you is extracted from your old IT equipment when it is resold.

FURTHER READING

As illustrated by the range of topics covered in this guide, keeping an IT network safe and secure can be a complex task and does require time, resource and specialist knowledge. However, there are a range of organisations offering advice and guidance appropriate to your business.

Get Safe Online (www.getsafeonline.org) A joint initiative between the government, law enforcement, leading businesses and the public sector to provide computer users and small businesses with free, independent, user-friendly advice that will allow them to use the internet.

Cyber Street (www.cyberstreetwise.com) Cyber Street is a cross-government campaign, funded by the National Cyber Security Programme, and delivered in partnership with the private and voluntary sectors. The campaign is led by the Home Office, working closely with the Department for Business, Innovation and Skills and the Cabinet Office.

Cyber Essentials (www.gov.uk/government/publications/cyber-essentials-scheme-overview). The Cyber Essentials scheme provides businesses small and large with clarity on good basic cyber security practice. By focusing on basic cyber hygiene, your company will be better protected from the most common cyber threats. Cyber Essentials is mandatory for central government contracts advertised after 1 October 2014 that involve handling personal information and providing certain ICT products and services. It has been developed as part of the UK's National Cyber Security Programme in close consultation with industry.

10 Steps to Cyber Security (https://www.gov.uk/government/publications/cyber-risk-management-a-board-level-responsibility). The 10 Steps define and communicate an Information Risk Management Regime which can provide protection against cyber attacks.

Action Fraud (www.actionfraud.police.uk) Action Fraud is the UK's national reporting centre for victims of fraud or financially motivated internet crime. Action Fraud records and refers these crimes to the police and provides victims with a crime reference number, support and advice.

If you would like to contact us please call 0303 123 1113 or visit www.ico.org.uk.

Information Commissioner's Office, Wycliffe House, Water Lane, Wilmslow, Cheshire, SK9 5AF.

APPENDIX 7

DIRECT MARKETING CHECKLIST

Businesses can use this checklist to help make sure their marketing messages comply with the law and don't annoy customers. It also includes an at-a-glance guide to the different rules on marketing calls, texts, emails, faxes and mail. It is primarily aimed at small businesses. For detailed advice, see our full guidance on direct marketing.

OBTAINING CONSENT FOR MARKETING

- We use opt-in boxes;
- We specify methods of communication (eg by email, by text, by phone, by recorded call, by post);
- We ask for consent to pass details to third parties for marketing, and name or describe those third parties; and
- We record when and how we got consent, and exactly what it covers.

USING BOUGHT-IN LISTS

- We check the origin and accuracy of the list;
- We check when and how consent was obtained, and what it covers;
- We don't use bought-in lists for texts, emails or recorded calls (unless we have proof of opt-in consent within last 6 months which specifically named or described us);
- We screen against the TPS; and
- We tell people where we got their details.

MAKING CALLS

- We screen live calls against the Telephone Preference Service (TPS);
- We only make recorded calls with opt-in consent;
- We keep our own do-not-call list of anyone who says they don't want our calls; and
- We screen against our do-not-call list.

SENDING TEXTS OR EMAILS

- We only text or email with opt-in consent (unless contacting previous customers about our own similar products, and we offered them an opt-out when they gave their details);
- We offer an opt-out (by reply or unsubscribe link);
- We keep a list of anyone who opts out; and
- We screen against our opt-out list

AT-A-GLANCE GUIDE TO THE MARKETING RULES

Method of communication	Individual consumers (plus sole traders and partnerships)	Business-to-business (companies and corporate bodies)
Live calls	Screen against the TPS Can opt out	Screen against the Corporate TPS Can opt out
Recorded calls	Need specific consent	Need specific consent
Emails or texts	Need specific consent Or soft opt-in (previous customer, our own similar product, had a chance to opt out)	Can email or text corporate bodies Good practice to offer opt out Individual employees can opt out
Faxes	Need specific consent	Screen against the Fax Preference Service (FPS) Can opt out
Mail	Name and address obtained fairly Can opt out	Can mail corporate bodies Individual employees can opt out

This only gives a very broad overview of the marketing rules. For detailed advice, see our full guidance on direct marketing.

APPENDIX 8

HOW DO I HANDLE SUBJECT ACCESS REQUESTS

Subject access code of practice
Checklist

How do I handle subject access requests?

Dealing with requests from individuals for personal information

Information Commissioner's Office

Ten simple steps to understanding and handling subject access requests

Is it a subject access request?

YES **Go to question 2**

NO Handle as part of your normal course of business.

Any written request by an individual asking for their personal information is a subject access request. You can choose to deal with it in one of two ways: as a routine enquiry, or more formally.

If you can, treat requests that are easily dealt with as routine matters, in the normal course of business; for example:

- How many cash withdrawals did I make from my account last month?
- What is my customer reference number?

The following are more likely to be treated formally:

- Please send me a copy of my staff records.
- I am a solicitor acting on behalf of my client Mr X and request a copy of his medical records. Appropriate authority is enclosed.

Do you have enough information to be sure of the requester's identity?

YES **Go to question 3**

NO Ask the requester for any evidence you reasonably need to confirm their identity.

Do you need more information from the requester to find what they want?

NO **Go to question 4**

YES Ask them **promptly** for the other information you reasonably need so you can find the information they want.

Are you charging a fee?

NO **Go to question 5**

YES You will need to ask the individual **promptly** to pay the fee.

The maximum fee you can charge is £10, unless the requested information is medical or education records – see chapter 5 of our 'Subject access code of practice' for more on this.

The 40 calendar days in which you must respond starts when you receive the fee and all the information you need to help you find the information.

Do you have the information the requester wants?

YES **Go to question 6**

NO Tell the requester you do not have the information they want.

Will the information be changed between receiving the request and sending the response?

NO **Go to question 7**

YES You can still make routine amendments and deletions to personal information after receiving a request.

You must not make changes to records as a result of receiving the request, even if the information is inaccurate or embarrassing.

Does it include information about other people?

NO **Go to question 8**

YES You will not have to supply the information unless the other people mentioned have given their consent for the disclosure, or it is reasonable to supply the information without their consent.

'If you decide not to disclose the other people's information, you should still disclose as much information as possible by redacting the references to them. See chapter 7 of our 'Subject access code of practice' for further guidance on this.

Are you obliged to supply the information?

YES **Go to question 9**

NO If all the information that the requester wants is exempt from subject access, then you can reply that you do not hold any of their personal data that you are required to reveal.

There are some circumstances when you are not obliged to supply certain information.

See chapter 9 of our 'Subject access code of practice' for guidance on the exemptions.

Does the information include any complex terms or codes?

NO **Go to step 10**

YES You must make sure you explain the codes so that the information can be understood. **Go to step 10**

Prepare the response

You must provide a copy of the information in a permanent form unless the individual agrees otherwise, or doing so would be impossible or involve disproportionate effort.

See chapter 8 of our 'Subject access code of practice' for more detail.

If you would like to contact us please call 0303 123 1113

www.ico.org.uk

Information Commissioner's Office,
Wycliffe House, Water Lane,
Wilmslow, Cheshire SK9 5AF

August 2013
Version 1

ico.
Information Commissioner's Office

INDEX

References are to paragraph numbers.